AF807772

MANAGEMENT UPDATE

The Answer to Obsolescence

MANAGEMENT UPDATE

The Answer to Obsolescence

JOEL E. ROSS

ROBERT G. MURDICK

amacom

A Division of American Management Associations

© 1973 AMACOM
A division of American Management Associations, New York.
All rights reserved. Printed in the United States of America.

This publication may not be reproduced, stored in a retrieval system, or transmitted in whole or in part, in any form or by any means, electronic, mechanical, photocopying, recording, or otherwise, without the prior written permission of AMACOM.

INTERNATIONAL STANDARD BOOK NUMBER: 0-8144-5340-6
LIBRARY OF CONGRESS CATALOG CARD NUMBER: 73-82720

FIRST PRINTING

HD
31
.R724

PREFACE

The world grows rapidly more complex, and mankind's bank of knowledge is on an explosive growth curve. It is ironic that such pressures force managers to focus on ever narrowing areas of business. Rarely does a manager take time to back off from his job and ask: "What is happening all around me? What rapid changes are occurring in business practice?" As a result, many managers paint themselves into a corner of obsolescence. They have failed to develop a general understanding of business, and their specialized knowledge is surpassed by younger, more recently educated people.

This book was written to give the manager a blink at the broad panorama of change in business. We foresee that it will be criticized as only a "blink," but we feel that a blink is often the sign of awakening.

THE AUTHORS

74-10423

CONTENTS

1

Managerial Obsolescence and the Need to Get Updated

"Greetings. You're obsolete!"

Although you may never be greeted that way by your boss, creeping obsolescence may have the same impact: displacement, early retirement, transfer or a pigeonhole until you take flight in boredom and frustration. You'll find a questionnaire for checking your own obsolescence on pages 8–9.

Not long ago most businessmen believed that the best preparation for a higher-lever management job was experience. Today that belief is held by only a handful of diehards. There is general agreement that higher levels of educational attainment and constant updating have become necessities for both top and middle management and for supervisory personnel as well.

Educational expenditures in American business are currently running at about $17 billion per year. Despite them, hardly a single company has been able to slow down the rate of managerial obsolescence. The executive director of The Forty-Plus Club of New York, an organization devoted to rehabilitating and placing unemployed executives who are over forty, says that a sadly high percentage of men have gone stale and are stagnating in their jobs. A company doctor corroborates that statement; he says the fire has simply gone out in about two out of three managers. An AMA paper concludes that the last day of college class is the last day of education for most executives. Specifically, "they exhibit little familiarity with advanced management techniques and barely recognize the advances made by the social sciences in such areas as communications, participation, motivation and other humanistic aspects of the business enterprise."[1]

The problem is not a failure to recognize obsolescence or admit that it exists. Most managers, as well as most engineering and technical people, view obsolescence in themselves and others as a serious and continuing problem in their organizations. The question is what to do about it. The over-thirty manager of today hears the footsteps of the accelerated generation, the junior managers who are updated and who are demanding and getting center stage. Experience may or may not be the best teacher, but it is certainly the slowest and most expensive one. The older manager—the one with all the experience—must first recognize the causes of obsolescence and then undertake a personal development program to avoid it both in himself and in his organization.

CHANGE: THE CAUSE OF OBSOLESCENCE

Once an individual, in his technical or professional development, falls below that required for effective performance, he is, for all practical purposes, obsolete. He will become more obsolete unless he takes corrective action to overcome his deficit in ability and knowledge that has been created by change; for it is change that causes managerial obsolescence. Change produces the discrepancy between job needs and managerial capabilities. With changes in technology, knowledge, and methods, the manager becomes obsolete unless he himself changes.

Almost all change results from the ever accelerating rate of advancement in human knowledge. For example, at graduation a university student, though better educated than when he entered, really possesses a smaller percentage of the total knowledge of the universe than he did when he began his freshman year. The situation in business is not so different. It is this advance in knowledge that produces changes in skills required, products, markets, procedures and processes, the functions of management, and a host of items related to the way the manager must perform his job.

Let's examine four types of change that directly affect job performance.

Business Environmental Change

No longer can the manager concern himself with operations solely within the firm. He should be aware of external change as well.

The *antibusiness mood* is growing in the United States. The public is turning sour on the American corporation and its profits, prices, and policies. This low esteem is new; formerly the public thought of businessmen as Horatio Alger characters who worked hard and deserved their successes. The writings of Ayn Rand were the postdeath of the great-man philosophy. Now the mood is changing and the overwhelming majority of firms will admit to a serious problem with their corporate image in the now generation. In an age of product recalls, cost overruns, and antitrust consent decrees, the common argument that business automatically benefits others—employees, customers, suppliers, and shareholders—no longer stands as sufficient justification for corporate existence. One of the natural outgrowths of this mood is the consumer movement (see Chapter 2). The public is no longer willing to tolerate what it believes to be an up-to-the-customer attitude by many firms.

Social responsibility is a relatively new but vastly accelerating concern for businessmen all over the nation. In 1969, when *Business Week* began its program of awards for business citizenship, involvement in social projects by corporations was so new that emphasis was on the pioneering nature of the projects undertaken by a relatively few companies. Now there is abundant evidence that businessmen have accepted that new role, albeit reluctantly. Research is now underway in many companies to establish some form of cost accounting that will permit the companies to budget and measure their social contributions. These contributions can include ecology and pollution control, development of underprivileged human resources, urban renewal, and other measures formerly considered outside the realm of corporate responsibility. It is no longer enough to measure social responsibility in purchases made or wages paid. (See Chapter 3.) The problem is to develop a new balance sheet showing social assets, social commitments, and contributed societal equity.

People Changes

Nowhere is there a greater potential for managerial updating than in the area concerned with the supervision and motivation of people. In fact, there is general agreement that the answer to increased national—and corporate—productivity lies in better management of human resources.

Many managers still belong to one of two schools: the autocratic or the paternalistic. The first is characterized by Henry Ford's comment,

"The average man won't really do a day's work unless he is caught and can't get out of it." The second school is represented by Theodore Vail (1845–1920), the founder and first president of AT&T. He not only incorporated the company but supplied its philosophy: "Provide your employees with security and their loyalty will guarantee service with a smile."

Each of these approaches to leadership may have been successful in its day, but neither reflects the views of modern behavioral science. We now have some significant information on human resources management that can result in increased productivity and worker satisfaction. If the manager wants to avoid obsolescence, he must become familiar with the state of the art in that field. Moreover, he should put the new, effective methods into practice. (See Chapter 4.)

Modern management theory and practice offer additional alternatives for *organizational development* and change to facilitate people productivity. Those alternatives are related to structure as well as work design. Organization charts and manuals may never be the same again. (See Chapter 5.)

Technological Change

We need only look around the home or workplace to see evidence of the fantastic changes resulting from the technological revolution. That revolution is not simply a continuation of the Industrial Revolution; instead, it is a vast and fundamental change in its own right. Its chief characteristics are the advanced mechanization and automation techniques that have been adopted and improved across a broad range of industries. Not only are products and supporting operations becoming more complex but the life cycle of products is being shortened as well.

The explosive change has been due in large part to increasing expenditure on *research and development,* and the great complexity of R&D demands new management techniques to cope with the planning and control of that expenditure. Similarly, the associated function of engineering is becoming more complex in a technical sense and its management is rapidly becoming more sophisticated. (See Chapters 11 and 12.)

Technology also results in significant product changes that not only increase the product mortality rate but also greatly shorten the time in which return from a given product must be optimized. That, in turn, either lengthens the time required to make decisions for future commitments of cash and other resources or increases the risk.

A second significant fallout from technological change in the *information explosion* and all it implies for management. There are various estimates of the resulting enormous expansion of information, but for our purposes we can say that the modern manager must keep abreast of the information required for increasingly complex decisions. That leads directly to the third major impact resulting from technological change, *the computer*. (See Chapter 8.)

Without the computer it would be impossible to store, process, and retrieve the vast amount of information that is necessary for modern management decision making. The computer offers the potential—and we emphasize potential—for becoming the most important tool of modern management. And the day will shortly arrive when the manager will simply be obsolete unless he has a minimal familiarity with that machine.

Change in the Process of Management

Management—the profession, art, science, practice, or what you will—is changing also. We are on the threshold of the systems age. That concept gives us three fundamental notions. The first is *information feedback systems,* a theory that explains the goal-seeking, self-correcting interplay between the parts of an organization. The theory is not entirely new, but it has only recently been applied to business thinking. A companion to it is the concept of the *automated or programmed* decision. Third, we have the techniques of *management science,* which permit the design of the decision rules that facilitate the systems approach to decision making. The computer, combined with management science, permits simulation of complex situations and the exploration of "what if" questions by management. (See Chapter 8.)

The basic functions of management—planning, organizing, and controlling—are also undergoing change. The classical, or structured, approach to them is giving way to the dynamic, integrative, and forward-looking systems approach. (See Chapter 6.)

All these changes have had considerable impact on the *technical functions* of marketing, production and operations, finance and accounting, and engineering and research. The salesman, accountant, engineer, production supervisor, or other specialist will find that constant change is a characteristic of the management of a particular subsystem of the organization. The departmental accounting head becomes obsolete because he fails to adapt to basic changes in the corporate financial function. Engineers become obsolete when their very specialized talents are no longer needed because a project has been canceled. Sales managers become obsolete when they can't keep up with the growth of a market, new marketing channels, marketing intelligence-gathering techniques, and modern human resource management. (See Chapter 10.)

PERSONAL OBSOLESCENCE

Although the changes described in the preceding paragraphs are largely beyond his control, the individual manager must adapt to them. If he can't, personal obsolescence will result. Despite noble-sounding policies, few companies view professional growth as a shared responsibility. Generally, it is every man for himself. In particular, when causes of obsolescence are to be found in his personal traits and how he operates within the organization, the manager must usually seek a solution on his own. He should be alert to the following symptoms:

Complacency. Widely recognized as one of industry's greatest problems, complacency usually results from euphoria or satisfaction with the status quo. The causes are several. For example, a manager who achieves sudden prosperity, either by promotion or otherwise, can become unaware of his new responsibilities. Alternatively, he can become apprehensive about measuring up to them and then become either arrogant or withdrawn to hide his fears.

Advancing age may bring a slowdown that can be both physical and mental. A job rut carved out by insistence on retaining outdated methods is a contributing cause of complacency.

Lack of confidence is a related problem that can occur when a man finds that his job has become too large or too complex and he is uncomfortable about keeping up with it. He notices his young subordinates asking difficult questions and pressing him for decisions on new and complex problems.

The organizational climate sometimes becomes more than he can handle. Superior-subordinate relationships head the list. Adequate communications don't exist; there is little or no direction; or there is no understanding or agreement about personal and corporate objectives. Complete frustration and resignation to the status quo can result. A little bird should tell the manager that he hasn't kept up with new organizational techniques, project management, and shared goal setting.

Organizational pressures and complexities also can lead to obsolescence when the manager finds them more than he can cope with. Political pressures, bureaucratic structure, methods changes, and increased corporate demands sometimes exceed the person's ability or desire to accommodate change. If they do, he may pass into a form of managerial menopause.

ESTIMATING YOUR OBSOLESCENCE

Earlier we noted that both managerial and technical personnel widely recognize personal obsolescence as a serious and continuing problem in other managers and within their organizations. But they are not so reliable in assessing their own obsolescence. Although the shortcomings of others are easy to see, personal shortcomings are often rationalized. Despite that, a reasonable assessment can be made by answering these questions:

Are you doing things differently today than you were two or three years ago? If your job is the same after that time lapse, the chances are that you haven't introduced any new ideas, methods, products, or changes. You haven't changed the output or the nature of the organization. In short, you haven't made changes, taken risks, or entered new ventures.

Have you achieved the promotion, recognition, or job satisfaction that is due you? If the answer is no, then ask this question: how is your company or your operation doing in comparison with other companies or similar operations? An objective examination of the answers to those questions may reveal that obsolescence is setting in.

Are you making progress toward achieving your goals? The answer to that question requires that you rigorously write down goals and avoid making excuses if you aren't achieving them. And it's not enough to say that a profitable business or a personal monetary reward reflects your total aspiration. Satisfaction with one of those goals or the status quo can be a major cause of obsolescence.

PERSONAL DEVELOPMENT: THE ANSWER TO OBSOLESCENCE

It is generally agreed that, once a manager becomes obsolete, there is very little that can be done except to relocate him, fire him, or give him a featherbed job. The answer to obsolescence lies more in preven-

PERSONAL EVALUATION CHECK FOR OBSOLESCENCE

PART 1

	Yes	No
1. Have your job responsibilities changed significantly in the last three years?	( )	( )
2. Have you attended an out-of-town management or technical meeting or seminar in the past two years?	( )	( )
3. Have you taken a university course (credit or noncredit) in management or in your own discipline within the last three years?	( )	( )
4. Have you participated in a workshop, seminar, or continuing education program in the last three years?	( )	( )
5. Did you receive a raise last year?	( )	( )
6. Are you comfortable with subordinates when they propose technical solutions to new problems? Do you understand the solutions?	( )	( )
7. Are you being assigned to new committees with increased responsibilities and more important decisions to consider?	( )	( )
8. Do your associates and subordinates regard you as a pioneer rather than a "statesman"?	( )	( )
9. Have your colleagues sought your advice within the past three months?	( )	( )
10. Can you explain to your wife's or subordinates' satisfaction such terms as Theory Y, MIS, time sharing, real time, marketing concept, exponential smoothing, management by objectives, PERT/CPM, transfer pricing, and organizational development?	( )	( )

If you have six or more no answers, you should check your obsolescence or check your pension plan

PART 2

	Yes	No
11. Are you being assigned more frequently to arranging for the company picnic, taking dignitaries on a plant tour, or conducting fund drives?	( )	( )
12. Have you forgotten most of what you learned in college or discovered that it doesn't matter any more what you learned?	( )	( )
13. Have you been saying lately, "We've always done it this way" or "What's wrong with the way we do it now?"	( )	( )
14. Do you subscribe to fewer than two professional journals or magazines, or do you habitually put off reading them?	( )	( )
15. Have you recently had the thought that you would rather stay home than get out and face your job responsibilities?	( )	( )
16. Do you have difficulty listing the five most important developments or discoveries in your industry in the last five years?	( )	( )
17. Are you snowed by the speakers at the conventions you attend?	( )	( )
18. If computer time were free, would you have difficulty in describing how you would computerize the five most important job responsibilities you have?	( )	( )
19. Are you drinking more cocktails per week now than you were five years ago?	( )	( )
20. Would you find it difficult or impossible to describe the contribution or philosophy of two of these men: Peter Drucker, Herbert Simon, Chris Argyris, Frederick Herzberg, W. W. Cooper, Robert G. Brown, Wroe Alderson, or Philip Kotler?	( )	( )

If you have six or more yes answers, you should check your obsolescence or check your pension plan tion than in cure. And the rather obvious answer to prevention is some type of personal development program. Although the organization can help by creating the proper environment, the ultimate responsibility is with the individual. That conclusion leads to two questions: What are the incentives for personal development? What action can you take?

Incentives

Incentives for personal development can be interpreted by the classic deficit and growth motives outlined by Maslow. Deficit motives are those basic to the organic and survival needs of the individual. Growth motives are the much higher ones that involve satisfactions and lend richness to life—the instruments of self-actualization. It is to the latter class that the incentives for personal development belong. They can be summarized as follows:[2]

1. *Opportunity* for increased responsibility and participation in higher-level decisions and operations.
2. *Recognition* by peers, superiors, and subordinates.
3. *Economic rewards* that reflect increased recognition.
4. A personal sense of *accomplishment.*
5. A personal sense of *power.*
6. A degree of *independence* from a restrictive job environment.
7. Increased opportunity for *advancement.*

What Action Can I Take?

Despite job pressures and constraints, each manager should have his own antiobsolescence program. A variety of components are available:

Self-education study at home or work demands individual effort and personal sacrifice, but it is the method employed by more managers than any other. It is convenient and flexible. It demands a high degree of self-discipline because, unlike the more structured approaches to learning, it depends solely upon the learner for reinforcement.

On-the-job learning is employed by almost everyone to some degree. Although this method of education has the advantage of direct orientation to the job, the subject matter and approach are rather restricted and there is no assurance that the learning process is general enough to combat obsolescence.

Seminars may be in the form of in-company educational programs, outside-company sponsored, or individually financed. They are organized around specific bodies of knowledge and provide the participant with potential professional contacts. Usually, however, a seminar is of such short duration that only a brief familiarity with the topic is achieved. Nonetheless, it can be used to combat obsolescence provided it serves as a foundation for future study and a stimulus to additional self-education.

University courses, which can be credit or noncredit, are part of a definite trend toward bringing professional education, particularly business education, to the practicing manager. If this approach is taken, the busy manager should be prepared to spend additional time on updating himself to compensate for the lapse in time since his college graduation.

Professional associations can be very effective in preventing obsolescence provided the member avails himself of the educational opportunities they present: publications, meetings, workshops, and seminars. In a move that is revolutionary for a professional association, the American Institute of Certified Public Accountants recently urged all states to adopt legislative and regulatory requirements for continuing education of CPA's who would otherwise become ineligible to practice public accounting.

WHAT IS THE ROLE OF THE COMPANY?

Despite any personal incentives for self-development, the individual manager will generally become discouraged unless his company creates the right climate. That would surely include a commitment to antiobsolescence programs in furtherance of the major objective of individual development. Indeed, it is not too much to expect that the company should adopt goals for human resource development that are second only to those of long-term profitability and growth. One set cannot be reached unless the other is also.

A company might include these specific program parts:

Set up an organizational environment that recognizes the need for self-development and establishes as a major corporate goal that of meeting the needs of its most valuable resources—people. Indeed, it would not be going too far to say that many industries that are oriented largely to science and technology are educational institutions.

Establish formal organizational policies that encourage personal development. They would include library facilities, educational reimbursement programs, in-company development programs, and a stated policy toward self-development.

As a part of the appraisal program include periodic review and development sessions that are directed specifically to obsolescence. Help subordinates work out a program for improved self-development.

Keep men on the move; don't let them stagnate in the same old job unless it's an admission of featherbedding or obsolescence. Move them periodically into new and more challenging assignments. If they are apparently stagnating and are not promotable, try to determine their interests and move them laterally to new jobs. If appropriate, move them from line to staff and into different functional areas.

Encourage people to work toward professional goals. The man who plots his career most carefully is least likely to become obsolete. Substitute objectives and goals for methods and procedures. Growth is a lifelong process; encourage people to set both short-range and long-range career goals.

In this chapter we have identified change as the number one reason for managerial obsolescence and have identified specific changes that are its major contributing factors. The answer to avoiding obsolescence is a personal development program to update yourself. The remainder of this book is devoted to a discussion of those topics. Our purpose is to update you on the latest developments that may have an impact on your job performance.

2

Consumerism: The Nader Syndrome

The ill repute of business would still flourish if Nader started doing commercials for General Motors.

MAX WAYS[1]

ITEM: One of the world's leading airlines is just finishing a ten-year effort to reverse its poor service image.

ITEM: A large oil company and its advertising agency are accused of false advertising by the Federal Trade Commission. Despite a balloon test conducted on TV by a former astronaut, the FTC says that the advertising contains false, misleading, and deceptive statements and that the company's additive does not reduce air pollution.

ITEM: A major pharmaceutical manufacturer, consistently ranked low in the industry by the public, voluntarily assured the FTC that it would refrain from misleading advertising for its decongestant. The FTC objected to such advertisements as the one portraying a woman, supposedly allergic to roses, holding a rose to her nose.

ITEM: The TV commercial claim that a certain health tonic is "a generally effective remedy for tiredness, loss of strength, run-down feeling, nervousness or irritability," is the basis of a $1 million suit charging violation of an order prohibiting false and misleading advertising.

P. T. Barnum's famous slogan, "there's a sucker born every minute," may once have been useful, but its time is past. Today's customer is more knowledgeable and shrewd, and he demands and gets greater responsibility on the part of both seller and manufacturer. As we write this chapter, hundreds of students on our own university campus bombard us with sales talks, posters, meetings, and student newspapers designed to recruit us for a growing student organization, The Public Interest Research Group (PIRG). The idea of PIRG, which was originated by Ralph Nader, is to enlist grass-roots support in combatting unfair and illegal business practices by local merchants. Support for the student branch was pledged by the office of the state attorney general, which issued this comment: "Their goal and the Attorney General's interest in the area of consumer protection are the same."

THE NEW CONSUMERISM

> *Ralph Nader didn't create consumerism. Consumerism was a movement in search of a high priest. Consumerism created Nader.*
>
> R.G.M.

Consumerism is not new to the business scene. The first consumer complaint probably took place in the Stone Age when someone traded a stone implement for an animal skin. But the current movement is notable for its intensity and breadth, and it shows no sign of subsiding. What exactly is this wave of frustration and aggravation? The noted marketeer Dr. Philip Kotler, in an excellent summary of the impact of consumerism on the functions of marketing, says: "Consumerism is a social movement seeking to augment the rights and power of buyers in relation to sellers."[2]

Although few sellers would agree, it is nevertheless a fundamental belief of consumerism that the buyers—the public—are being denied their basic rights. Since the issue is critical, it is worthwhile to examine the rights and limitations of both seller and buyer.

Seller Rights	*Seller Limitations*
Right to introduce any product in any size and style.	Cannot be unnecessarily hazardous to health or safety. If it must be hazardous, proper warnings and controls must be used.
Right to put any price on the product.	No discrimination among similar classes of buyers.

Seller Rights	*Seller Limitations*
Right to advertise in any way.	Can't be defined as unfair competition.
Right to formulate any message concerning the product.	Must not be misleading in content or execution.
Right to finance sale of the product.	Subject to truth-in-lending and usury laws.
Right to introduce any buying incentive scheme.	Subject to all preceding limitations.

Buyer Rights	*Buyer Limitations*
Right not to buy any product.	Hazards and warnings must be clearly printed on the containers of such products as drugs, cigarettes, and cleaning fluids.
Right to expect the product to be safe.	
Right to expect the product to be as represented by seller.	Sales slip is sometimes required; time limit is set in some cases.
Right to return any product that is defective or fails to meet seller's claims.	

If you keep in mind that consumerism is a movement of consumer advocates and not businessmen, you can better understand the public's view that the balance of power lies with the seller rather than the customer. The seller's argument that the customer has all the power he needs because *he can refuse to buy the product* is no longer acceptable. The consumer advocates say that the buyer isn't getting the information he needs about the product because advertising is deceptive. Often the seller isn't delivering the warranty, safety, and performance he promised. In addition, much of the buying public isn't equipped to read and understand the tricky phrasing on packages or in advertising.

What additional rights do consumer advocates want? Basically there are three:

The right to be informed. Five specific shortcomings about which there has been a great deal of discussion and action include true interest cost of a loan (truth in lending), true cost per standard unit of competing brands (unit pricing), true ingredients (ingredient labeling), nutritional quality (nutritional labeling), and product freshness (open dating).[3]

The right of protection against questionable products and marketing practices. This is a reaction to the let-the-buyer-beware philosophy of the past. Consumer advocates say that the customer hasn't the ability or the time to understand the complex information about a product and so there must be some group or government agency to help him. The expansion of government agencies and the issuance of new powers to existing ones reflect this right. The most notable action in support of it is the passage of laws affecting the safety of automobiles.

The right to have products and practices that will increase the "quality of life." Consumerists say that, in addition to being convenient to the consumer and profitable to the company, products, packaging, and market practices must be life-enhancing. The more notable effects of this right have been the regulation or promotion of product ingredients (detergents, gasoline), packaging (biodegradable containers), and the establishment of consumer representation within the policy-making councils of the company (board of directors).

If you are a businessman (seller) and believe that the consumer movement is a serious challenge to the *traditional* rights of business, you are correct! However, the traditional rights are not today's rights. Consumerism is here to stay. Even if the protest phase of the movement should end, and there is evidence that it will, the corporation of today and tomorrow must operate within the constraints that have thus far been established by consumerism. Some of them are the truth-in-lending, truth-in-packaging, and auto safety laws, the Office of Consumer Affairs and the Environmental Protection Agency, and the greatly increased powers of the Federal Trade Commission and Food and Drug Administration.

THE WHY OF CONSUMERISM

Except for professional athletes, Ralph Nader is one of the few living Americans who is a hero to any great number of people. Why is this somewhat radical, left-of-center, young man a hero? Is it, as Professor George Lodge of the Harvard Business School says,[4] because "Ralph Nader is performing an extremely useful service to the community. He throws light on the real problem, the basic problem, the radical problem. It is that the whole community, not just business, is trying to live according to an outdated ideology."

Whatever the reasons, there has been no shortage of people willing to identify them. Here is a smorgasbord of explanations for consumerism advanced by a variety of sources. Select from this menu or add a dish of your own:

1. The widening gap of understanding between business and the public.
2. A sudden and dramatic shift in human values.
3. A gap of unrealized expectations between business and the public.
4. Consumer counteraction to the growing misuse of power by business.
5. A gross misconception of business on the part of the average citizen.
6. A changing ideology that accentuates public rather than individual property rights (for example, General Motors belongs to the people).
7. The mass media coverage of such bad reactions to consumerism as General Motors' attempt to "investigate" Ralph Nader and spontaneous store boycotts by housewives in search of a better deal.
8. The politicians at all levels who picked up consumerism as a vote-getter.
9. The many old and new organizations that act in defense of the consumer.
10. The youth, ecology, and antiestablishment movements.
11. An increase in the production of shoddy merchandise.
12. A more educated public that is identifying shoddy merchandise, whether there is more or less of it.

THE IMPACT AND THE DILEMMA

The impact of consumerism can best be seen in its effect on the appliance industry. Over a billion appliances are owned in this country, and Americans keep buying more. Yet the industry is called a merchandising jungle and a massive service headache. Established manufacturers are pulling out; retailers are dropping lines; and servicemen are backing away. Nobody is happy—not the manufacturers, not the retailers, not the servicemen, and certainly not the customers.

The entire bag of consumer complaints is embodied in appliances. There is a lack of safety (power mowers that trim fingers and toes as well as lawns), an abundance of well-hedged warranties ("what the bold print giveth, the fine print taketh away"), complexity (one GE refrigerator has 63 operational components, including 2 relays, 3 solenoids, 5 thermostats, 6 motors, 11 switches, and 12 heaters). Added to that is the frequency and cost of repairs. You may have heard a variation of the story of the New York lawyer who, when billed for $42 for a one-hour in-home TV repair, complained, "I'm a lawyer and I don't get $42 an hour." Replied the repairman, "Yes, I know. I used to be a lawyer myself."

The pressures behind the new demands place the company squarely on the horns of a dilemma. No major corporation can survive without taking account of and responding to consumerism. On the other hand, no company that attempts to meet *all* consumer demands can survive either. The businessman is faced with the classic tradeoff problem. Business history, as well as his own survival, will be depend on how well he resolves it. He must achieve the optimum mix of two conflicting forces. One is the familiar competitive marketplace that is reflected in the traditional focus of decisions, operations, and company policy. The other is the emerging public sector, which includes the government, the general public, and specific publics such as consumer advocates and the consumers themselves.

PRODUCT SAFETY

The board chairman of a lawn mower manufacturer claims he saw two men trying to cut a hedge with a power mower. "It's impossible to invent an idiot-proof machine," he says. A leading vacuum cleaner company that has had its share of liability troubles is putting together in writing all of its product safety standards and making them a part of top management policy. "In the past," its president says, "we would wonder who in their right mind would pick up puddles of water with the vacuum cleaner. Now we say, 'Don't pick up puddles of water with the vacuum cleaner.' "[5] Ford Motor Company swallowed hard and recalled 436,000 cars—largest in its history—to install a retainer plate on the rear-axle bearing to keep the axle from pulling out of the car. The cost exceeded $30 million. *Automotive News* likened the plate installation to installing a cowbell on a car "so when it rolls over, there is a warning signal."

According to the National Commission on Product Safety, an estimated 20 million persons injure themselves in the home each year with consumer products—four times as many as are hurt in highway accidents. In fact, consumer concern with home safety is surpassing consumer concern with automobile safety. That is logical considering that 30,000 Americans are killed, 110,000 are permanently disabled, and 585,000 are hospitalized annually as a result of incidents involving consumer products.

Despite those horrifying statistics, the ratio of injuries to appliances has actually gone down. If the home accident rate experienced in the 1930s had prevailed in 1970, there would have been 57 percent more fatal home accidents than actually occurred. That there were not is due in part to greater safety manufacturing requirements. For example, one major manufacturer states that its automatic washer complies with over 350 safety requirements of UL Standard No. 560 and its electric space heater with some 500 safety requirements of UL Standard No. 573.

Manufacturers complain that you can't make a foolproof product. There seems to be an overwhelming compulsion on the part of housewives to open the lid, reach in, and either take something out of the clothes washer or put something in. They say that up to 95 percent of household injuries could be prevented by changing human behavior, not the product. That claim notwithstanding, the public and the government continue to press for greater safety.

PRODUCT LIABILITY

The old saw, "let the buyer beware," is outdated; now it's "let the manufacturer and the seller beware." Today the consumer doesn't say, "I've got a lemon." He says, "I'll sue."

Some years ago, a manufacturer of washing machines was sued by a housewife who was injured when her compulsion to open the lid of her machine had predictable consequences. The jury insisted on a demonstration of the unit at the height of its spin cycle; it then found for the manufacturer on the ground that either the housewife accepted the risk of sticking her hand into that whirling mass or she was negligent.

It is very unlikely that a jury would reach such a verdict today. A revolution in product liability is taking place. In 1960 there were fewer than 50,000 such liability cases in the courts. By 1975 the figure is expected to pass the million mark. Consider this sampling:

- A woman who developed a blood clot after taking the pill collected $250,000 from Searle.
- A hospital cook in New York collected $550,000 when he came down with polio after taking Sabin polio vaccine.
- $930,000 was awarded by a Cook County jury to an Illinois housewife who was blinded by an exploding can of Drano.
- A $150,000 judgment was made against the manufacturer of a vaporizer that tipped over and scalded a child.
- A $32,000 settlement was made by a retailer for breach of warranty when a blouse he'd sold caught fire near a kitchen stove and burned the woman wearing it.

The possibility of such suits has caused food and other manufacturers to conduct costly recall programs. One pharmaceutical firm spent $8.5 million to recall intravenous-feeding bottles. A soup company spent $5 million to recall two kinds of soups processed in only one plant. One of the most publicized cases was that of Bon Vivant vichyssoise. When a customer died of botulism after eating a can of it, the cost of recalling all products and the bad publicity drove the company into bankruptcy.

The year 1916 saw a drastic change in the philosophy of privity of contract. Originally, the effect of privity was to allow lawsuits only between the purchaser and the direct seller; the 1916 change was to permit the purchaser to sue the manufacturer as well. A man named MacPherson had lost one of the wheels from his new Buick while driving at 15 miles per hour. He was injured, and he sued Buick for negligence—claiming that the wheel had been defective—and won. Since that time purchasers have been able to sue anybody in the distribution chain from the manufacturer down. Although the approach was seldom used until recently, it has gained in favor because of the changes in marketing methods. In recent decisions courts have ruled essentially that, since the world of merchandising is no longer one of direct buyer-seller contact but is one of advertising, labeling, packaging, and such, the buyer must depend upon those representations to be truthful. The effect of the movement has been to make the manufacturer virtually the insurer of his own products.

Ten reasons have been advanced for the product liability revolution and the tremendous increase in legal activities:[6]

1. Since packaging prevents proper inspection of the merchandise, the courts have placed the responsibility on the vendor and the manufacturer to represent the product truthfully.

2. The complexity of today's products (for example, TV and Hi-Fi) precludes proper buyer appraisal. The buyer cannot judge safety, quality, price, suitability, and other characteristics.

3. Because of the explosion of advertising expenditures, the consumer is subjected to such a barrage of appeals and persuasions that he can't make a rational purchase choice.

4. Most transactions between seller and buyer are now impersonal; they are conducted between strangers and uninformed clerks.

5. The emergence of national distribution networks has further impersonalized transactions, and some manufacturers are relaxing their design and safety standards as a result.

6. The plethora of new products and innovations (7,000 to 9,000 products in the average supermarket) doesn't permit any degree of product knowledge. The consumer is confused and can't make rational choices between alternatives.

7. Rapid product innovations and the demand for new products cause honest errors in safety and design.

8. The success of some attorneys who specialize in the product liability area has encouraged others to enter the field.

9. The new consumer movement has had wide public acceptance.

10. Claims, awards, and settlements have encouraged more injured parties to seek redress. Product liability claims are skyrocketing.

MARKETING AND CONSUMERISM

Although corporate executives have long realized that their markets were somehow intertwined with "society," only very recently has a great deal of conscious thought been given to a reconciliation of what happens in the market with what happens in society. Indeed, market planning is increasingly contingent on that reconciliation. The idea is so new that it hasn't been adequately treated in textbooks.

The marketing concept anticipated the potential of consumerism. General Electric was implementing it in the early 1950s (as described in its internal manual "Introduction to Product Planning," PUB/MS8-7) before many companies were aware of what it was all about. The concept rests on three premises: (1) the customer is king,

(2) emphasis is properly placed on increasing profits, not sales, and (3) product planning should be carried out by cross-functional teamwork. It has been given a modern definition by Philip Kotler: "The marketing concept calls for a *customer orientation* backed by *integrated marketing* aimed at generating *customer satisfaction* as the key to attaining long-run profitable volume."[7]

As expanded by Kotler and others, the *new* marketing concept adds *long-run consumer welfare* to customer satisfaction. Sears, Roebuck and Co. is a modern outstanding example of successful application of the concept. Says its president, "To be successful in this business you've got to look after every customer." In other words, the marketer should serve not only the consumer's desires but his interests as well. Since his desires and long-run interest may conflict, the corporation is faced with a dilemma. The successful company will resolve the dilemma in favor of a "societal marketing concept" that recognizes the importance of long-run consumer welfare. That concept can form the basis for profitability through the introduction of needed new products and the adoption of a companywide consumerist orientation. Consumerism also has an immediate effect on the functions of sales, advertising, and warranty and service.

Sales

The top door-to-door salesman of all time sold cosmetics. His approach was simple. He greeted the housewife who opened the door with five little words: "Girlie, is your mother home?"

A somewhat similar approach catapulted an encyclodepia–reference book company into fame and earnings in the middle sixties. Its sales force used such pitches as "I'd like to talk with you about improving your child's education." The profits were handsome until the FTC accused the company of high-pressure selling. Then the company found that the soft sell was hurting it badly. The FTC suggested that telephone "qualifying" practices and misrepresentation of the salesman as a survey researcher were deceptive. The Commission first proposed that the salesman present a card such as the one shown here and get the housewife to sign it before he entered the door. When the company complained that such a procedure would wreck its business, the FTC relented on the signature.

The encyclopedia case is just one of many undertaken by the FTC. Many businessmen are confused and wonder just what constitutes "un-

ENCYCLOPEDIA INC.

____

(Salesman)

I agree to permit this salesman to enter my home, understanding that his purpose is to persuade me to acquire a set of encyclopedias.

____

NOTICE TO CONSUMER

It is illegal for the above-named salesman to enter your premises until after he has

(1) presented this card to you and
(2) you have signed it in the above space

If either condition is violated, then you may cancel any contract at any time up to 10 days after the date of your receipt of all of the publications, merchandise, or services contracted for, excluding the receipt of yearbooks or research service.

fair and deceptive" selling practices. Meanwhile, FTC's size and influence are growing and the agency is devoting more of its attention to consumer protection. As Gilbert Burck of *Fortune* says, "Inoculated with the New Consumerism, the fifty-seven-year-old Commission is prancing around like an adolescent."

Other companies are feeling the heat in their personal selling methods. Some auto dealers are telling their salesmen to cool it and to tout fewer "executive" cars. Some appliance dealers are actually giving their salesmen short courses in consumerism.

Advertising

Advertising is under even greater attack than personal selling methods. Companies that rely on advertising as a persuasive form of salesmanship are being accused of purveying false and deceptive information. Some are even being forced to recant publicly. The FTC, having found that the Continental Baking Company was falsely advertising its product ("Profile Bread will help you lose weight"), ordered the company to spend 25 percent of its advertising budget for six months on advertising that states "Profile Bread is *not* effective in weight reduction, contrary to possible interpretations of prior advertising."

Although most corporate executives would probably agree that the antiadvertising campaign of the new consumerists and the FTC has gone a bit too far, they would no doubt also agree that, by its very nature advertising is open to abuse and misinterpretation. Except for the better mail order houses, want ads, advertising of simple products (the claims for which consumers can and do check), and advertising directed to professional buyers, much advertising is misleading at best and fraudulent at worst.

Some advertising is false either intentionally or mistakenly. A major food manufacturer advertised that its quick snack food, which was to be heated in a toaster, contained at least as many nutrients as a breakfast of two eggs, two strips of bacon, and two slices of toast. The company subsequently signed an FTC consent order prohibiting it from making false nutritional claims for that or any other consumer food product.

Some advertising is deceptive and borders on the false. An example is the newspaper ad that offers a "like new" rebuilt vacuum cleaner for $19.95. The advertiser has no intention of delivering; his sole purpose is to get the customer into his store and trade him up. All too commonly, large department stores offer a heavy price reduction on a sale item. When the shopper shows up, she finds that only a few units were offered and have already been purchased—probably by employees.

In a drive against deceptive TV commercials, the FTC obtained an affidavit of discontinuance from the manufacturer of a laundry detergent. The commercial showed a man wearing a stained shirt pouring detergent into water rising around him as he stood, fully dressed, in some sort of tank. As the water receded, the shirt appeared to emerge free of its stain. The FTC said its investigation showed that the shirt had been cleaned not by the televised immersion, but by normal laundering. But as anyone who has attempted to buy an advertised $1999 car for $1999 will testify, deceptive advertising is subjective in definition. It is therefore difficult to curb.

Some advertising is zero advertising. "I'm handsome; I use Slurp after-shave; and you will like it too." At the time this book was written, no one had suggested curbing the free speech in that type of advertising. Although the statement contains no product information, it does identify the product. However, the classic example of the zero advertiser is the individual who, in a classified ad, said "This is your last chance to send in your $2." Although the postal authorities could not find any specific violation of law, they were able to apply enough pressure to end a lucrative "business."

To conclude these remarks, we feel safe in predicting that advertising will continue to take its lumps. Increased public anger and concern can be expected. Those feelings will be taken out not on advertising agencies, but on the corporations that market the products. Finally, it may be increasingly difficult to convince people to buy on the basis of a promotional claim.

Warranty

Remember the good old days of 1,000 miles or one month, whichever occurred first? A landmark case in warranty is that of the New Jersey housewife who was injured when her two-week-old car went out of control and struck a wall in 1960. Despite the fact that there was no evidence of manufacturer negligence, the jury was directed to return a verdict for the driver. Later, upon appeal, the New Jersey supreme court held that, "under modern marketing conditions, when a manufacturer puts a new automobile in the stream of trade and promotes its purchase by the public, an implied warranty that it is reasonably suitable for use as such accompanies it into the hands of the ultimate purchaser."[8] The case was the forerunner of others that have established additional rights for the consumer. Warranty can be express or implied. *Express warranty* is an unequivocal claim to the buyer that the product has certain characteristics and that certain other claims are made for it. The warranty is not limited to a card or other such document but may include labels, packaging, and express warranties in advertising. The manufacturer is liable for an express warranty even though the purchaser doesn't buy the product directly from it.

Implied warranty is a greater problem. You imply, by the act of selling it, that a product is fit for the ordinary purpose for which it was intended and is likely to be used. Moreover, if you provide a customer with a product that you claim meets his needs, that act is an implied warranty. Thus, if you put yourself in the hands of a used car salesman and he trades you up to a motor home, his statements are implied warranties of the fitness and utility of the motor home to fulfill the purposes for which you bought it.

Again, we can turn to the FTC for evidence of increasing warranty problems and the policing of advertising claims surrounding them. The FTC ordered a dozen automakers to substantiate more than 100 advertising and warranty claims made for their 1973 models. The automakers subsequently submitted documentation in support of those claims, but Bess Myerson, who was then New York City's consumer affairs commissioner, said it was found that 20 of the 54 replies were irrelevant, grossly inadequate, or contradictory to the claim.

Executives of one of the top three automakers are wondering what has to be done to appease the customer. Their man-in-Detroit program, organized to give the customer a speedy channel to the top, a vice-president, has backfired. One hundred seventy-five customers took them up on their offer to complain to the top, but they also complained to Ralph Nader about their treatment when they got there. All that happened, they claim, was that their complaints were bucked back down to the dealers where they started. Nader said the company's program was only a "sales gimmick."

ROLE OF GOVERNMENT AND COURTS

A Mexican-American group filed suit against the California Highway Commission charging that adequate environmental impact studies and map relocation plans had not been made in connection with construction of an Alameda County freeway. The court not only enjoined construction of the freeway but subsequently directed the California Highway Commission to pay the lawyers' fees for the case and the expenses of expert witnesses. Following that precedent-setting ruling, which was appealed, came a flood of similar cases. The implications are potentially revolutionary. Government agencies and businesses may have to not only defend themselves against suits but pay the plaintiff's legal costs as well.

The mighty investigative and regulatory forces of the U.S. government, operating through the agency of the FTC, engage in proceedings to stop the unfair and deceptive advertising of Wonder Bread and Hostess cakes. Why? Because the vitamin and mineral supplements of those products are emphasized in advertising and the manufacturer is therefore appealing to guilt feelings. When the American mother encounters an advertisement for Wonder Bread, she buys the product to assuage her guilt for not feeding her children more nutritious food. And since Wonder Bread and Hostess cakes are no more wholesome than many other baked products, the advertising is deceptive and unfair, says the FTC.

The time will probably come when liability will be imposed on the manufacturer whether or not there was a defect in the product. The forerunner of that can be seen in the current widespread movement to no-fault insurance.

The zealots of the new consumerism have turned to both the courts and government regulation in order to achieve what they think is equity. The fight has taken on the attributes of a mass movement. Courts have become more "lenient." City and state agencies by the hundreds strive to outdo each other in developing and enforcing new regulations. Politicians and reformers harass the agencies for more. The prospect is for still more of the same. It could lead to a regulatory monster.

Meanwhile, the corporation must live with the trend and add consumerism and the regulation it implies to the ingredients of the marketing mix and the cost of its product.

ENVIRONMENTALISM: A RELATED ISSUE

In addition to the right to free choice, the right to a safe product, and the right to be truthfully informed, the public has come to expect as its right that the corporation will not violate the principle of a safe, clean, and healthy environment by its operations. Except for popular wars, few issues in history have so caught the fancy of the American public as ecology, or environmentalism.

Nobel Prize winners, presidential advisers, and respected scientists predict a variety of disasters from another Great Flood to a failure in oxygen supply due to pollution of the seas.[9] The famous "doomsday report" of M.I.T., entitled *Limits to Growth,* has had enormous impact in many nations around the world. The report concluded that the world's exponential rates of population and industrial growth cannot be sustained for more than another 100 years, even if advances are achieved in birth control, food production, natural resource output, and pollution control.[10] There was considerable joy among zero-population-growth advocates when it was announced that in 1973 the United States had finally achieved a birth rate that would stabilize its population.

All those events are aberrations of the new concern with environmentalism. It is difficult to separate the truth from the fear appeal arguments. Despite the difficulty, we can be assured that the issue will continue to be of major concern to executives, government officials, and the public alike.

The confusion over ecology is demonstrated by the off-again, on-again approach to the manufacture of laundry detergents containing phosphates. By the early 1950s the housewife had adopted the phosphate detergent and relegated soap to a small share of the market. Lever Brothers, whose Rinso White had been the country's best-selling soap, tried to avoid the inevitable, but "Rinso White or Rinso Blue; soap or detergent, it's up to you!" failed to hold back the Tide. Rinso White was All washed up.

In the late sixties a dispute arose over the possibility that phosphates may be harming the environment. The crescendo of protest resulted in a variety of phosphate-free brands, but their heyday was brief. The Surgeon General cautioned that some phosphate-free detergents were hazardous to human health. At the time this book was written the situation was confusion on the part of housewives and counterclaims among the experts in limnology, the study of fresh water. In a satire on the phosphate problem, *Fortune* designed the acceptable detergent and named it UTOPIA. The package proclaimed that UTOPIA was "free of everything" and promised the following results: "Washes whitest . . . cleans lakes too . . . keeps your washing machine young . . . flameproofs clothing . . . harmless if swallowed . . . cheap."

The economics of ecology is also an unknown factor. Environmentalism is costly, but we have few yardsticks to measure performance of cost. The potential for serious company problems will hurt the smaller company the most. The majority of small company presidents list ecology as among their very top problem areas. Because those firms are less influential, have less money, and are less flexible, they stand to lose the most.

Whatever the cost of operating companies to obtain a clean environment, it will be great. According to a McGraw-Hill estimate, these are the required industrial investments in billions of dollars: electric utilities, 3.24; iron and steel, 2.63; petroleum, 2.12; paper, 1.84; and nonferrous metals, 1.62. In some of those industries, the environmental expenditures will comprise a significant fraction of the money spent on capital equipment. For example, in the paper industry, each $5 spent for new plant and equipment must be matched with $1 to control air and water pollution.

Can industry afford to do it? Can industry afford not to do it? Although the answer to neither question is entirely clear, it appears that the answer to the first one is affirmative, since ultimately the cost is passed on to the consumer. Take the steel industry. Although it fought for seven months to delay its publication, a Booz, Allen & Hamilton report for the President's Council on Environmental Quality concludes that the steel industry can afford to spend $2.4 to $3.5 billion by 1976 to control air and water pollution. That would necessitate a price increase of 1 percent per year, borrowing to the hilt, forgoing expansion, and holding the line on dividends in order to raise capital for the equipment. *But the steel industry can do it.*

Despite the debate on the varying aspects of ecology, one thing is clear to all. Industry, and the public, must clean up the environment. It is none too early for the individual firm to start planning and acting.

CORPORATE REACTION

Many diehards remain, but in general companies are taking action in response to the consumer movement. A selected few would include Whirlpool Corporation, which pioneered the toll-free number to answer complaints. Mobil Oil automatically suspends monthly finance charges until it resolves a complaint about a credit purchase. General Electric and Westinghouse have reorganized their service operations to make them more accountable to customer needs and have installed scorekeeping systems to make sure that complaints are acted upon quickly. Polaroid gives a dissatisfied customer a new camera even though the warranty period has expired. Automobile companies tell their customers, "We listen" and "Call me toll-free in Detroit."

Other actions designed to close the gap between company and consumer include the commitment by Mobil Oil of major advertising dollars to its long-term highway safety program "We want you to live," the publication by First National City Bank of *Consumer Views* and annual reports in three languages, the Quaker Oats proposal for a comprehensive program of advertising self-regulation that led to the establishment of the National Advertising Review Board, and the American Airlines fight for youth fares and its catering to the special needs of Spanish-speaking passengers on the San Juan run. Further, Sears, Roebuck and Co. changed its finance charges on revolving credit from the previous-balance to the average-daily-balance method. Giant Food Inc. became a pacesetter in consumerism by open dating, unit pricing, and nutritional labeling. Coca-Cola established a new position, director of consumer affairs, and filled it with a woman. Avon Products became the first cosmetics manufacturer to disclose its ingredients.

Not all companies have been so positive in their actions, at least according to the consumerists. An electric utility—the only one to do so—absolutely refused to give information to the Council on Economic Priorities and also was cited by the EPA administrator as costing the government between $1 and $2 million to get it to comply with pollution abatement. A manufacturer and automotive supplier closed a plant and moved to Mexico with no explanation or attempt to relocate workers. It constantly carps at wage laws and pollution regulations and encourages stockholders and employees to go to the polls and vote against those who are "dictating social change." A steel company has consisttently blocked efforts on pollution control and is now facing criminal action for discharging industrial waste into harbors and rivers. A national manufacturer and land developer has been ordered by a court to stop "false and misleading" sales practices in twenty areas in one state. A liquor distributor takes umbrage at an insurance company's advertisements that campaign against drunken driving. A major oil company that has had 37 spills in less than five years is known for the large sums of money it spends to defeat proconsumer legislation. A number of children have cut lips from licking the rip-off top of a canned instant pudding. The food manufacturer says, "They should learn better."

In one survey conducted by *Business and Society Review,* an attempt was made to rank a number of companies according to their consumer practices. Two hundred and fifteen individuals and groups engaged in monitoring consumer practices were asked to "compare corporations (36 on enclosed list) according to their social responsiveness and accountability to the public interest." The forty-nine who responded ranked as highest in their industries, Sears, Roebuck and Co., Safeway Stores, Inc., Johnson & Johnson, General Mills, and S. C. Johnson & Sons. There appears to be a significant degree of correlation between consumer accountability and financial performance. Perhaps the better-performing companies can afford to cater to consumerism.

HAS CONSUMERISM GONE TOO FAR?

If Ralph Nader is the high priest of consumerism, Milton Friedman is the rugged spokesman for the opposition. The well-known right-wing economist recently suggested: "If it's cheaper for the corporation to put the effluent in the water and pay the tax than it is not to pollute or to clean up the river, then that is what should be done."[11]

We can only speculate about the extent to which the anticonsumerist view prevails in executive washrooms, but there is evidence of a growing questioning of the movement. It seems that in some cases the argument has come face to face with the inescapable economic law of diminishing returns. If a soft drink manufacturer spends $\$x$ to insure that the chance of a fly being in one of its bottles is one in 5 million, can it afford to spend $\$2x$ to improve the chances to one in 10 million? At what point will the consumer, the public, and the government be unwilling to pay the extra price for the small gains involved? The anticonsumerists also argue that:

1. There's no free lunch. The cure for environmental damage can be as bad as the disease. The additional electrical energy and other requirements for the clean-up also cause pollution.
2. The consumer doesn't always act in a rational and responsible manner.
3. Expenditures on pollution are lost in the sense that there is no multiplier effect. Expenditures for pollution control equipment provide only one job for every hundred that would be provided by an equivalent expenditure for production facilities.
4. We are rushing too fast into ecology control. Witness the pollution controls on new automobiles.
5. The cost of consumerism (product liability, warranty, improved engineering) will raise the price beyond what the public will pay. It will hurt our foreign trade.
6. The growing "reforms" demanded of business and the fear of liability and government regulation inhibit innovation, change, and technological advances.

THE BRIGHT SIDE OF CONSUMERISM

From the corporation point of view the argument for consumerism lies in the long-run effects. There is little doubt that many companies will incur short-run costs that will not be recaptured by compensating profits. In that sense they will be losers. But the company that has an executive who can think in terms of long-run objectives rather than short-run payoffs can profit.

Aside from the arguments that (1) consumerism is enduring and there is no choice but to get with it and (2) what's good for consumerism is good for business, there is the overriding possibility that consumerism can open new avenues for profitability. For the innovative company, the negatives can be turned into positives, the problems into opportunities. That attitude is summarized by Peter F. Drucker: "Consumerism actually should be, must be, and I hope will be, the opportunity of marketing. This is what we in marketing have been waiting for."[12]

Consider the potential payoffs from two strategy alternatives, namely, building a competitive edge from a consumer orientation and finding new opportunities in product-service development. The thrust of corporate strategy should be devoted to building a unified sense of direction around product-service differentiation. It is necessary to establish a corporate identity, niche, image, personality, or strategy that takes maximum advantage of market opportunity and optimizes company resources in the process. The innovative company can embrace consumerism as a fundamental part of its strategy. The adoption of a companywide consumer orientation can open up new opportunities or strengthen a sagging image. Sears, Roebuck and Co. provides an excellent illustration. The world's biggest and most consistently profitable retailer has made consumer satisfaction *the* basic ingredient of strategy.

There will be profit and growth opportunities in new products and services. As the public becomes more sophisticated, more socially conscious, and less subject to seduction by advertising, it is demanding and buying different products. It wants products that are salutary, safe, ecologically oriented, and relatively reliable in operation. Nonpolluting gasolines, phosphate-free detergents, biodegradable packaging, appealing and nutritious foods, and noninflammable materials are among the possibilities.

In summary, the consumer movement has potential opportunities for the company that attempts to implement the new marketing concept: What's good for consumers is good for business.

SUMMARY: HOW TO LIVE WITH CONSUMERISM

The new Consumerism has far-reaching implications. The movement can have positive (profitable) or negative (increased cost) effects. We summarize our ten recommendations for coping with it and opening up new opportunities.

Don't fight it. Consumerism is here. It's an enduring characteristic of the business scene. The consumer has three legitimate rights: to be informed, to be protected against questionable products and marketing practices, and to have products and practices that increase the quality of life. Admit the legitimacy of those rights and cater to them.

Assimilate it into corporate strategy. Make consumer orientation a basic part of the company image and of managerial philosophy. Use it to differentiate your product or service, and you will have a competitive edge. It pays off.

Adopt the new marketing concept. Marketing has evolved from the sales concept, to the marketing concept, and now to the new marketing concept that incorporates long-run consumer welfare as an ingredient.

Organize for consumerism. Put somebody in charge—a committee, a vice-president, a new department. Don't relegate consumerism to a powerless staff officer or to public relations. Make it a way of corporate life.

Communicate with the customer. Cut red tape, appoint an ombudsman, install a toll-free line, or take whatever action is necessary to provide an authoritative source of satisfaction for the customer who has a complaint. Do something to reduce the impersonal, bureaucratic, don't-care image.

Check your advertising and selling. If it's false or misleading, change it. If it's palliative or offensive, review it. Does it inform the customer? Does the product perform as advertised? Is your sales force engaged in hard sell to the extent of misrepresentation? Are you selling to a market segment that can't afford your product or benefit from it?

Review product safety. Is safety built in to a reasonable standard of design? Make sure the purchaser and seller are notified of potential hazards and operating instructions. Consider organizing separately for safety by getting safety, design, and quality control out of the production department.

Review "oppressive" liability potentials. Take a look at recent legislation, court decisions, and industry practices. Such a review might indicate product redesign, labeling changes, or different packaging or advertising.

Clean up the environment. If your operations or your products are polluting the air, water, or atmosphere, do something about it. Not only is that the socially responsible thing to do but failure to do so can hurt your image and your profits.

Investigate new product opportunities. For the fast-thinking company there are profit and growth opportunities in new products and services that cater to the needs of consumerism and environmentalism.

3

Social Responsibility or Corporate Chauvinism?

Most of the talk [about corporate social responsibility] has been utter hogwash. . . . The question is, do corporate executives, provided they stay within the law, have responsibilities in their business activities other than to make as much money for their stockholders as possible? And my answer to that is, no, they do not.

MILTON FRIEDMAN[1]

A large corporation not only may engage in social responsibility, it had damn well better try to do so.

PAUL SAMUELSON[2]

How can two of the twentieth century's most respected economists have such different attitudes toward an issue of such immense importance? The answer, of course, is that corporate social responsibility, like many other public issues, is viewed in widely diverse ways and generates some rather strong opinions.

Few businessmen enjoy a better reputation than Irwin Miller, chairman of Cummins Engine, and so his comment on Milton Friedman's antiresponsibility statement is worth attention: "I find highly offensive the argument of a well-known economist that the business of business is to do business. You can call it a rule of thumb that where corporations do more than the law requires you have a good society."[3] His statement fairly well reflects the pro-social-responsibility views held by—or at least voiced by—an increasing number of chief executives and other businessmen. The anti-social-responsibility party is somewhat less vocal and outspoken. The maxims and clichés of bygone days are no longer popular, at least for general public consumption.

"Frustration" is the best word to describe the feeling of many executives who are faced with taking specific action in response to the social responsibility syndrome. That frustration—and apprehension—is reflected in the testimony of Donald Kendall, chairman of Pepsico Inc., before the Federal Trade Commission: "The distrust [of advertising and free enterprise] is taught . . . taught often and all too well by men whose intentions for our country are either curious or unknown to me. . . . I think the ultimate target is free enterprise itself."[4] A lot of people are wondering what *is* going on.

Whatever your individual views, you will no doubt agree that a consensus regarding social responsibility is developing. But consensus alone holds no answers for these questions: What is social responsibility? Why do I, as a businessman, have to be concerned about it? What are the forces behind it? What should I do, or not do, about it?

We hope to provide answers to most of those questions in this chapter.

WHAT IS SOCIAL RESPONSIBILITY?

An investigation of the nature of social responsibility might begin by finding what social responsibility *is not.* In a May 1972 address to the annual meeting of stockholders in Memphis, Tennessee, Harold Geneen, chairman and president of ITT, gave the following definition of social responsibility:[5]

> But let me suggest that the overriding and most important social responsibility of our Company is to provide *independence* to the employees who make up our group, and to provide it through soundly conceived, productive and economically secure jobs.
>
> They [the employees] have a place to stand and a place to sit, and a roof over their heads—which might not be there if it were not for ITT. *I submit that this is our first and most important social responsibility.* [Italics are Mr. Geneen's.]

Now, Mr. Geneen is our nominee as one of the top managers of the decade, and ITT as one of the best-managed firms in the world, but we submit that his opinion about social responsibility is not sound. Why? Simply because nobody is going to buy it—not the stockholders, not the general public, and certainly not the employees. The days of the benevolent employer are gone.

What *is* your social responsibility if it is not providing jobs for your employees? Since the "public" is a somewhat indefinable group that speaks with no single voice, it is not easy to say specifically what it expects from corporate behavior.

T. Vincent Learson, former IBM chairman, is a man who states his views succinctly. In his opinion the U.S. public currently expects major corporate enterprises to "shape up or to ship out" on four fronts: the employment and training front, the environmental front, the consumer front, and the community well-being front. If we start with Mr. Learson's comments and add our own, we can summarize current thinking on corporate responsibility under six headings:

Minority employment. Business is expected to provide jobs for the various minority groups who have traditionally been discriminated against by hiring practices. Moreover, those persons are expected to have equal opportunity to be promoted on their merits. Blacks, women, the physically handicapped, the long-time unemployed, and ex-convicts are among those minority groups.

EXAMPLE: Jeno Paulucci, a maker of frozen pizza and other snacks, was named 1972 employer of the year for his performance in hiring handicapped workers. Over half of his 1,600 employees are classified as handicapped or disadvantaged.

Training and education. Corporate responsibility now requires that the company expand its employment and personnel practices to include the training of individuals who are otherwise unemployable.

EXAMPLE: General Motors, the nation's largest industrial corporation, has responded with impressive social actions in all the identifiable areas. As one example, the company has opened a center in Philadelphia to train 1,000 auto mechanics per year.

Consumerism. The growing concept of consumer rights now includes the right to be heard, the right to have reliable information upon which to base product choices, and the right to have a safe, reliable, product that performs as warranted. Both the manufacturer and the seller have a responsibility to fulfill these rights.

EXAMPLE: When Levi Strauss & Co. went public in 1971, its prospectus stated that "social responsibility is a matter of strong concern on the part of management." Among the many actions the company has taken to implement that concern is the creation of a product integrity department headed by a member of the board of directors. The department reports to the president, bypassing production and marketing.

Environment. The public is expecting more and more action on the part of business to protect our environment—air, water, and landscape. The expectation is particularly specific as it relates to pollution resulting from company operations.

EXAMPLE: RCA has instituted a companywide drive to organize all employees for environment improvement. More than 15,000 employees at 27 plants in 7 states have been recruited for antipollution projects. One ecology optimist is Arjay Miller, former Ford head and now Dean of Stanford's Graduate School of Business. "Technology will solve our environmental problems. . . . If analysts had projected London's transportation system at the turn of the century, the streets would now be eight feet deep in horse manure."[6] Ironically, an article entitled, "Heaping It On: Plastic Refuse Begins to Mount in the U.S.; The Efforts to Recycle It Prove Difficult," appeared about the same time.[7]

Community involvement. The corporation is expected to be a good citizen of the communities in which it operates. That involvement can include improvement of schools, housing, cultural and recreational facilities, health facilities, and government machinery.

EXAMPLE: Ralston Purina has been a leader in the rebuilding of St. Louis; $2 million of company funds went into the development of La Salle Park, a "new town in town" that borders Checkerboard Square. The company has also contributed resources and manpower to aid community projects. Charitable contributions of more than $1 million per year go to support institutions "affecting the greatest number of people." The company has set up an office of urban affairs to coordinate such programs.

Products. In addition to other consumer considerations, business has a responsibility to supply products and services that will satisfy new or expanding wants and contribute to a better life.

EXAMPLE: Giant Food Inc., only twentieth in size among retail food chains, has become the pacesetter in protection of the customer.

When meat prices soared, Giant stores blossomed with posters advising their shoppers to "buy something else." Other programs, including one of refusal to stock products that are unsafe or are unfairly packaged, have paid off handsomely in profitability.

Commitment. The public expects something more than lip service and token responsiveness to social demands. It wants social responsibility incorporated into company strategy and assigned to an organization that can exercise it.

EXAMPLE: Quaker Oats does not relegate social responsibility to a powerless staff officer, but instead assigns it top management attention. The company is one of the few to have a comprehensive social action progress plan that is updated annually and financed with a company budget.

Although the preceding list does not include all aspects of social responsibility, the businessman who is meeting all or most of the expectations can be comfortably assured that he is socially responsible.

THE RATIONALE

The classic comment, "The public be damned," has been attributed to Cornelius Vanderbilt. Few tycoons would have the courage to voice that sentiment today.

For a long time businessmen have operated on the assumption that market forces were the major factors in shaping business decisions. The question has been, "What will be the impact of my decision on the competition, the consumer, and the supplier?" Today, it is clear that business decisions are being affected increasingly by nonmarket forces as well. The company is shaped by consumers who react to the quality, price, and packaging of its products, by its employees, by other companies with whom it competes, and by government regulations. As never before in history, the collective standards of society are shaping both the character and the operations, in market and nonmarket environments, of individual firms.

In short, the rationale for accepting social responsibility as a fundamental determinant of business behavior and decision making is that the action makes good sense. It is essential to corporate longevity and profitability. Those are the economic reasons. The noneconomic reasons are the same as those for individual responsibility. After all, the corporation is nothing more than a collection of individuals. In this connection we can let several corporate chief executives speak for themselves. Their comments were made to *Fortune*.[8]

"One of the greatest responsibilities of the corporate executive is to ensure the climate that makes it possible to grow in the future, and that means the whole environment."

"Society is the platform from which we work. We have got to be engaged in social matters."

"In the fabric of society, unless you make a contribution to enhance human values, your institution is in danger."

"I got over a long time ago the feeling that business exists only to make a profit."

THE CAUSE: CHANGING SOCIAL BEHAVIOR

Exhortations to the businessman to become socially responsible are heard from all sides. The voices include federal agencies, public critics such as Ralph Nader, and industry leaders such as Henry Ford and David Rockefeller. The Committee for Economic Development (CED), which is composed of 200 leading businessmen and educators, issued a policy statement entitled "Social Responsibilities of Business Corporations." The Commitee declared that the self-interest of business requires that firms play a part in meeting the problems of society. A consensus has developed. What has caused it? Here we will attempt to summarize four contributing factors.

The Antiestablishment Syndrome

The corporation position is similar in some respects to that of the university, the public education system, the church, war, the city, and, in fact, the many social institutions that affect the quality of our lives. We seem to be living in an age of negativism. Almost all major issues are approached with such negative phrases as anti-Pentagon, antiestablishment, antipollution, antibusiness, and antilabor. Even government agencies seem obsessed with saying no; the bureaucracies find it much easier to give reasons for not doing something than to get something done. What happened to the can-do spirit?

We doubt that negativism has been the fault of business. Although business has had some recent subtractions from its public esteem—as for example, by the Wall Street slide, Lockheed, IOS, Yale Express, and the ITT incident—the real reason for much of the hostility toward it is that it has become something of a scapegoat for the youth movement people, the consumer-ecology movement people, and a general public that is uneasy about the performance of traditional institutions.

Those developments have caused the image of the corporation and the businessman to be altered rather drastically. Formerly thought of as grown-up all-American boys, businessmen are now held in low esteem by a clear-cut majority of Americans. The situation is recognized by corporations themselves. An AMA survey found that about two of three companies feel they have serious corporate image problems. *Business Week* reports that the man in the street is disenchanted with business and convinced that corporate management cares only about its own pay and earnings per share. Moreover, the central reason for the disenchantment is the increasing dissatisfaction with institutions and leaders who don't deliver. In many cases business is only the convenient whipping boy.

Failure of the Great Society

In 1902 Samuel Gompers expressed the aspirations of labor in a classic formula: "Workers want more, and when we get that more we shall insist upon again more and more and even more."

During the Depression of the 1930s a popular political slogan was "a chicken in every pot." Today, although the sixties have passed into history, the Great Society's promises of more for everyone and equality for everyone have left the general public with plenty of unfulfilled expectations and material for recrimination. The traditional American ideal of self-sufficiency has been largely dispelled by assumptions that citizens have "rights" to public aid of many kinds. By and large, the expectations of the Great Society have not been fulfilled.

Those who want more will frequently go to great lengths to get it. A&P, with a profit margin consistently under 1 percent on sales, has had serious repercussions from its attempt to deal rationally with Operation Breadbasket, an economic arm of the Southern Christian Leadership Conference. Reverend Jesse L. Jackson, national chairman of Operation Breadbasket, has promised his organization "will cut the margin of profit at 600 stores" in order to achieve its goal of forcing the company to hire more blacks. General Electric is sued by women employees and the International Union of Electrical, Radio & Machine Workers (IUE) on the charge that the company shows sex bias by refusing disability pay in maternity cases. "After all," they reason, "if a man hurt his finger, he'd get paid weekly disability benefits." Class action suits by a variety of other special interest groups have become commonplace.

The point here is that established institutions, including government, have not delivered on the better life and the "more, more, more" that has been promised. On the other hand, there is mounting evidence that social reformers, sometimes unkindly and erroneously called do-gooders and bleeding hearts, are beating a retreat from some of their pet theories. During a decade of unparalleled prosperity and unprecedented efforts to solve welfare problems, welfare enrollments tripled. As poverty declined, crime—which, according to reformers, is a result of poverty—increased. Public housing has been nothing short of a disaster. Manpower training hasn't made a dent in unemployment, and the various actions intended to advance school integration have done little to increase tolerance but have quite possibly reduced academic performance. Yet demands for more public largesse continue and criticisms of business increase. What *is* going on?

Other Reformers

John Kenneth Galbraith has had many professional triumphs and is an economist not to be dismissed lightly. It was his program for wage and price controls that the Nixon administration faithfully adopted. He explains the social responsibility belief in terms of the traditional and emerging views of the public corporation. The traditional American view is that the corporation has the right to be free from interference, a right that is protected by the corollary right of privacy. Honesty is maintained by the competitive forces of the marketplace. Competition will, in the long run, do what's best for everyone.

The view emerging in the 1970s is at odds with the traditional view. It is that, at some stage in growth and power, the private corporation becomes a public institution. The argument runs that such firms as Lockheed, Penn Central, and AT&T are so bound up with the government that the line between private and public is indistinguishable. Consider the impact of General Motors, with annual sales that are greater than the GNP of Norway and Greece combined. According to a group at Yale law school, it achieved its present size and prominence by the practice of contrived obsolescence introduced by Alfred P. Sloan. The Yale reformers say that substantial annual model changes constitute unfair competition and promote monopolistic imperfection of the marketplace; they want the Justice Department to take steps to prevent them. Whether or not their allegation is reasonable, GM effectively sets automobile prices throughout the nation, negotiates wage contracts that indirectly affect the entire national workforce, establishes safety features and emission standards that have enormous impact on safety and ecology, and makes decisions on what it will make and where, from what, and with whom that have national and international implications greater than those of many government decisions. If you buy that notion of the evolutionary or emerging corporation, you will see the tendency of the corporation to become assimilated with and regulated by the state and influenced by the public. Galbraith argues that the tendency is irreversible. The message is that companies must learn to live with public investment.

There is no shortage of people and organizations willing to keep score on corporate actions. The Council on Economic Priorities, the Project on Corporate Responsibility, the Church Project on United States Investments in Southern Africa, the Professionals for Responsible Corporate Management, the American Baptist Board of Education & Publications, the Council for Corporate Review, and an untold number of other government and quasi-government agencies are willing to keep the company honest. Two of their favorite tactical devices are the stockholders' vote and the stock purchase, or nonpurchase.

Measured by their quantitative impact on stockholder voting, the reformers' influence is not large. In only a few cases have reform proposals amassed even the 3 percent vote required to guarantee proxy statement inclusion. But that statistical measure is misleading and underrates the influence. The small voting voice with which the reformers speak is coming through loud and clear and is getting widespread attention, and in some cases it produces no little embarrassment for corporate management. "We are a flea on the elephant's back at this point," remarked the director of the Corporate Information Center of the National Council of Churches of Christ.[9] "Defeat was expected. But we keep nibbling away. It raises the consciousness eventually. The dialog has started. The issues are now joined." Another group promises, "Our next move is into the board room." Paul Samuelson warns,[10] "You are naive if you look only at the number of proxy votes the Nader movement is able to mobilize against management. The leverage of such movements is not to be found inside the corporate ballot box, but in the minds of men."

A growing number of highly respected organizations are influencing corporate social responsibility by the way in which they invest their funds. First National City Bank says that "a company's sensitivity to its corporate responsibility is now an integral part of the bank's investment criteria." The bank's investment portfolio is not small; its Investment Management Group manages in excess of $14 billion and is keenly interested "in how companies are responding to environmental issues, to the consumer movement, and to pressure for social reform."[11] In addition to banks, an increasing number of other portfolio managers invest only in "socially approved" stocks. Some mutual funds are adopting that policy, and others are being formed for the specific purpose. In other cases, trusts, foundations, churches, and universities have instructed their fund managers to seek out opportunities among socially responsible firms.

While many of these actions seem to be relatively unimportant when taken individually or collectively, the leverage possibility is fantastic. Imagine your chagrin and potential public embarrassment if your stock were delisted by a reputable investor or if you were required to solicit proxy voting power on a contested social issue.

A growing number of reporters and reform organizations are attempting to catalog, rank, or score companies on their involvement in social issues. For $50 you can purchase from Human Resources Network, Inc. (a nonprofit organization) a three-volume set of *Profiles of Involvement,* which lists over 500 action projects of almost 200 of the nation's largest corporations. In each issue of *Business and Society Review,* a recent successful entry published in Boston, there is contained a "Company Performance Roundup" that attempts to summarize notable company achievements and failures in areas of public concern.

The Boston periodical, in its inaugural issue in the spring of 1972, reports the results of an interesting survey. Questionnaires were sent to 800 readers who consisted primarily, but not exclusively, of corporate staffers working in the urban and public affairs areas. Respondents were asked to rate 45 companies on their social programs. Results were, of course, subject to the shortcomings and methodology of any opinion survey, but they do provide us with a measure of the thinking of social-performance-conscious employees from a good cross section of big com-

Table 3-1. A study of ratings of companies on their social programs.

BEST AVERAGES*		FINANCIAL INDEX†	WORST AVERAGES		FINANCIAL INDEX
Chase Manhattan	4.3	20 of 26	Kroger	2.0	20 of 38
First Pennsylvania	4.2	2 of 26	LTV	1.9	44 of 44
IBM	4.0	2 of 10	Texaco	1.8	6 of 28
GE	3.9	2 of 18	A&P	1.8	32 of 38
Sears	3.8	16 of 46	Swift	1.7	34 of 37

* The highest possible average is 5.0; the lowest possible average is 1. Xerox and Levi Strauss were not among the 45 listed companies, but, the write-in vote placed them at a higher average than any of the companies listed here.

A subsequent survey of business school students ranked firms with the best averages as Xerox, First Pennsylvania (bank holding company), IBM, Cummins Engine, and Prudential Insurance. Those with the worst averages were Commonwealth Edison (Chicago), LTV, U.S. Steel, Standard Oil Co. of California, and Con Edison (N.Y.).

† The financial index relates the firm's five-year (1968-1973) return on equity to that of other firms in the same industry. Hence, Sears ranks sixteenth from the top of 46 firms in retailing.

Source: *Forbes* "25th Annual Report on American Industry," January 1, 1973.

panies in the nation. Results are shown in Table 3-1.[12] We have added, as a matter of interest, our own measure of the financial performance of the companies. As you can see, there is a significant correlation between the appraisals of social consciousness and those of financial performance.

ANOTHER CAUSE: MISCONCEPTION OF BUSINESS

How much of the swift decline in public esteem of business is due to ignorance and misconception on the part of the public? The answer is quite a lot! Max Ways of *Fortune* thinks that business must do a better job of explaining itself because "what little the American public knows about business is some fifty to seventy-five years out of date. The public image of the big businessman is about where Theodore Dreiser, Upton Sinclair, and the cartoonists of fifty years ago left him."[13]

Survey after survey has shown that the general public has long held wildly erroneous notions of business operations. Here are some of the fictions, along with the facts:

Fiction	*Fact*
After-tax profit as a proportion of total sales is around 28 percent. Company stockholders believe the average is 23 percent. The average man considers it fair to make 10 percent.	The 28 percent is more than five times the profit levels of recent years.
Distribution in U.S. corporations is about 40 percent to employees and 60 percent to net profit. One-third of the people believe the most practical way for workers to improve their standard of living is to get more out of company profits rather than increase productivity.	Department of Commerce figures report the actual two-way split for all companies in their U.S. operations is about 90 percent to employees and 10 percent to net profit.
Employee pay and benefits can be increased about 9 to 10 percent per year without increasing production costs enough to cause a price increase.	Federal guidelines say that pay-benefits increases of more than 3.2 percent will be inflationary and push up production costs and selling prices.

Those are only a few of the gross misconceptions that lead the general public to view the businessman as a money-grabbing, insensitive, oppressive, inhuman ogre with an up-the-public attitude. Yet business managers have done little to correct this view. They have depended on public relations to paper over mistakes and change public opinion. They have too often refused to talk about problems openly and frankly. They have engaged in "creative bookkeeping" and reported one thing to the public and another to the SEC or to Internal Revenue. Advertising has produced claims that even children find unbelievable.

The reluctance of business to talk and act in a straightforward way has also widened the credibility gap with youth, employees, and the general public. In short, the American corporation needs to do a better job of explaining itself. Part of the answer lies in putting its economic cards on the table, face up.

SOCIAL RESPONSIBILITY IS HERE TO STAY

Predicting the shape of things to come in the social or economic sector is a chancy occupation. However, evidence is substantial that the social responsibility movement will continue and increase in power. Opinion Research Corporation, of Princeton, New Jersey, reports that (1) the pressure to limit corporate profits will continue, (2) costs and prices will move upward as a result of the environmentalist movement, (3) consumerism will force companies to deliver what the public expects, and (4) further government intervention is certain unless business dispels public mistrust.

Economist John K. Galbraith has stated that a new social regulator is born: "countervailing power." Consumerists, environmentalists, and other aggrieved groups are emerging in response to, and will ultimately neutralize, the market power that has been acquired by large firms.

Economist Paul Samuelson says that the prerogatives of the businessman are shrinking:[14] "He will discover that hundreds of traditional ways of making business decisions will simply no longer be available to him. Society will expand business's responsibilities and take an increasing part in deciding how they are to be met."

George Lodge, a professor at the Harvard Business School (the man who ran against Ted Kennedy for the Senate in 1962) is gaining increasing acceptance for his notion that the basic Lockean ideology of America—the rights of individualism, individual property rights, unhindered competition, and the limited role of the state—are shifting now to the more recent concept of rights—the rights to survival, income, and health. In other words, the enjoyment of your property rights is subject to the needs of the people who work for you and the entire community. Lodge has had a mixed response, however. While both he and Richard C. Gerstenberg were attending a Conference Board meeting, he asked Gerstenberg whether GM is property and, if so, who owns it. The GM chairman replied: "You are one of those troublemakers, like one of those Nader types."

Additional evidence comes from all sides. The U.S. Chamber of Commerce concludes, "Consumerism is on the march as never before. . . . You can't afford the luxury of standing pat." Moreover, one has only to keep score on government legislation and the growing number of agencies set up to prescribe and police social responsibility. All evidence points to the conclusion that social responsibility is here to stay.

HOW NOT TO REACT TO SOCIAL PRESSURE

Daniel Yankelovich, a widely respected attitude researcher in business, says that, in trying to meet the problems of social pressure, businessmen made three errors:[15]

First, they regarded the demands of the public sector as a moral issue of what business ought to do as a good citizen rather than as a practical issue of what it had to do in order to survive and prosper. Second, with some notable exceptions, they regarded the social responsibilities of business as of marginal importance in comparison with day-to-day operations. Finally, they decided how much they should do to fulfill their social responsibilities was largely optional.

If those errors fairly represent the attitudes of businessmen, then the specific actions taken to overcome the problem of social pressure are likely to be in error as well. Some of the actions and attitudes that *should not* be taken and held are the following:

Don't Be Self-righteous

The reaction of some steel executives to the Clean Air Act of 1970 and a string of stiff state laws has been described as paranoid. Although some companies have responded positively, *The Wall Street Journal* reports that "others have seemed to react much the way that southern school boards responded to the Supreme Court's desegregation decisions in the 1960's."

In contrast, while successfully battling air pollution problems at three of its own plants, Union Carbide has become a major manufacturer in the environmental control industry. Things were not always that way. Once featured on the cover of a national magazine as "America's Most Polluted Company," Union Carbide shaped up considerably in the ensuing years. It got its black eye by having a self-righteous attitude and being unwilling to communicate with public and government agencies and respond effectively to demands for improvement plans. The attitude of the head of a government air pollution control agency was, "The regulations say they will do it or we'll have a piece of their hide. They know it."

Clichés of the past are not appropriate for the present. The chairman of Tenneco, Inc., whines, "I keep saying that a basic good that Tenneco performs is meeting its payroll . . . and we pay dividends to a quarter of a million shareholders whose investment makes all this possible." Harold Geneen, the incredible manager who runs ITT, responds to criticism, "I submit that this [provision of independence to the employees] is our first and most important social responsibility."

The performance of these two executives in meeting social responsibilities is certainly above average, but the point here is that indignation, clichés, and a return to protestations about the so-called rights of business are not going to get acceptance. Right or wrong, the public isn't too much interested in rights other than its own.

Don't Make Blanket Denials

Business should take the offensive to deny an untruth that is indeed an untruth. However, the credibility gap between government, business, and the public has become so great that flat denials of accusations have almost become an admission of some guilt. Ford Motor Company officials announce they are "surprised and shocked" by a wide-ranging lawsuit charging the company with making the air around its giant River Rouge plant filthy, smelly, and hazardous to health. ITT denied the Dita Beard and document-shredding events and later suffered a great deal of embarrassment and loss of public image. Presidential cabinet members denied allegations that were later proved substantially correct by publication of the Pentagon papers. The later dismissal of charges against Daniel Ellsberg and Anthony Russo, the defendants in the Pentagon Papers trial, has helped reduce White House credibility to its lowest point in history. Is there a message here for business?

The trouble with flat denials, assuming that they are not totally justified, is that they can boomerang. Nor is "business as usual" sufficient justification for what the public thinks are antisocial actions. Today's business is *un*usual.

Don't Use Muscle or Paper Over Mistakes with Public Relations

Rhetoric of the public relations kind is an inexhaustible resource; the chief executive can squander it freely and have no noticeable effect on profits. A great deal of it has nothing to do with real company objectives, and both the employees and the public know it. Although the corporate director of public relations still has a business role, it is probably a serious mistake to assign him the task of responding to social needs. People, including employees, are quick to sense what is actually important to management.

Companies have widely press-agented their good earnings and other accomplishments when things have gone right, but line executives should be willing to talk candidly about the bad as well as the good. Consider ITT's public relations fiasco, which may have long-range effects on the whole of U.S. business. Variously alleged to have schemed to block the election of President Allende of Chile, to have had insider stock tradings with company executives before the announcement of a consent decree by the Justice Department, and to have influenced the Republican National Convention, the company issued flat denials, shredded company documents, and pressured the press in efforts to cover what may have been entirely innocent affairs. *Business Week* reported that "even sophisticated businessmen and investors are talking of the damage done to the reputation of business in general, describing ITT's recent conduct as arrogant and conscienceless."[16] But the biggest boomerang of the decade was thrown by GM when it attempted to investigate Ralph Nader's personal life. (That event was later topped by the White House's ill-conceived attempt to investigate Daniel Ellsberg.)

Don't Use Secrecy

When companies withhold information about operations, the public expects the worst. Mobil Oil and IBM are among the companies that aroused the ire of church groups by their investments in South Africa. Actually, neither company had any apologies to make; indeed, both are pacesetters in their policies in this country. And both were let alone by the pressure groups after the right information was furnished, but not before they received some bad publicity that could have been avoided.

The right to secrecy of information has long been a jealously guarded prerogative of business. The government prescribes minimum disclosure regulations, and that is usually what the corporation discloses—the minimum. But from a practical standpoint, how much harm could fuller disclosure do?

Many companies withhold from their financial statements information that they routinely report to the SEC. Take, for example, the case of Form 10-K on which the SEC requires information about sales and earnings by product line. Ogden Corporation, which was having trouble on a Navy contract to build destroyer escorts, reported in its financial statement that the trouble "caused Ogden not to recognize any profit on the 20-ship contract" for 1971. However, on the 10-K report turned in, a $729,000 loss for the year was shown.

At least one of the big eight accounting firms, Touche Ross & Company, insists that its clients include 10-K information in their annual reports. That action probably reflects widespread dissatisfaction with current accounting practices and financial reporting procedures.

Plan Ahead

Fortune reports that a visitor to the Detroit office of the chief executive of an automobile company asked why no one had anticipated the problems associated with the redesign of the automobile around antipollution devices. After a few moments' reflection, the chief executive said, "Issues don't get dealt with until they become issues."[17] Is that an argument for planning?

A GE executive draws the analogy between the businessman and Harry Houdini wrapped in chains, handcuffed, nailed in a coffin, under 30 feet of water: he has only himself to blame; he did it to himself in the process of trying to make a living; he is supremely confident he can get out of the mess by himself. Despite his confidence, a certain amount of suspense is generated among onlookers. Finally, no one is supposed to offer help until it is too late.[18]

Planning social action involvement is advisable for the same reasons that any other type of planning is advisable: it offsets uncertainty, it focuses on company objectives, it's more efficient, and it avoids crisis management.

THE SOCIAL AUDIT

If normal financial accounting practices cause debate, what will the social audit cause when it becomes widespread? The idea of a social audit to provide a yardstick for corporate social actions has captured the imagination of reformers, consultants, and businessmen alike. The American Institute of Certified Public Accountants has appointed an eight-man committee to develop "standards and techniques for measuring, recording, reporting, and auditing social performance." A number of management consultants such as Arthur D. Little are helping clients develop a technique of auditing.

Up to now there has been little reason for corporate executives to record and report such activities, let alone provide measures for all to compare. Because social actions have no visible effect on the bottom line and because they provide no basis for promotion, pay, or other internal evaluation, there has been little reason to have a system.

Do You Need a Social Audit?

If you don't intend to engage in social actions in any organized way or establish any social objectives, then you don't need a social audit. But if you plan to do either of those things, you should make an audit for the following reasons. Further information is given in a book by Dan H. Fenn, Jr. and Raymond Bauer.[19]

1. It is a way to appease outside critics. If you have a system of measurement, it will answer many of the questions that are being asked. The number one question is usually, "Is the company really trying?"
2. The use of some form of social audit is almost certain to grow, particularly in the large firms. The audit can be helpful for internal measurement, for use in annual reports, and for a variety of other purposes.
3. If you are going to engage in them, your social activities, like all company operations, will need some system of internal planning and control.
4. There is some evidence that the few companies that have adopted the social audit have corporate attributes of lively, imaginative, and courageous leadership.

Is It Feasible?

The social audit has been called "an attempt to measure the immeasurable," and therein lies the problem. No reliable measures have been developed for just what responsibilities the company is expected to assume, for just how much should be done in any one field, and on what issues the company should take a stand. Despite those difficulties, a growing number of companies large and not so large are making the attempt. Among them are Chase Manhattan, IBM, Kimberly-Clark, Exxon, Coca-Cola, BankAmerica Service Corporation, AT&T, and Arthur D. Little.

At the time this book was written, however, no specific balance sheet, accounting system, or guidelines had been widely adopted. Each company must develop its own system that is dependent upon its own social objectives. Two or three systems in the early stages of development are variations of the Stanford Study, a method used by The Commitee for Corporate Responsibility at the Stanford Business School. The analysis is based on three dimensions. The first is a breakdown of firms within an industry or other convenient division. The second is the identification of areas of concern for the industry (for example, consumerism, personnel practices, or environment). The third is a composite rating of the action of the individual firm in areas of concern as compared with that of other firms in the industry. Naturally, the method has its shortcomings, the foremost of which is the selection of areas of concern. Moreover, the ratings are subject to bias and the quantification itself is subjective. However, it is a start.

Fenn and Bauer recommend a four-step approach:[20] (1) Inventory the social activities that have an impact on the company. (2) Examine and explain the circumstances that led up to those activities. (3) Evaluate the activities and programs that are most relevant. (4) Assess the ways in which the activities mesh with the objectives of the firm and of society. Shulman and Gale would take the approach of identifying the constituencies of the organization, which might be employees, consumers, suppliers, communities, society in general, and competitors, and then analyzing all business decisions to determine the way in which they affect those groups.[21]

The major drawback in any scheme of social accounting is the difficulty of quantifying social information. The best approach seems to be the use of some scale that compares like firms within an industry.

SUMMARY: A GUIDE FOR SOCIAL ACTION

To the company executive who wants to deal successfully with corporate social responsibility, we offer ten suggestions:

Recognize that social responsibility is real. The demand for corporate action in the new business climate is not a passing fad; it is here to stay. New forces, other than conventional market forces, are having an impact on corporate operations. Don't react to criticism with self-righteous indignation.

Set goals and objectives. Companies can operate within a wide range of philosophies. Henry Ford II told stockholders, "I believe that the social responsibility of the corporation today is fundamentally the same as it has always been: to earn profits for shareholders by serving consumer wants with maximum efficiency. This is not the whole of the matter, but it is the heart of the matter."[22] Other executives see things differently. Bank of America says, "The corporation, by virtue of its own enlightened self-interest, the conscience of its officers, and expectations of the public, has a role to play in solving contemporary ills."[23]

Whatever your goals in society, you should make them clear. No company can do everything, and there is always the danger of dissipating your effort. Pick and choose among the demands being made on you or set a new course of action of your own. Don't wait for the boom to fall.

Get commitment and involvement. As in any program or change, if you don't get the commitment of the top man, forget it! One or two speeches isn't enough. But if the word gets out that the top man is serious, then many more people will get serious. Involvement of others, from the board to the employees, is required. Social action is something that few people get excited about, because it interferes with normal operations. Moreover, people don't normally get rewarded or measured by their participation. That's why one company president bases his pay raises and bonuses on achievements in specific social programs such as hiring and training minority groups.

Organize. Don't overstructure your social responsiblity effort to the extent of frustrating it, but do make organizational provision for it. And that doesn't mean assigning it to the director of public relations or a powerless staff officer in an isolated cubicle. Also, don't make it a maverick assignment so that responsible persons shy away from it. The man responsible should be a corporate executive close to the chief executive. As Nicholas Katzenbach suggested, responsibility has to begin with the "greening of the board room."

Set policies. Your policies reflect the fact that you mean business, and both employees and the public can sense when you don't mean business. Policies are concerned with product, operations, finance, marketing, and personnel.

Find out what the public wants. Many corporate managers will admit that they are insulated from their customers and the public; communications is largely through paperwork and impersonal procedures. A growing number of companies are breaking down the walls through special studies, opinion surveys, and face-to-face talking. There is need of a new rapport between business and its public. A department store in Philadelphia has set up a series of consumer advisory boards drawn from the ranks of ordinary shoppers. A Colorado meat processor and distributor has appointed a committee for the 1970s to bring in outside views on his company's performance in the area of social responsibility.

Help dispel the misconceptions of business. Use financial statements, company media, and other available communications to tell the story. The average citizen has an incredibly erroneous conception of business—its profits, its distribution of wealth, and how its managers think. Internally that is also true of employees.

Don't paper over mistakes with public relations. Guard against PR or advertising that could be misinterpreted. Don't expect the media to print your story as you write it. Remember that public relations as an end in itself is dangerous—it can boomerang.

Use a form of social audit. Although yardsticks are inaccurate and comparisons are difficult, some measure of your performance is necessary. If you are going to engage in programs of social action, internal planning and control are as necessary as in other programs. Despite its probable lack of precision, develop your own approach to auditing the company's social responsibility.

Recognize that stockholders won't like some things that might have to be done. A very small minority of stockholders are interested only in dividends and earnings per share. The possible alienation of that group may be the price you have to pay for survival and prosperity in the new society.

4

Organizational Development:

Enlightened Leadership or On-the-Job Retirement?

The Navy has reached a point where we can no longer drift with the tides and winds of change totally oblivious to the demands of our youth, the needs of our civilian society and the dignity of our personnel. . . . The Navy's problem today is not one of discipline but one of enlightened leadership.

ADMIRAL ELMO R. ZUMWALT
Chief of Naval Operations[1]

Coming as they do from an officer in an institution whose organizational innovation and progress are measured in millimeters, Admiral Zumwalt's words are revolutionary. We get the feeling that *all* organizations had better keep in step with the times or perish for lack of willing yeomen. Organizational development (OD) consists in developing better leadership, involving people so they find self-fulfillment in productivity, and providing the facilitating formal organization structure for these two processes. The results of effective OD are high productivity and employee satisfaction. In this chapter we will point out new concepts and practices in the OD processes.

VALUE OF HUMAN RESOURCES

Recently a dozen executives of large corporations sat around a conference table analyzing employee turnover costs for a company. On the basis of recruiting, hiring, and training, the final figure that appeared on the blackboard amounted to 75 percent of the company's net profit before taxes in the year before. Having recovered from their astonishment, the executives responded in typical fashion by attacking the figures themselves rather than considering the possibility that people on board do have a high dollar value. Because people aren't listed on the balance sheet as an asset and turnover costs don't appear on the P&L report as an expense, the executives couldn't believe that people are valuable.

Companies often invest thousands of dollars on training and education at every level of the organization yet adopt policies that encourage quits, "clear out the deadwood," fail to recognize and promote from within, and create an atmosphere of apathy. Salvageable employees in whom the company has made large investments are regularly lost.

What are some companies doing to increase profit through OD? In Chapter 7 we discuss how the R. G. Barry Corp. (Ohio) is attempting to value human resources on the balance sheet. Between 4 and 8 percent of the U.S. work force are alcoholics who cost business up to $10 billion in absenteeism, poor decisions, and scrapped work. Du Pont and Eastman Kodak have used their special knowledge to rehabilitate alcoholics. New programs have been put into effect by such companies as Lever Brothers, American Airlines, American Motors, and Hughes Aircraft.

Another comtemporary business problem is drug addiction. Kemper County Mutual Insurance Co. believes that it, like alcoholism, is an emotional illness and can be treated successfully. Kemper was the first company to announce that it would hire rehabilitated drug abusers. It sensitizes management, through seminars and films, to detect changes in performance of ex-addicts that indicate a relapse. The medical and psychological staffs are then brought into action.

Many blue chip companies today have programs for hiring ex-convicts. Such programs are little publicized, but obviously they prevent a great waste of human resources.

Other areas of waste of human resources that are receiving a lot of attention today are the underutilization of women, blacks, and handicapped people. Despite the fanfare, however, progress in those areas has not yet been substantial. A little more special attention paid to such potential workers could well result in big payoffs for a company.

BEHAVIOR AND MOTIVATION

> *We might as well recognize the difference between educating the elite and motivating the slobs. We need to admit that some people are the elite, most people are slobs, and let organization theory develop differently for each class.*
>
> A sociologist, about 1959

The view that far greater productivity can be achieved by releasing the potential of every individual is, of course, the antithesis of the pessimistic sociologist's view. A summary of research in basic behavioral disciplines and applications of OD in actual firms will update the manager.

People Are Different—From Each Other

The one principle of human behavior that all can accept is that every person is different from every other person. Both the busy manager who tends to treat all his subordinates alike and the sophisticated one who tries to structure them into three or four classes will encounter a steady stream of dropouts—turned-off employees.

Behavioral and perceptual differences among individuals are produced by physical attributes, mental capabilities, life experiences, culture, and age. Often with age comes a reinforcement of experiences and attitudes that leads to resistance to new methods and ideas. Not only does behavior differ among people but the pattern of behavior of the individual himself changes with time.

Basic Needs of People—Updated

Psychologist A. H. Maslow developed a classification or "hierarchy of needs" to explain the motivation of people. From most basic to highest developed need the needs are:

1. Physiological—hunger, thirst, and sex.
2. Safety, stability, and security.
3. Affiliation, belonging to a group.
4. Self-esteem (ego need) and esteem of others (social recognition).
5. Self-fulfillment—achieving all that the person desires and is capable of.

Daniel Yankelovich and others have summarized new trends in needs that affect behavior. In our country today, we think and act like affluent people. That means we seek (need):

Greater physical self-enhancement through cosmetics, dentistry, surgery, and colorful clothing.
Individualized life styles, or "doing your thing."
Meaningful work, personal creativity, and self-expression.

At the same time there is a reaction against materialism and complexity and people seek:

Antimaterialistic pleasures and social goals.
Simplified living, return to nature.
Distrust of tradition and slogans and confidence in science.
Smaller business and government units in belief that bigness is not so good.

New values are replacing both the puritanical and the Horatio Alger ones. The values that now underlie motivation are:

Pleasure for its own sake.
Liberal sexual attitudes.
Greater freedom of expression on all topics in all media.
Blurring of the sexes.
Living for the present.
Acceptance of drugs.
Relaxation of self-imposed standards in working and in studying.
Rejection of hypocrisy, challenge of authority, and cynicism toward widespread corruption.
Rejection of family unit if unsatisfactory.

Theory X and Theory Y

How do we establish an organizational climate in which people will produce? Douglas McGregor said that the way management behaves toward its people is what counts and that, in turn, the way management behaves depends upon its assumptions. Further, according to McGregor, managements in practically all companies act upon the "nonpeople assumptions" inherent in the rational, controlled, and tightly structured organization. People are assumed to be primarily economically oriented and basically lazy. The following summary explains further what McGregor called Theory X.[2]

Theory X indicates that efficiency will be high when:	*Theory X assumes that:*
Authority flows down a chain of command in which each employee has only one boss.	Most employees would rather be directed and have little desire for responsibility.
Work is divided into small narrow tasks.	Motivation occurs only at an economic level. The worker is resistant to change in work content.
Span of management is kept small.	People must be closely supervised. Men are by nature indolent.
Work is carefully specified and the worker is hired to fit the job.	People can be considered alike as units of production. No differentiation of jobs to take advantage of different interests and talents is desirable.

McGregor's own view was that people are quite different from the picture given by Theory X. He believed that giving people more responsibility, more freedom, and more satisfactory sets of tasks would stimulate them in their work. That he called Theory Y.

Theory Y implies that efficiency will be high when:	*Theory Y assumes that:*
Authority and communication flow in both formal and informal systems.	Employees are social beings who can work together for company and personal goals.
Work is varied and enriching.	Everyone has some degree of creativity. Workers are motivated by needs above the economic level.
Span of management is as broad as possible as long as major objectives are achieved.	People desire self-fulfillment through directing their own activities and setting their own objectives.
Tasks are grouped into different meaningful jobs to accommodate individual talents and capacities.	Employees achieve their fullest potential when their aspirations and job challenges are matched to their capabilities.

Argyris: Control and Motivation

Chris Argyris of Harvard University investigated the conflict between the individual's needs and the formal organization's characteristics.[3] He found that the formal structure and emphasis on control patterned after classical organization theory are in direct conflict with the needs of healthy mature people. Classical theorists and most managers have assumed that employees are apathetic, lazy, or dependent. All the trappings of an engineered organization are necessary: manuals, organization charts, job descriptions, incentive systems, procedures, inspections, and progress reports.

Argyris concluded that people react to tight controls by evasion or other resistance and that management responds with even tighter controls. Employees gradually become frustrated, apathetic, aggressive, or hostile. The answer, he believes, is a reality-oriented management that adapts the organization structure and management style to the situation and the aspirations of the employees. He gives an account of the successful application of his theories by three companies.[4]

Motivation and Hygiene Factors

In our affluent society, employees have satisfied lower-level needs such as desire for food and shelter. Note that *satisfied* need is not a source of motivation; it is the higher-level needs that proliferate into many *learned needs* that provide motivation. Frederick Herzberg has refined the concepts of Maslow, McGregor, and Argyris by identifying specific factors under the control of management that are important to motivation. He found that there are two types of factors, which he called hygienic factors and positive motivators. Hygienic factors consist of poor working conditions, poor policies and administration, reshuffling of tasks, incentive systems, and salaries. Those factors must be of high enough quality that employees are not completely frustrated, but improving them greatly brings about little change in productivity. Positive motivators, on the other hand, consist of:

1. Removing controls of the employee but holding the employee accountable for results.
2. Giving a person a complete, natural module of work, not just adding and subtracting tasks.
3. Granting the employee additional responsibility and job freedom.
4. Making periodic reports available so that, on their basis, the em-

ployee may initiate corrective action instead of being directed to take it.

5. Introducing new and more difficult assignments so that the individual may learn and grow.

The positive motivators and hygiene factors are diagramed in Figure 4-1.

The implications of Herzberg's research are clear. Management must achieve at least a minimum satisfactory level of factors such as salary, physical environment, and organizational relationships. All must be present; paying very good salaries, for example, will not by itself motivate people to work harder. Management must offer the positive work motivators shown in Figure 4-1.

INFORMAL ORGANIZATION: SILENT PARTNER OF THE FORMAL ORGANIZATION

Formal and company organizations share communication, control, and motivation. The informal organization is the social one that forms spontaneously when two or more people are associated with each other over a period of time. The total informal organization is made up of subgroups based upon:

Location within the plant or office.
Occupation or like-skilled people.
People with like outside interests.
Special issues—employees joined together in some cause such as resisting a new policy or an old manager.

Informal organizations have as an important characteristic the establishment of their own norms. New members of a group must conform to the established norms or face pressures varying from suggestions to dirty tricks and violence. Employees see their work groups as mutual protection societies—us against them. Group norms may restrict productivity or increase it.

Giant Food Stores, Carlisle, Pennsylvania, decided to put the psychologists' ideas about norms into practice. As Lee Javitch, president of Giant Food, explained it, the first step was to identify the present norms. Ten norm clusters were then targeted. Employees were encouraged to speak freely and help in the development of new norms. Here is one

Figure 4-1. Factors affecting job attitudes.

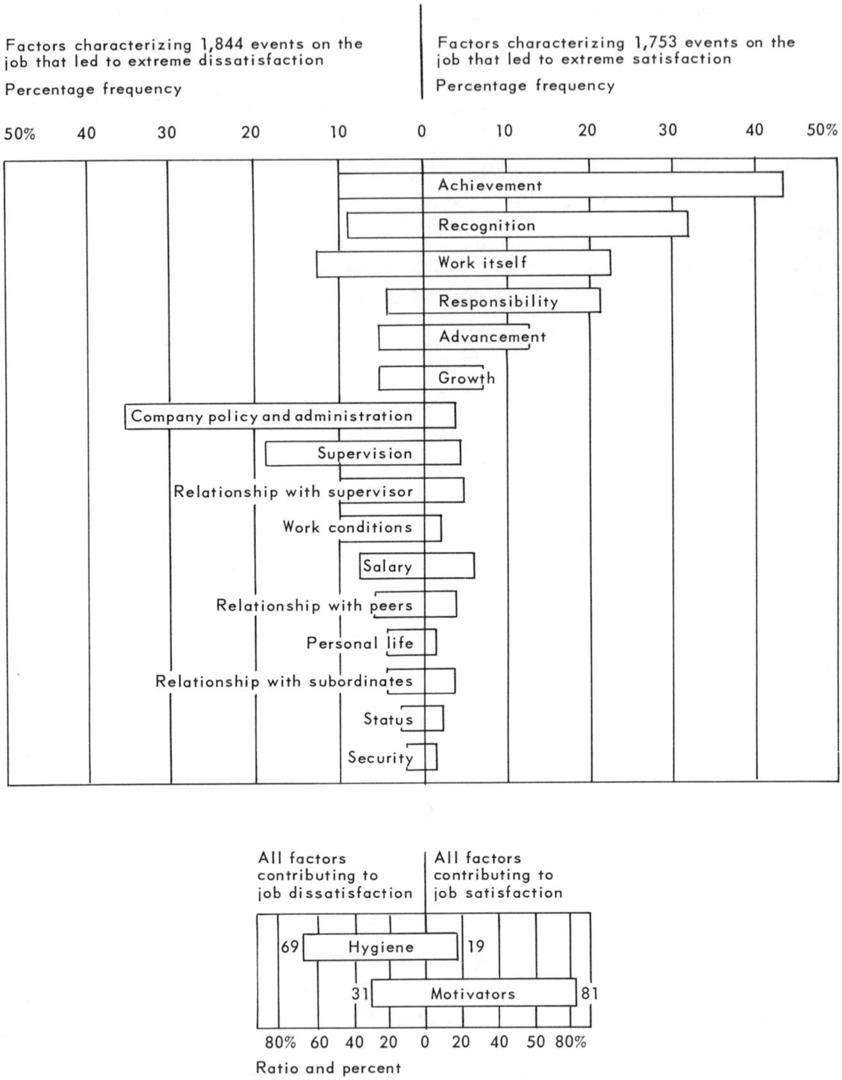

SOURCE: Frederick Herzberg, "One More Time: How Do You Motivate Employees?" *Harvard Business Review*, January-February 1968, p. 57.

result: By substituting peer group pressure and by setting up shrink teams in the stores, shrinkage dropped from $3,700 per month to about $600 per month.[5]

WHO'S THAT STRANGER IN OUR GROUP—A COMPUTER?

- Your check is a punched card.
- Your weekly report on inventory is a computer printout.
- Your engineering aide is a time-sharing computer terminal.
- You receive computer reports, analyze them, and pass them back to someone in the computer room.
- You record sales at a checkout counter on a terminal linked to Atlanta, New York, Chicago or where else.
- As a bank teller you record transactions on devices linked to computers.

As electronic computers have become omnipresent, if not omniscient, in the organization, resistance to them has undoubtedly lessened. Does such an automaton in the midst of humans affect OD? Yes, in two ways. The first is in its impact on formal organization structure; the second is in its impact on development and motivation of people.

Companies followed two different lines with regard to motivation. Many of them viewed computers as a means of reducing the labor force and then faced resistance in introduction of computers and demoralization of the remaining employees. Others viewed computers as a means of giving their employees more responsible jobs with increased intellectual content and less routine. Employees were trained and upgraded. They were made to feel part of glamorous new professions. Motivation on the job was increased by their awareness of new opportunities for learning and advancement, or at least increased power over their work situation. The speed of output and the marvels of things the computer can do will provide a fascination to workers in the future.

RESISTANCE TO CHANGE; NEW TENSIONS

One of the greatest causes of low productivity is resistance to change. In the shop, it may mean slowdowns and sabotage; in the executive suite, it may mean the termination of a top executive. Dr. Donald F.

Heany, in an address at Stanford University, described the "one hundred different ways" General Electric tried in an effort to introduce quantitative modeling for financial decision making within its operations. After two basic approaches failed, GE has now succeeded by a combination grass-roots and top-down approach. Briefly, "agents of change," people with skills and interests in quantitative modeling, were used in a diffusion process. At the same time, attempts were made to create a climate favorable to change by means of seminars for managers at all levels.

There is deep-seated belief that worker satisfaction and productivity are incompatible. "UAW Will Emphasize Escape From the 'Job' in 1973 Contract Talks" is a front-page story of *The Wall Street Journal*, December 8, 1972. Perhaps the most irrational beliefs of rational organization theorists is that formal organization requirements dominating people requirements will yield greater productivity. New values of people in an affluent society are imposing severe strains on that classical belief. Resistance to change in organizational development and old management myths held by U.S. managers parallel the union belief that work must be boring and must be avoided.

Misunderstandings and fears of job insecurity, as well as just plain inertia, cause resistance to change. I. W. Abel, president of the steelworkers union, agreed during the 1971 negotiations to collaborate fully with management in an attempt to increase productivity. Steel companies were being seriously hurt by lower-priced imports. After 18 months, the program was a complete failure. Scattered strikes resulted from activities of the plant productivity committees. The conclusion has been that poor communication, lack of understanding by the workers of the external threat, and old suspicions of workers about management caused resistance to new practices. The workers were simply not motivated to increase their output.

The purpose of OD, of course, is to redesign work and the work environment. Change becomes desirable in such a situation because it produces greater satisfaction for the individual in leading a more productive life.

GROWTH OF PROFESSIONALISM

Large companies, although not always the big profit makers, are usually the leading innovators. To remain competitive, they have been continually upgrading their requirements for young people hired as potential managers. B.A. degrees are giving way to M.B.A. degrees, and more highly trained specialists are being hired. The growth in computer use has increased the number of professional opportunities for thousands of junior college graduates.

Professional work requires greater freedom from supervision. OD *must* obtain personal commitment from its professionals, since missed opportunities due to lack of motivation are not easy to identify. Professionals require continued education to keep them abreast of their fields, and that places a specific requirement on company policy and OD. Constant intellectual renewal through contact with outside professionals is an important aspect of their motivation.

Managers will find an increasing independence among professionals, whose loyalty will be more toward their professions and their colleagues. That will lead to greater power equalization within the organization. However, the organization will benefit from those changes by increased creativity and a greater freedom of expression of ideas.

LEADERSHIP IN THE ROUND

Admiral Hyman Rickover was a successful manager. Here is the basis of his methods:

1. The interests of the project must come before the interests of any member of the project.
2. Problems must be made visible to all levels of management immediately. Hiding a problem in the hope of solving it before it becomes serious will lead to dismissal of the person responsible.
3. The leader must be involved in the work. Every manager has to know exactly the status of all work in his organization at all times.

A different type of leader is Don Shula, coach of the Miami Dolphins. Shula manages to get total commitment from every player and concentrates on only one thing, the immediate game ahead. He has a complete awareness of everything going on during a practice play, and he corrects each man's errors in a quiet businesslike way. He lets the players know that he expects those corrections to be made before the game, and the players rise to his expectations.

Leadership means providing the values and focus of action for members of the organization. It also means developing the organization to achieve the maximum output willingly. Successful leadership has been

Table 4-1. Four models of organizational behavior.

CHARACTERISTICS	AUTOCRATIC	CUSTODIAL	SUPPORTIVE	COLLEGIAL
Basis	Power	Economic resources	Leadership	Mutual contribution
Managerial orientation	Authority	Material rewards	Support	Integration and teamwork
Employee orientation	Obedience	Security	Performance	Responsibility
Employee psychological result	Personal dependency	Organizational dependency	Participation	Self-discipline
Employee needs met	Subsistence	Maintenance	Higher order	Self-realization
Performance result	Minimum	Passive cooperation	Awakened drives	Enthusiasm
Morale measure	Compliance	Satisfaction	Motivation	Commitment to task and team

SOURCE: Keith Davis, "Evolving Models of Organizational Behavior," *Academy of Management Journal,* March 1968, p. 29.

shown to be a function of (1) the forces in the leader, (2) the characteristics and types of needs of the subordinates, and (3) the situation.

Four models of leadership and related organizational behavior are shown in Table 4-1 as ranging from autocratic to collegial. Autocratic and custodial are by far the most common models in business practice.

Robert R. Blake and Jane S. Mouton developed and tested a means for measuring a manager's orientation or style that they called the Managerial Grid®. A manager is rated for his concern for production and his concern for people on a scale of 1 to 9 for each. Ideally, a manager should achieve a (9,9) rating: work is accomplished by committed people in a relationship of trust and respect.

IMPLEMENTING AN OD PROGRAM

To start with, it may be impossible to set up an OD program in most companies. We may be doomed to be victims of Western theology and a puritanic heritage that dictates that work be penance, not fun. To illustrate that, contrast the behavior, dress, and effectiveness of the company softball team at the game and on the job. Studies have shown that there are many ways to implement an OD program. "Experts" and researchers disagree on such a basic question as whether top management commitment is necessary. "Our experience in this study indicates that a clear-cut commitment at the top of the organizational unit to a particular OD program is not necesssary for a development program to succeed!"[6]

It appears that OD is best implemented by a hodgepodge of techniques chosen as appropriate for a particular organization. Further, the ones to be chosen cannot usually be determined in advance, but must be selected in an experimental process. Some of those techniques are discussed in the following paragraphs.

Top Management Commitment

Management must be made aware of the dollar and cents value of people simply so it won't act irrationally. For example, terminating 10 percent of the employees to cut costs is absurd if those employees are the cause of twice their salaries coming in as revenue. Further, top management commitment would seem to be necessary just to obtain the resources, including manpower, to institute the OD program. In addition, the workers reflect to some degree the values of management with regard to on-the-job relationships. Too heavy-handed involvement by top management in OD implementation may lead to suspicion and resistance by people in the organization, however.

There should be some rough plan as to the OD teams or consultants, the groups to be worked with first, the supporting educational and training programs, and measurements of progress. Management should not expect much impact from the program for two to five years.

Establish Good Flow of Information

If you can take a few randomly chosen employees aside for ten minutes each and get them to tell you honestly what prevents them from performing their best on the job, you have the basis for a good communication system. On their side, employees must be supplied with up-to-date information about how their jobs fit into the company's competitive position. They need to be kept regularly informed of company problems.

Information on opportunities for training, advancement, and job changes must be provided promptly. Regular weekly meetings of small groups of employees with managers concerned with a mutual problem may institutionalize the information flow.

Job Enrichment

Bankers Trust of New York found that, in the stock transfer department, turnover was high, production and quality were low, and employees viewed their jobs as dull and repetitive. Following several seminars for supervisors, motivators were introduced one at a time. Each motivator consisted of giving another task and greater responsibility to the clerical people, thus relieving the supervisor of those tasks. Finally, instead of work being assigned at random, each employee was given a module or independent area of responsibility.

Job enrichment might seem more feasible in office work than on an assembly line, but Eugene A. Cafiero, group vice-president at Chrysler Corp., is risking his future by introducing it. Relaxation of tight discipline, bringing workers together to solve output problems, and putting trust in workers has led to some repercussions from the unions and some from management, but Cafiero has much the same philosophy as Admiral Zumwalt.

The fact that more and more companies are experimenting with it indicates that job enrichment must have some merit. The old methods simply aren't working, as consumers will tell us. When companies are going down the drain anyway, trying to plug the drain becomes worthwhile.

Don't Keep Your Organization Structure Frozen in Concrete

In classical management practice, a person is hired for a permanent position. Why not just the opposite? Why not assign a man to a team or work group until a major task is completed and then rotate him to another job with new problems and new relationships? As a matter of fact, just that has been done in engineering projects for several decades. The people who perform well on one project may get key spots on the next one. Competition between projects may stimulate high output as well. As people try different temporary jobs, they may find hidden skills and interests. Instead of being fixed at all levels, organizations could be problem-oriented at the lower ones. There should be a closer relationship between formal and informal organizations.

Adapt to Workers' New Desire for Freedom

Absenteeism has been reduced by making the workplace less neo-penal. Some companies have taken out the time clocks. Staggering hours for the regular shift to reduce traffic and allow workers a choice over an hour or so of when they report to work has been tried.

Flexible workweek arrangements have become popular in Switzerland. Kurt Wagner, a 45-year control man, always leaves early in summer so that he can work in his garden. Fritz Soltermann, an engineer with the same company for 23 years, likes the flexible-hour system because now he can have lunch at home with his wife and children. Under the sliding work schedule, an employee can report to work anytime between 6:30 and 8 A.M., take lunch up to 90 minutes between 11:45 and 2 P.M., and leave between 4:00 and 6:00 P.M. Absenteeism has been reduced. Employees have an increased feeling of individual responsibility. The system obviously is more difficult to apply to production workers on an assembly line. Finally, the 40-hour 4-day week is another approach to giving employees more freedom in life style.

SUMMARY: GET YOUR BIG GAINS IN PRODUCTIVITY FROM OD

1. Old methods of rigid organization structure, tight supervision, and autocratic control by power are causing increasingly lower productivity, employee resentment, careless workmanship, and even sabotage.
2. Management needs to evaluate, measure, and develop its human resources as it customarily does its physical resources. Employees must be counted as assets, not expenses.
3. Unsatisfied needs motivate employees; with every satisfied need, dozens of learned unsatisfied needs arise. Make sure you look in the direction of changing values of the upcoming generations.
4. McGregor, in his Theory X and Theory Y, says to treat people as responsible humans and get away from assumptions that they are indolent, prefer to be directed, and must be closely supervised. Argyris also says there is a basic conflict between the tight control in business

organizations and the needs of mature individuals. In essence, *let loose on the reins.*

5. Herzberg has shown that many factors such as compensation, security, status, and company policy do not motivate people; they merely satisfy them (hygienic factors). In contrast, opportunity for achievement and recognition, the work itself, and responsibility are motivating factors.

6. The goals of the formal organization and the norms of the informal organization must be matched. Norms of the informal organization may be changed by participative seminars and communication of company problems.

7. The computer has many impacts on the organization. Recognize them and develop your employees to handle new opportunities.

8. Resistance to change can sink an OD program unless the program is properly implemented.

9. The growth of professionalism will in the future force management to share its power with the professional sector of employees.

10. Enlightened leadership seeks a balanced concern for production and motivation.

11. To implement an OD program:
    (*a*) Utilize experts.
    (*b*) Form a plan.
    (*c*) Get top management dedicated to its success.
    (*d*) Establish open communications between all people in the organization by means of small group meetings.
    (*e*) Make jobs bigger, more challenging.
    (*f*) Give people more responsibility for *how* things are to be done. Emphasize feedback for self-control, not supervisory control. Emphasize employee accountability for results, but don't abdicate your management responsibility for control.

5

Structuring for Productivity, or People in a Box

With the behavioralists and humanitarians to the left, orthodox doctrine to the right, and top management just down the hall, it would be natural if organizational planners developed at least a slight case of schizophrenia.

Business Week, January 6, 1962

So what's new?

1972

In Chapter 4 we noted that the two major outputs of the organization are productivity and member satisfaction. Major inputs are the individuals, the groups, and how they react to the "socio-work environment" of the company. Because those inputs operate within the formal organization structure of the company, we will point out new trends in structure. We are interested primarily in how we can improve the satisfaction-productivity output through the organization of work and people.

There is certainly a decreasing satisfaction with the classical hierarchical organization structure. Both researchers and businessmen are saying that the bureaucratic structures are creaking under the weight and complexity of today's pressures in business. Some of the shortcomings are identified as the rigid organization lines and authoritarian style of a bygone era that seem increasingly out of touch with today's reality.

How can we improve things in 1974?

Of all the recent problems in business and government, the most far reaching is the productivity of American industry. It is of practical and immediate concern to the multinational corporations, to both the large and small firms that must compete against foreign imports, and of course to the consumer. All indications are that it could become the most important business problem for the remainder of this century.

There are two main aspects of productivity. The first is the matter of foreign competition. The second, and related to the first, is the fact that the declining rate of increase in productivity is a primary cause of monetary problems and inflation. With regard to foreign competition, the picture is getting increasingly dim. According to chairman Richard Gerstenberg of General Motors, "Productivity in manufacturing was increasing at an average annual rate of only 2.1%—well below the long-term average. At about the same time, productivity was increasing 5.3% in Germany, 6.6% in France, 7.9% in Sweden, and 14.2% in Japan [during the latest five-year period for which statistics are available]."[1]

If improved work output from both professional and production workers is the answer, exhortations won't get it. Organization and management might. Former Secretary of the Treasury John B. Connally has said that "the rest of the world is at work while we're worrying. They're out-working us, out-thinking us, and out-planning us." If that is so, then the major responsibility for a solution lies in the laps of managers. To quote chairman Gerstenberg of GM once again, "Better productivity results from better management." Eugene A. Cafiero, another automotive executive and a top man at Chrysler, put it even more succinctly, "We've got to stop bossing and start managing."

That argument is not to imply that increased productivity cannot be achieved through a third avenue: increased investment in engineering and technology and improved capital goods. We question, however, just how much farther we can go in that direction. For example, in the automobile industry, the investment per hourly employee has become more than five times that of the early fifties. Have we reached a plateau? Getting that extra amount of productivity from capital equipment may prove as elusive as getting it from increased worker motivation. That opinion is endorsed by 3M's chief executive, Harry Heltzer, "You can't press the button any harder and make the automated equipment run any faster. In a rising cost spiral you've just got to find ways of pressing it more intelligently."[2] Among those more intelligent ways of pressing the button are innovative forms of organization and methods of managing.

ORGANIZATION AND HUMAN RESOURCE MANAGEMENT

Let us propose a hypothesis: Managers, by and large, have overlooked or underemphasized two major sources of increased productivity that may hold more potential than improvements in hourly pay or labor output. The first of these is the salaried side of the company, that broad area known as white collar and middle management. One company that examined it was Hercules Incorporated, the chemical giant. It reached the conclusion that those groups are getting overcompensated in relation to their attributable productivity gains to a greater extent than hourly workers. Other companies and studies have found that in general those groups are growing relative to direct labor; they exceed 60 percent in many cases. Moreover, few of them work to any standard of performance or under any productivity measurement system, and it is widely estimated that they seldom top much over 50 percent of their potential.

A possibility of immediate improvement in work lies in stimulating and helping lower and middle managers to do a better job. Frequently those people are so bogged down in procedures, paperwork, red tape, and other trappings of current organization structure that they put more valuable work aside. They have little time left for the more productive jobs of planning, communicating, and motivating. Jobs are so narrowly defined and supervision is so close that motivation is killed. That aspect of OD has been discussed in Chapter 4.

The second source of increased productivity is the organization structure, the framework that facilitates OD and guides company operations. We made the point in Chapter 4 that most managers are handling their physical and financial assets reasonably well but are overlooking the human resource. It is pertinent to point out again that a careful analysis of the costs of the human resource would very likely lead to its better management and organization.

Consider some tentative but realistic figures. Despite the difficulty of placing a dollar value on human resources, most managers would agree that the cost of building their human organization from scratch would be at least 3 times payroll. Since most payrolls average somewhere near 8 times earnings, this means that the "asset size" of the human organization is about 24 times earnings. It now follows that if we can increase productivity by about 5 percent (by lowering the costs of turnover and hiring and by improving output through better organization and motivation), we can more than double earnings!

While most executives are familiar with this type of accounting for physical assets, few are willing to apply it to the management of their people asset. For example, many would be shocked to learn that turnover costs (recruiting, hiring, training, lost time, etc.) can sometimes equal 50–100 percent of after-tax profits. As a mental exercise you might try computing the cost of your own turnover and then estimating what a 10 percent reduction would do for earnings. We think you will find that the investment will earn you more than your return-on-investment target for other capital expenditures.

Are such gains worth trying new approaches to organization?

THE CLASSICAL ORGANIZATION STRUCTURE

The classical, or bureaucratic, hierarchical organization continues to be the most common corporate structure. It is easily understood; it is traditional; and it works reasonably well. Other organization structures are modifications of the classical one. Or to say it another way, the classical structure provides the foundation on which adaptations are constructed.

The key words are "structure" and "formal." The basic tenets of the classical structure are specialization of work (departments), span of management (nobody supervises over six subordinates), unity of command (nobody reports to more than one boss), and chain of command (authority delegation). Methods of departmentation are function (sales, operations, finance), territory (sales districts), product (product groups), customer (retail, industrial, manufacturing), process (welding, cutting, assembly), and service (maintenance, shipping, labor crews). The whole structure takes on the shape of a pyramid.

The manager determines work activities to get the job done, writes job descriptions, and organizes people into groups and assigns them to superiors. He then establishes objectives and deadlines and determines standards of performance. Operations are controlled through a reporting system. Finally, the manager plugs people into the boxes; and if they don't perform as directed, they are pathological!

How do we arrive at a bureaucratic, pyramidal structure? The answer lies in an understanding of how a company grows and develops. In the beginning communication is simple and effective because activities and communication channels are few in number. But as operations grow in size and communications become more complex, proper coordination and direction demand written directives and procedures. Communication is between offices and not people. More growth means more complexity, and that calls for more policies, procedures, and further formalization. In time the abundance of systems, procedures, and regulations demands greater departmentation and more staff people to coordinate operations. The classical structure has arrived! The tendency toward structure and formality can be observed by anyone in either a growing or a mature organization.

Despite the criticism so frequently leveled at it, the classical structure will probably be around for a long time to come. There will be modifications and additions, but the basic form will survive. Not long ago the Fellows of the Academy of Management, a group of distinguished senior management professors, attempted to forecast the shape of the organization of the future.[3] The result was a 75 percent probability prediction that the dominant organizational structure in 1985 would be the classical pyramid. Harold Smiddy commented, "There will always be experiments, exceptions, etc.—and a continuing deluge of academic clap-trap, largely irrelevant, passing as research—but reality will show little widespread change in the periods [1985–2000] at issue here."[3] Ernest Dale, another respected theorist and consultant agreed, "Despite the suggestions of the behavioralists, the pyramidal structure is still overwhelmingly used by the majority of business firms and other organizations—and will continue to be!"[4]

One characteristic of the present pyramidal structure is the rather tight hold the man at the top has on the reins of authority. Frequently the structure is patterned after the needs and desires of that man. It is interesting to note how often the customs and rites of the business are also. At Phelps Dodge they have a compulsion about clean desks at the end of the day. National Cash Register Company formerly unlimbered the girls in the typing pool with ten minutes of morning calisthenics. At Hallmark Cards each employee is entitled to free coffee, tea, and milk twice daily. At Goodyear, 200 management Santas distribute 30,000 toys at an annual Christmas party. And at IBM, although they have stopped singing such fight songs as "Ever Onward, Ever Onward," they still wear the white shirts that go back to Thomas Watson, Sr. He believed that IBM salesmen should look like their banker customers.[5]

OTHER THEORIES OF ORGANIZATION

The most persistent criticism of the classical organization structure comes from the behavioral scientists. Although the behaviorialists have some difficulty in recommending specific workable alternatives, their basic claim is that the classical organization is too mechanistic and therefore tends to overlook human nature and the needs of people. Some, such as Chris Argyris of Harvard, maintain that such organization "trappings" as structure, procedures, and controls actually violate human wants and inhibit productivity. Others say that the pyramidal structure, although perhaps suitable for a stable environment, is unable to accommodate the change that is so characteristic of modern organization.

We will shortly describe the contingency model that tries to incorporate the best of all worlds, but first we will look at two other emerging concepts that show the trend of current thinking.

The Behavioral Model

In the behavioral model an attempt is made to overcome some of the mechanistic-structural objections to the classical organization. The model assumes the objective of economic-productivity output as given, but it adds a new dimension, namely, employee satisfaction. The satisfaction, which presumably leads to greater productivity in turn, is a function not so much of structure as it is of individual perception and personal value systems. Essentially, the idea is that the pyramid should be modified to provide:

1. A more democratic attitude by managers.
2. More participation in major decisions at lower levels.
3. Decentralization of decision making as far as possible.
4. Less emphasis on hierarchy and authority delegation.
5. Less narrow specialization of work tasks.

The argument is that those modifications will improve worker satisfaction and hence productivity.

Most managers react to the behavioral model in one of four ways: with skepticism, with a pretense of apparent acceptance but with an actual intention to manipulate people and decisions, with general agreement but confusion on how to implement the model, or with a true desire to adopt the model as a modern way to motivate people in the company. The skeptics will find little comfort in the conclusion of Harlan Cleveland, who has had a distinguished career in business, government, and higher education. His view fairly well represents the behavioralists when he says, "The pyramid structure of less than a generation ago must be replaced by 'horizontal systems' in which control is loose, power diffused, and centers of decision widespread."[6] The receptive manager might respond, "Great! But how do we do it?" Frustrated managers who are making honest attempts to apply the model will probably agree with George A. Spater, president of American Airlines, who says that business is still in the Stone Age when it comes to applying the behavioral sciences.

Although the participative approach is fairly widespread in such organizations as universities, unions, and voluntary groups (have you ever gone to a PTA meeting?), it is embryonic and still evolving in industry. Indications are clear, however, that the approach will gain greater acceptance. Old-line classicists probably choked on the news that a major issue in the 1973 UAW contract talks was life on the assembly line and the need to let the workers become involved in decisions regarding their tasks.

Some top-level managers pay lip service to behavioral ideas, and others seem to be genuinely committed. Eugene A. Cafiero, touted by some as the future top man at Chrysler, is one of the latter. His philosophy and actions are summarized in his comment, "Let responsibility extend down to its lowest practical level and give authority to go along with it. The lowest level in my mind, in a lot of cases, is the guy right on the line."[7]

Other companies that have taken action to involve workers and let them participate in decisions regarding their work and to reduce the specialized and monotonous nature of the job include AT&T, where selected typists can now research, compose, and sign their own letters without supervision. Another is Motorola, where female hourly workers who formerly performed very specialized tasks (for example, wiring or soldering) on a walkie-talkie assembly line, now assemble the entire product and approve its final checkout. At Chrysler, assembly workers in selected plants are authorized to reject substandard parts, work sitting instead of standing, and paint their own machines in any color, including psychedelic.

There is a lot of talk and much speculation on the behavioral approach to improving organizational productivity, but the state of the art today can be described as limited and experimental. The companies that have tried to modify their organizational approach in that way are few, and most have done so on a trial basis. We think the approach will have accelerating acceptance because it makes good economic sense and because the workforce, including lower and middle management, will demand it.

The Organic Model

The organic approach to organizational design is behavioral in nature but goes one step further in that it addresses itself to the structure and the specialization of tasks—classic fundamentals. Warren Bennis, its foremost proponent, argues that classical structure is too rigid to adapt to the frequent changes caused by modern technology. To accommodate that change, organizations should be composed of temporary task forces that change their membership and composition as needs change:[8]

> First of all, the key word will be temporary. Organizations will become adaptive, rapidly changing temporary systems. Second, they will be organized around problems-to-be-solved. Third, these problems will be solved by relative groups of strangers who represent a diverse set of professional skills. Fourth, given the requirements of coordinating the various projects, articulating points or "linking pin" personnel will be necessary who can speak the diverse language of research and who can relay and mediate between the various project groups. Fifth, the groups will be conducted on organic rather than on mechanical lines; they will emerge and adapt to the problems, and leadership and influence will fall to those who seem most able to solve the problems rather than the programmed role expectations. People will be differentiated, not according to rank or roles, but according to skills and training. . . . Though no catchy phrase comes to mind, it might be called an *organic-adaptive structure*. [Italics added.]

Generally speaking, the organic approach to organization and productivity has had moderate acceptance, although its use is accelerating. In many ways it overcomes the traditional objections to bureaucracy expressed by Robert Townsend: "It strangles profit and stifles people." The organic approach provides more freedom of action and less narrow specialization. We will examine the organic model further when we discuss the task force–project management–matrix management type of organization later in this chapter.

CLASSICAL STRUCTURE: RIGHT OR WRONG?

The dangers inherent in the classical structure, with its trappings of systems, formality, and controls was very well expressed by C. Peter McColough, chairman of the Xerox executive committee: "I think the greatest fear we have about weakness is that as we grow, and we're already very large, we will get the big-company syndrome—and we will become slow and cautious, people will be afraid to make mistakes, and we'll build up barriers and fail to communicate."[9]

Criticizing the bureaucracy is getting to be a profitable vocation; witness *Parkinson's Law, The Peter Principle,* and *Up the Organization.* Some of the charges leveled at the classical structure are:

- It is too mechanistic and ignores major facets of human nature.
- It is too structured to adapt to change.
- Its formal directives and procedures hinder communication.
- It inhibits innovation.
- It pays the job and not the man.
- It relys on coercion to maintain control.
- Its job-defensive behavior encourages make-work.
- Its goals are incompatible with those of its members.
- It is simply out of date with the needs of the seventies.

Many of those criticisms have a basis in truth. Except for the small organization, the classical structure appears to be the easiest effective way to cope with complexity. Bureaucracy, with all of its "evils," is an organizational requirement when we go beyond the face-to-face stage of communications. And therein lies a paradox. In order to maintain our distinctly human form of social organization, we must employ an organizational form that negates much of what is desirable in the human form.

The major arguments in favor of the classical approach are:

- It has overwhelming acceptance by practicing businessmen.
- It works.
- It is easily understood and applied.
- It isn't set in concrete—it can accommodate modifications such as the behavioral or organic ones when the need arises.

A careful evaluation of recent business events tends to support the claims of utility of classical methods. The reader will recall the conglomerate era of the late sixties when LTV Corp., Litton Industries, Gulf & Western, and other conglomerators were having a field day with "free-form management," a style characterized by loose controls and a high degree of decentralization of authority. For a while, it appeared that doing without some of the classical standbys such as performance standards and controls was having some success, at least if we could judge by Wall Street's reaction. Events have proved otherwise, however. Almost without exception the return has been to operations, not conglomerate decentralization. Tight controls are back in favor.

That view is given further support by two outstanding companies, ITT and TRW. Although both are conglomerates, neither fell for the typical conglomerator free-form management and financial manipulations. Instead, they stuck with the old-time religion. Both retained the essential fundamentals of classical planning and control. Each maintained strict reporting procedures that required substantial involvement on the part of division managers. Each insisted on accurate projections. And each established an enviroment of reporting informality that made the best advice in the company accessible to everyone. In short, they used the proven classical methods with the necessary adaptation for human involvement to make them work.

Boise Cascade, whose 1968 annual report described the company as "an environment relatively free from job descriptions, organization charts, and other inhibiting restrictions," was the darling of the young MBA's of the period. Now that operations have turned sour, the company has scrapped some of the free-form methods and returned to tighter controls. LTV Corp. transferred authority, people, and control "downstream" in the free-form days. The company now finds some degree of recentralization necessary. It has discovered that the name of the game is operations, not delegation.

ORGANIZATION CHART: HELP OR HINDRANCE?

Robert Townsend, of *Up the Organization* fame, equates organization charts with rigor mortis and recommends that charts be drawn in pencil and never formalized, printed, or circulated. His rationale is that a chart tends to demoralize people because nobody likes to think of himself as below other people.

The opposing argument, which can be found in most management textbooks, is that documentation of the organization structure provides a means of communication, helps avoid overlap and duplication, and lets people know their reporting relationships.

It is perhaps unfortunate but true that some form of organizational documentation is necessary. That does not necessarily take the form of a chart, but some definition of job responsibility, relationships, and structure is desirable. Some of the alternatives are discussed in the following paragraphs.

Line and Staff

Probably few concepts in management have caused more debate and ill feeling than the theory and operation of line and staff. Marshall McLuhan, the director of the Centre for Culture and Technology at the University of Toronto who threw Madison Avenue into a frenzy over his communications theories, speculates that "today's organization, with its line and staff, is as out of step with what is happening as a 19th century military organization."[10]

Linear Organization Chart

For those who oppose the pyramidal form of charting, the linear organization chart may satisfy a minimal need for specification of responsibilities. Developed in the early sixties, this technique of mapping the managerial hierarchy is useful when there is a need to show a relationship between functions and responsibility quickly and concisely. It is illustrated in Figure 5-1.

The Circle

The circle form of organization charting overcomes Townsend's objection that "nobody likes to think of himself as below other people." Genesco and C.I.T. Financial are two companies that have used the approach successfully.

The chart consists of concentric circles. The top officers comprise the inner ring (the hole in the doughnut), and staff specialists in such areas as engineering, systems, R&D, legal, and personnel comprise the second ring. Those specialists do not report to any particular hierarchy of managers but are accessible to everyone.

Figure 5-1. Linear organization chart.

	Board	President	VP Marketing	VP Operations	VP Finance	Division Manager	Plant Manager
Corporate Strategy	A	A	B	B	B	E	E
Long-Range Plans	B	A	D	D	D	D	E
Development Plan	C	B	D	A	C	D	E
Financial Plan	D	A	D	D	C	B	B
Market Forecast	E	D	A	E	E	E	F
Capital Budget	C	B	D	D	C	D	E
Organization Development	E	B	E	E	E	E	E
Project Control	E	E	E	E	E	E	A
New-Product Development	E	E	B	E	C	E	E
Plant Construction	E	D	E	A	C	D	A
R&D	E	D	D	E	C	E	E

A Direct responsibility
B Overall supervision
C Approve finance
D Approve plan
E Notify
F No need to consult

The third ring consists of line managers, divisional managers, or operating departments that do not report to any single officer as they would under a divisionalized setup or a pyramidal structure. Thus, everyone sees himself working in a circle, and the feeling of structure and constrictive lines of authority is reduced.

The Ladder

The ladder organization is designed to show proper staff relationships and, incidentally, get more productivity from specialists. In the pyramidal chart the staff departments are shown just below the chief executive;

in the ladder chart they are placed vertically alongside. Du Pont is a well-known user of the ladder approach.

The ladder organization works somewhat like a management consulting group. Specialists (consultants) can move about the organization at any level and go to the spot where they are needed most without the usual delay of protocol and reporting relationships.

Fragmentation at the Top: The Plural Executive Office

The organizational entity called "the office of the president" goes back to 1955, when Ralph Cordiner of General Electric designed it as a partial solution to the problem of presiding over a company that had just completed a gigantic decentralization move. The problem then was the same as it is today: How do you give a manager independence at the operating level and yet maintain some degree of control at the corporate level? How do you help the decentralized operating level plan for the future? And how do you stretch the talents of the chief executive so that he can oversee the operation?

Cordiner's office of the president consisted of himself, the chairman, and five group vice-presidents assisted by ten staff vice-presidents. All seven line members had the authority to speak for and assume "the posture of the president." Both moves—decentralization and the office of the president—were widely copied by other companies.

The reasoning behind the office of the president is simple: The responsibility of the chief executive to maintain control over a complex decentralized operation must be divided. No one man at the top in these days of change and complexity has the time, the knowledge, or the energy and experience to properly oversee the many tasks and subordinates that are his responsibility. Despite such techniques of delegation as decentralization, profit centers, staff specialists, and computer systems, it is still difficult for one man to handle the job. Boise Cascade, Bache & Co., General Mills, Mead, Borden, Chase Manhattan, Pet, Caterpillar Tractor, Scott Paper, Singer, Ampex, and Continental Can are among the companies that have an office of the president. Even the job of vice-chairman, traditionally a ceremonial one with limited authority, is rapidly being upgraded as companies seek help for the top man. Richard Gerstenberg of GM and John D. deButts of AT&T are among former vice-chairmen who have been promoted to the top job.

Despite indications that many top-level decisions will be made by an executive team or plural executive, there are second thoughts about the office of the president. Among the doubters is Peter Drucker, the widely respected management professor and consultant. He thinks the concept might work *if:*[11]

1. Each member of the office knows his position vis-à-vis other members in the group and all members work to keep the entire group informed.

2. It is understood that the entire organization has no appeal from the decision of any one member. The office must speak with the voice of the president.

3. Members of the office are carefully selected to insure that they don't fortify each other's blind spots.

An excellent example of how *not* to organize the office of the president was furnished by Najeeb E. Halaby when he was chairman of Pan American. Instead of naming a president, as some members of the board demanded, Halaby elevated four men to the title of group vice-president. None of them had been with Pan American as much as a year and a half, and only one had an airline background. The four men were his office of the president, and he let it be known that all four were in contention for the presidency. He attempted to delegate operational responsibility to the "groupies," as they were known throughout the company, without assigning definite responsibility and authority. The result of the entire effort was low morale, declining operations and profits, and the ultimate ouster of Halaby.

CENTRALIZATION VERSUS DECENTRALIZATION

Divisionalization and other forms of organizational decentralization have been popular since 1950 or so. If a company has a logical breakdown of products, services, customers, or geography, the natural tendency is to decentralize. General Motors and General Electric are among the major companies that started the trend in the fifties, and the movement has become one of the popular subjects of debate in business schools since that time.

There is little doubt, at least in neoclassical theory, that decentralization is the way to organize. It develops subordinates, improves morale and productivity, and helps provide an organizational climate that more closely resembles the behavioral model that we seek. On the other hand, there are a number of prerequisites to decentralization: capable subordinates that can handle the job, a good system of planning, and a modicum of control.

A number of companies that have gone the decentralization route are having misgivings that are due, in part, to the way in which decentralization was managed. Some took a laissez-faire attitude toward division managers or those in charge of decentralized operations: "Show me a profit or return on investment and no questions asked." That, of course, invited trouble. First, as any manager knows, there are many creative bookkeeping ways to make sure that short-run profit goals are met. You can fire staff people, delay needed maintenance, or manipulate the valuation of such assets as inventory and accounts receivable. The manager may well think to himself, "Who cares about the day of reckoning? I will be promoted and transferred by that time."

Another danger in total decentralization is the managerial behavior that is encouraged. Sometimes a manager will go like a house afire, putting the screws on people and pushing them to maximum effort in the short run without commensurate rewards. When recession or other adversity comes, he can't cope because of the lack of a human resource backlog. Managers who operate that way hope they will have been promoted elsewhere before the effects catch up with them.

Despite the potential dangers in complete decentralization, the trend in that direction continues, particularly in the multiproduct, multinational, multidivisional, or conglomerate type of operation. Such companies as Honeywell Inc. and Litton Industries retain the corporate staff functions of organization and executive personnel, financing and investment objective, compensation and benefit policy, accounting controls, basic research and corporate ventures, public affairs and public relations, and legal and patent matters. The remaining operations are delegated to autonomous divisions.

The pressure for recentralization is now coming from two directions. First, many companies are finding that operations must be controlled and are returning to more centralization. Second, the development of sophisticated computerized management information systems makes centralized control of complex operations more feasible. Recently Motorola, the broadly based electronics manufacturer that prided itself on its casual and friendly atmosphere and its one-man organization, found that some control had to be returned to headquarters. Robert W. Galvin ("Bob to you"), the chairman and chief executive, announced a new layer of management at the corporate level. That layer includes group vice-presidents and the usual accompanying staff specialists.

For the manager who is concerned with just how far he should decentralize, the following "equation" may supply an intuitive feel:

Style of organization depends upon D, P, S, T, M, C, and E

where D = decisions to be made, their cost and impact
P = corporate policies that guide decisions and operations
S = size and complexity of the company's operations
T = tradition and history of corporate management, management values, and philosophy of management
M = managerial manpower availability
C = sophistication of control system
E = environment (complexity and changes over time; need to take a systems approach to the whole)

EMERGING CONCEPTS: THE TEAM APPROACH

If we recall that the essential characteristics of the organic model are "temporary," "flexible," and "accommodating to change," then the task is to find a structure that can operate within the pyramid of classical organization. That approach, which we shall call the team approach, takes on a number of modifications. The one called project management is widespread; matrix management and venture teams are evolving. The use of all three is accelerating.

The team, or plural, approach to problem solution and management is nothing new; indeed, committees and other coordinative devices have been with us for centuries. However, the team approach that was popularized by the Navy's Special Projects Office's use of PERT in the Polaris program is finding increased use in nondefense applications. Indeed, some form of team organization promises to be the major innovation in dealing with complexity and change during the coming decades.

Project Management

Assume that you have a plan that requires the coordination of two or more functional departments, that is, accounting, marketing, finance, engineering, and operations. It may be the development and design of a new product, a program for deeper market penetration of an existing product, a cost reduction program, acquisition of or merger with an outside company, a management development program, new financing, construction and location of a new plant, overhaul of your company, or any one of a multitude of complex programs. How do you organize to accomplish the job?

The first inclination is to form a task force or a committee, the device that tends to emerge when one department has difficulty in coping with a problem. Committees are usually found in firms in which the incapacity of the organization structure to deal with change has been admitted. The shortcoming is that the committee is rarely given the power to make decisions and implement plans of action. In fact, ineffectiveness and win-lose dynamics are attributes of committee "decisions." That type of body, with its diffused power and lack of specific individual responsibility, is not appropriate for decision making. Therein lies its weakness.

Another solution might be to assign responsibilities for the various parts of the task to an operating manager of one of the functional departments. Here the problem is that serious top management involvement is necessary to resolve conflicts and to assure that all steps are coordinated and taken. The approach is disruptive.

A third approach might be to establish a project manager with complete, undiluted authority for all aspects of the project. That is the organizational device being used in aerospace and a variety of other industries with accelerating frequency. Its use will grow as we move away from process production systems into unit production and service output.

The central idea is to assign one individual, the project manager, the responsibility for planning, work scheduling, budgeting, and controlling. His job is to insure that the task or the project is completed within the established standards of time, cost, and technical specifications. Two forms of project management organization are the matrix and the line. Matrix management is by far the more common. Line organization is more effective, but it also requires considerably more skill in meshing projects.

Matrix Project Management

Matrix organization gets its name from the fact that a number of project managers exert planning, scheduling, and cost control over people who have been assigned to their projects while the functional managers exert line control (technical direction, training, compensation) over the same workers. There is shared responsibility for the worker, and the worker must please two bosses.

A simple matrix arrangement is shown in Figure 5-2, and the organization of a typical project in one of the nation's top aerospace firms is shown in Figure 5-3 to demonstrate the concept in practice. The program manager is essentially a "contractor" who "hires" personnel from the line organizations. His funds are obtained when the company bids on a project successfully.

Two excellent examples of project management in operation involve Honeywell Inc. and Texas Instruments. When General Electric decided to quit the computer business, Honeywell acquired the pieces. It set up 20 managerial task forces, made up of about 200 people from both its own staff and G.E.'s. Operations involved the integration of manufacturing, marketing, engineering, field services, personnel, software, and the inventory of actual product lines. Honeywell's chairman called it a textbook exercise in how to merge painlessly.

In the case of Texas Instruments, project management is a way of life; it has been carried to its ultimate degree of sophistication. Broad company objectives are broken down into a series of strategies and methods for achieving them. Those strategies, in turn, are translated into several hundred tactical action programs (TAPS). Each TAP has a project management system.

Line Project Management

In the line project management organization, each employee has only one home—the project to which he is assigned or an auxiliary service group. Usually a number of projects are active at the same time but

Figure 5-2. Matrix organization: workers in a box.

	Marketing Manager	Engineering Manager	Financial Manager
Project Manager A	5	2	1
Project Manager B	2	7	2 ← Number of personnel assigned
Project Manager C	1	3	1

are in different stages of their life cycles. As new projects build up, people are transferred from the projects that are approaching their ends.

The project manager has complete responsibility for resources of money and men. He contracts for auxiliary services such as centralized testing in an R&D organization or special staff assistance in a business venture program. He is held accountable for meeting specific time, cost, and performance goals. Figure 5-4 shows the top levels of management in a division that developed prototype nuclear power plants.

Venture Teams

"The greatest challenge facing most corporations today is the development and marketing of new products or services that will produce a profit in the face of increased risks of failure," says a manager in the marketing research firm of a leading consultant. The venture team is a recent organizational innovation to meet the demand for a breakthrough in product marketing. As in the case of so many tasks in the classical company, the functional structure inhibits innovation. Booz, Allen & Hamilton, The Conference Board, and the U.S. Senate antitrust subcommittee are among those whose concern with product innovation has led to the conclusion that traditional functional organizational obstacles must be overcome.

The venture team is somewhat like the project-matrix management approach in that its personnel resources are obtained from the functional departments. Other similarities include organizational separation, the team of multidisciplinary personnel, and the goal-directed effort directed to the achievement of a single result—product development and introduction. The venture team also may have a flexible life span wherein a completion time is loosely defined by broad time and financial goals.

A study of 24 large companies showed that members of venture teams were generally well accepted by a cross section of the organization (see Table 5-1, p. 93). Without such acceptance, the venture manager's job would indeed be difficult. Table 5-2 (p. 93) shows how the venture manager interacts with various members of the organization.

For companies that are committed to growth, and for those whose success depends upon the marketing of existing products and the development of new ones, the venture team approach offers a promising alternative to the operations traditionally found in marketing departments.

Figure 5-3. Typical program manager in areospace industry.

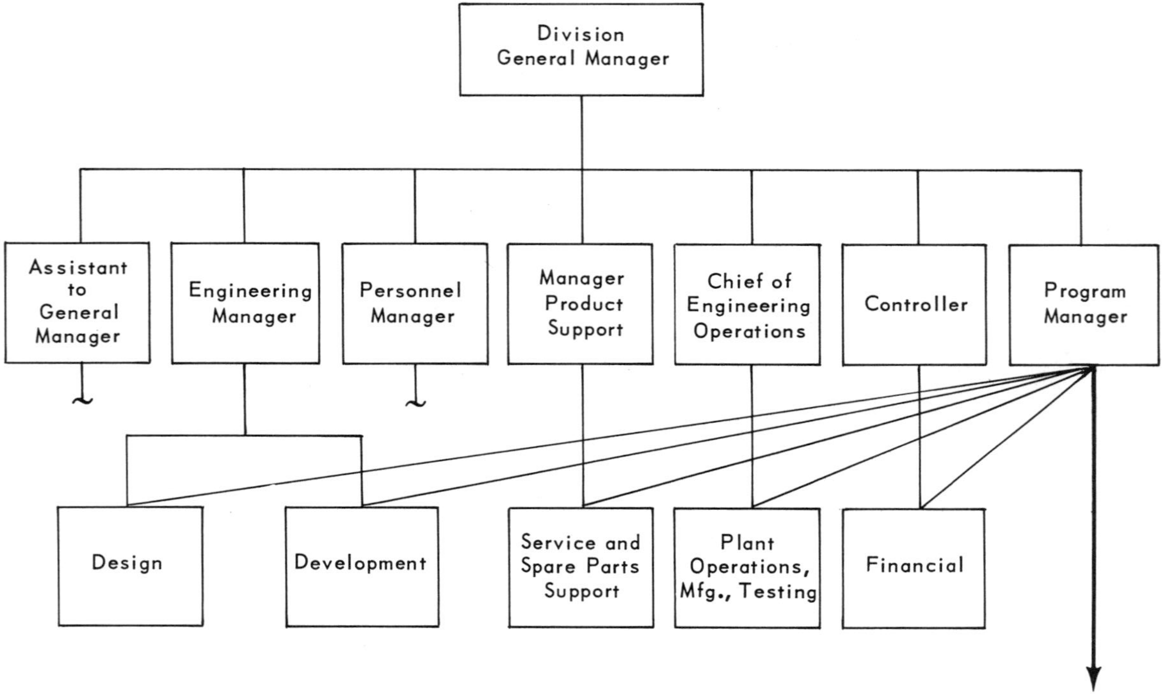

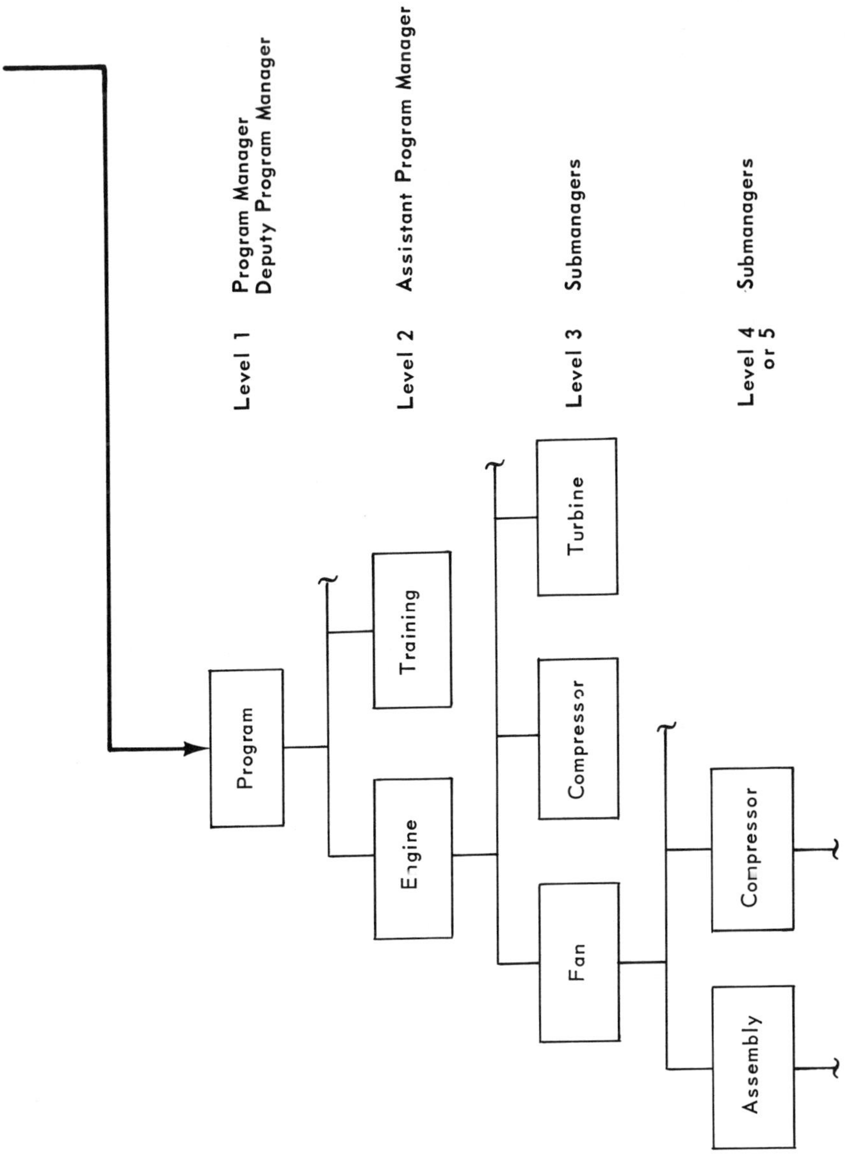

Level 1
Program Manager
Deputy Program Manager
Level 2
Assistant Program Manager
Level 3
Submanagers
Level 4 or 5
Submanagers
Program
Training
Engine
Turbine
Compressor
Fan
Compressor
Assembly

Figure 5-4. Line project organization.

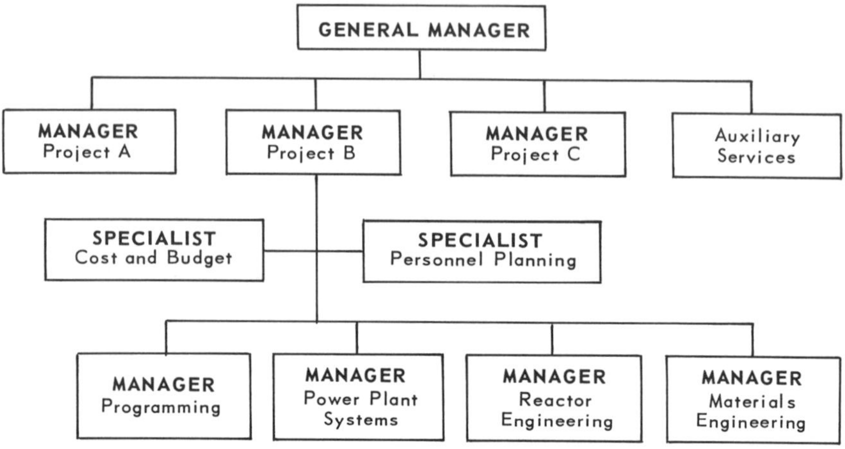

EMERGING CONCEPTS: THE CONTINGENCY MODEL

Thus far we have examined the classical pyramidal form of organization structure, modifications of it, and a number of related approaches, behavioral and organic. Unfortunately, all of these concepts taken together do not provide us with a workable systems approach to organization. The contingency model attempts to do so. It represents the latest thinking and research.

The contingency model seeks to answer this question: What factors, forces or variables should be considered in deciding how to design an organization structure? The most important of them are the following:[12]

The manager. Corporate personality, strategy, policies, and plans reflect the personal, social, and ideological goals of the top management group, frequently of the top man himself. It follows that top management is the most important variable in shaping the company's organization structure. Organizations don't have objectives; people have them.

Taken together, the value system and philosophy of management of managers provide the greatest impact on organizational design. How do the managers view individual freedom to make decisions as opposed to normal authority channels within the company? What is their feeling toward leadership? How do they view the interaction between the company and its external environment?

Table 5-1. Acceptance of venture management by others within the organization.

DEGREE OF ACCEPTANCE	PERCENT
Extremely well received; enthusiastically	8
Well received; cooperatively	52
Received with some reservations; no overt opposition	16
Not fully accepted by some functions; "waiting to see"	12
Not received by most functions concerned; open hostility evident	4
No comment	8

Table 5-2. Cross section of a venture manager's daily activities.

ACTIVITY CLASSIFICATION	PERCENT OF DAY DEVOTED
Planning ventures–proposal development	25
Organizing–negotiating–liaison	10
Directing	10
Controlling–analyzing	15
Attended meetings	20
Other (patent work, correspondence, internal and external public relations)	20

SOURCE (both tables): Kenneth A. Jones and David L. Wileman, "Emerging Patterns in New Venture Management," *Research Management,* November 1972.

The work. Since accomplishment of tasks to achieve organizational goals is the primary reason for organizing, it follows that a fundamental determinant of structure is the nature of tasks. The work determines such considerations as span of control, authority delegation, and the extent to which an organic as opposed to a bureaucratic structure is adopted.

A growing body of research evidence relates technology to organization design. Different technologies seem to have different management content. At the risk of oversimplification, we can probably conclude that in low-technology, stable, continuous-process industries, there is less need for adaptive organizations.

The environment. The factors in the environment of a firm include the social, political, economic, and technological ones and also those related to product and supply markets. This environment is complex; and the more a company interacts with it, the greater its impact on the organization design.

The greatest environmental interaction probably occurs in connection with the availability of resources and capital, the products or services marketed by the company, and the competition anticipated. Other market considerations are the changing demand for the company's output and the technological or other factors that may change demand.

It isn't difficult to see why a stable environment, such as that of the steel industry, would demand a different pattern of design and behavior than an uncertain and changing environment, such as that of the computer industry.

The individual contributors. Because an organization structure is nothing without people to man it, the human element is an essential factor. We now have a growing and perhaps conclusive body of evidence that increased productivity and other desirable outputs can be achieved by adapting the structure to accommodate the needs of organizational members. That is not academic clap-trap, but practical business sense. Because Chapter 4 dwelt on it, the point will not be discussed here.

What does all this suggest and what practical use has it? To us it suggests that the right structure is a function of the interaction of four variables each of which must be balanced against the effect of the others and against the desired output of the organization. The ultimate complex and dynamic structure can be represented as in Figure 5-5.

No one style of organization design is universally appropriate, nor does Figure 5-5 provide the answer. What we have attempted to elaborate is a model of design that contains the most important factors to consider, a checkoff list if you will.

SUMMARY: BUILDING AN ADAPTIVE ORGANIZATION

Howard Wesley Johnson, president of M.I.T., argues that change is permanent and that educational institutions must prepare the potential

Figure 5-5. Factors in organizational design.

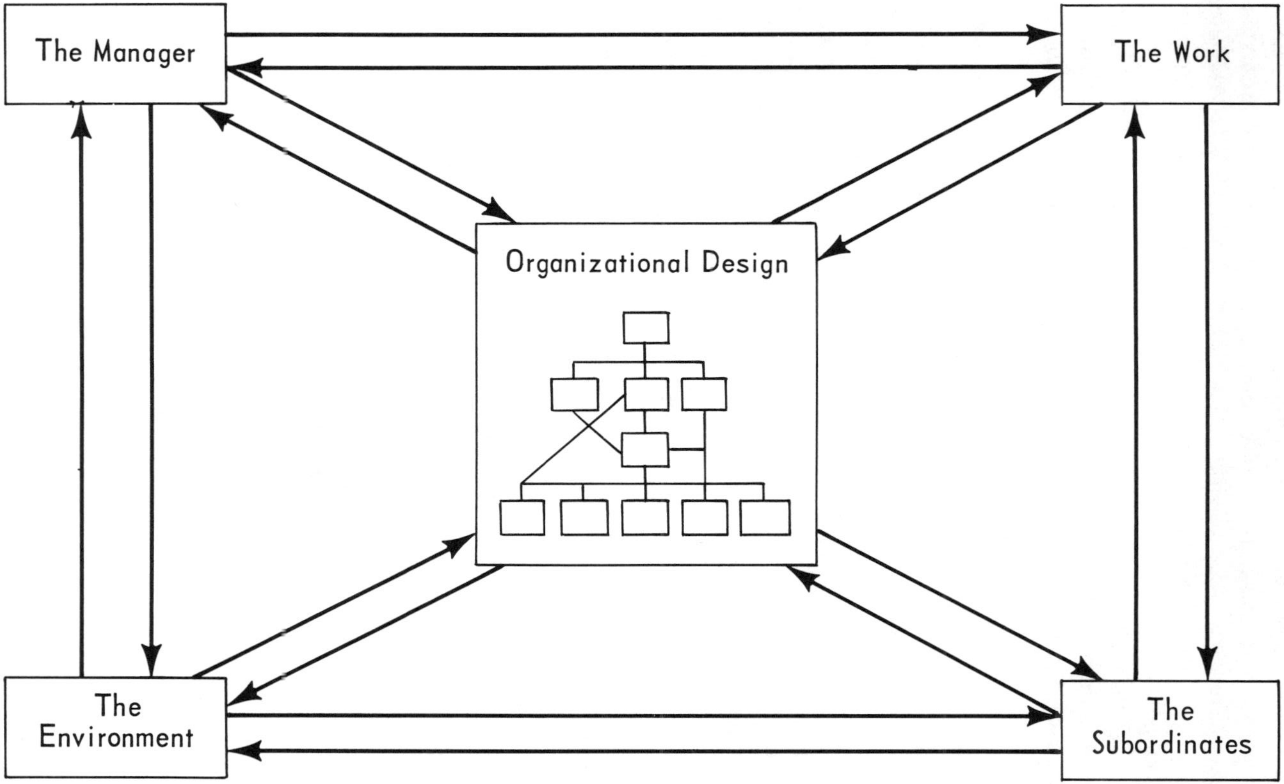

and existing manager for it. Organizations must adapt to it. Entrepreneurship and innovation must be fostered. Joseph C. Wilson, the late executive committee chairman of Xerox, concluded that the greatest strength of a company is the spirit of innovation and adaptation to change.

To close this chapter, we supply a few questions for your own use in determining the vitality of your organization and the need for a review of its design. Your answers will indicate your adaptability.

Human Resource Management

1. Do you blame most of your productivity problems on labor?
2. Have you identified the output and costs of the nonhourly workforce including white collar and lower and middle management? If so, are those groups working to a standard and can you identify changes in their productivity?
3. Do you know what a 5 percent increase in productivity of each category of worker would do for profits?
4. Do you have a program for identifying the value of your human resources and the costs associated with them in much the same way as other assets?
5. Do you have a true management of human resource program, not just a personnel department that maintains records?

Organizational Rigidity

1. Have you checked out your structure in the last year?
2. Except for adding appendages as the need arises, have you made a significant change in structure during the last 3 to 5 years?
3. Do your people cling to old ways of working after they have been confronted with new situations?
4. Are the older managers living in the past and passing their thinking along to the younger men?
5. Is institutionalism setting in?
6. Is your reputation one of safety, security, and a nice place to work?
7. Has the management group developed a low tolerance for criticism?
8. Does company esprit depend upon one or more outdated rites?
9. Does your entire operation depend on tight controls?

Organizational Design

1. Do you feel that line-staff conflict is nonexistent and that staff specialists are doing their job?

2. Do you feel you have achieved a delicate balance between decentralization and centralization?

3. Have you reviewed the situation to see whether some form of team organization would work?

4. Are you willing to delegate and let subordinates make mistakes?

5. Have you reviewed the relationship between the determinants of organizational design (managers, work, environment, individual contributors) to see whether you have a good mix that fits your structure?

6

The Systems Approach to Planning and Control: 2 + 2 = 5

syn·er·gism *the simultaneous action of separate agencies which, together, have greater total effect than the sum of their individual effects.*

Webster's Dictionary

The management fad of the 1940s was human relations; the 1950s favored organization; and the 1960s spawned management science. Yet none of those movements have the potential impact of the systems approach, the buzzword of the 1970s.

The central concept of the systems approach is *integration of the parts.* Every manager has an intuitive feel for it but knows that it seldom exists in his organization. One frustrated chief executive lamented, "Marketing is selling what engineering can't design, what production can't deliver, and to customers that finance won't give credit to anyway!"

A major reason for lack of company integration is that most managers are concerned with their individual (department, division, unit) goals at the expense of companywide objectives. That is not surprising, because managers get positive feedback and rewards of pay increases and promotions for optimizing their own restricted operations. The accountant believes that his true objective in manufacturing is the preparation of the cost control report, whereas in reality his job is to improve production planning and cost control. The engineer designs the product in complete ignorance of product policy or marketing strategy. The sales manager pursues his objective of increasing sales by a given amount without regard to market segmentation, profitability of customer or product groups, and overall corporate strategy. Shop foremen hoard parts because they are rewarded for shop output and not for inventory management.

The common tendency to identify problems and seek solutions in terms of individual units rather than overall company objectives leads us to our principles of the organizational subsystem:

1. Managers owe their *loyalties* to particular organizational units rather than the whole enterprise because of their fear of what will happen if their units don't survive.
2. Managers *promote* their own organizational units at the expense of the whole enterprise because they can't be held responsible for failure of the whole.
3. Managers tend to *identify* with their specialties or particular units because they see them as critical to the survival of the entire enterprise.

Some way must be found to relate individual performance to total company performance. The systems approach to planning and control can provide a good start.

THE PROS AND CONS OF SHORT-RANGE PLANNING

Short-range plannning (frequently called operational or annual planning) is almost always financial in nature; that is, it expresses goals and performances standards in financial terms. A number of devices have been used in an attempt to achieve a higher degree of organizational integration. Variously called profit center planning, management by objectives, planning and control for profit, and return-on-investment (ROI) planning and control, each approach identifies the determinants of profitability and establishes a system for planning and controlling them. Most of the approaches are either a direct descendant or a variation of the Du Pont system, which was pioneered in the early 1900s but was not widely adopted until the profit center concept became popular in the fifties and sixties.

The basic notion is to decentralize profit responsibility to profit centers, where standards of performance for sales, turnover, and cost of sales are established. In turn, those elements are broken down into measurable and controllable components such as investment (fixed assets, inventory, accounts receivable, and cash) and cost of sales (direct labor, overhead, selling, transportation, and administration). The elements are, naturally, integrated with the income statement.

Short-range financial planning has several advantages. It makes identification and control of profit determinants of separate organizational entities easier. Its use as a common denominator for comparison purposes and as a yardstick of performance and presumably as a motivator has been widespread. And as a side benefit it has provided techniques for evaluating and auditing capital investment proposals.

Multidivisional companies have almost uniformly gone to some variation of profit center planning and control. Many have command centers or elaborate chart rooms backed up by sophisticated computer operations. Such a company is AMF, the very successful diversified producer of industrial and leisure time products. In the bowels of its 29-story headquarters building in New York is a chart room that displays variance charts on each profit center and more than sixty diversified divisions. Included in the basic information are budget variances in dollars and percents in the areas of total budget, volume, price, product mix, cost variables, fixed cost–shipping volume, over- or underabsorbed overhead, production volume, operating expenses, nonoperating income and expenses, and inventory turnover. AMF's chairman Rodney C. Gott cited the chart room and "our abiding emphasis on the control and operation of our business" as reasons for the corporation's success.

Short-range planning became a finer instrument of planning and control in the very recent past as tools and techniques became refined. Companies whose sales are dependent on rapidly changing variables, for example, Jantzen, the bathing suit manufacturer, update sales forecasts weekly to plan and control production. AMF's system is successful because of its ability to react quickly to problem areas. Program evaluation and review technique (PERT), a tool of program-project management, has given way to the more sophisticated graphical evaluation and review technique (GERT), a tool that permits iterative planning and control.

However, despite the necessity of using it in some form, short-range planning doesn't go far enough toward giving us the integrative approach we seek. Shortcomings generally fall into these classes:

Accounting costs. These are historical and rarely reflect current costs, replacement costs, or comparative costs of different operations.

Assignment of costs. It is difficult to assign responsiblity to specific individuals.

Beating the system. Deferring maintenance, postponing R&D, firing staff personnel, and a variety of creative bookkeeping measures are available to the manager who wants to make sure that his short-range objectives are met.

Short-run nature. Because of the focus on annual financial results, such factors as maintenance, employee development, social responsibility, and contribution to long-range objectives are not measured.

INTEGRATION THROUGH LONG-RANGE PLANNING

Few recent developments in management have had the growth and widespread acceptance of long-range planning (LRP). The research and literature surrounding it have been multiplied by professional planning groups, universities, and corporate planning directors. Planning horizons have been extended to five, ten, and even twenty years as firms in the natural resource (mining, oil, paper) and manufacturing industries attempt to chart a course for the future. Courses and seminars on planning are proliferating as more and more companies attempt to predict the future by assessing the impact of the external environment of the firm.

Long-range planning is a difficult task because it is concerned with the distant future. It is made more difficult by the tendency of most managers to concentrate on the short run—today's problem. A well-known planning consultant concludes that "long-range planning is a discipline which is almost incompatible with the temperment of the American business executive." Despite that, LRP is necessary not only for removing some of the uncertainty of the future but also for providing direction, an integrative element for the organization.

How are goals and activities integrated by planning? Consider the hodgepodge of external factors, artifically established organizational components, natural systems of business activities (production, logistics, financial, information, behavioral, and so on), and physical and human resources. Planning is the system that weaves those factors together into a tight fabric. Without planning, to continue the analogy, we would have a twisted mass of threads instead.

Aside from the obvious reason that it saves you money, LRP is supported by a strong systems argument. First, it forces you to define and focus on your objectives because you can't plan without them. Second, good plans provide a subsequent means of control. Third, LRP tends to integrate the organization into a system. Finally, if you don't plan, your competitors who do so will eventually put you out of business. Of the 25 top industrial firms of 1920, fewer than 15 retain their rank. Three (Armour, Swift, Pullman) are no longer in the top 100, and 2 have been acquired or gone bankrupt. Coming out of nowhere to replace them are such firms as IBM, ITT, Tenneco, Continental Oil, and Eastman Kodak, all known for their planning systems.

STRATEGIC PLANNING

Although short-range (operational) and intermediate-range (developmental) planning are nothing new to most medium-size and larger firms, strategic planning is not widespread and is still evolving in concept and practice. It differs from the short-range plans in three respects: (1) The formulation of company objectives is an integral part of the planning process. (2) The scope, both of time and environment, is much broader. (3) The effects are much more pervasive and more enduring.

If there is a single characteristic that distinguishes a well-managed firm from a poorly managed one, a successful company from an unsuccessful one, it is strategic planning. A strategy is essential. It comprises the company image, the niche, and the competitive edge; it is the integrative element that provides a unified sense of direction to the organization so that it can compete successfully with other firms. It defines your product/market scope and the nature of your business. Without a strategy, integration is impossible.

Year after year the correlation between outstanding results and strategic planning is proved. Except for a few notable exceptions such as ITT and TRW, the conglomerate movement and the individual conglomerates failed because of a lack of total systems (integrative) strategy. Many chose pyramidal growth as their objective without too much regard for making and selling a product at a profit against entrenched competition. Operations were secondary. When the financial chain letter ran out, the managers realized that strategy should have had something to do with operations.

Some food chains, retail chains, utilities, and manufacturers have had poor results because their strategies failed to adapt to changing residential and buying habits of the U.S. consumer. The major U.S. steel companies found themselves in a precarious position vis-à-vis Japanese steel companies because of their failure to do their strategic homework and adopt the new processes of the competition in Japan. They failed also to recognize the importance of technological research and capital investment.

On the positive side, we can list dozens of success stories that are directly attributable to correct strategy. Among them are Xerox (aggressive marketing and go-go attitude), IBM ("we sell solutions and service, not just computers"), ITT (sound justifiable acquisitions financed with cash and placed under tight planning and control), Walt Disney (find a niche and fill it), Eastman Kodak (product reliability), Sears (customer is king), S. S. Kresge Co. (upgrade, discount, experiment), and J. C. Penney (upgrade, innovate, research).

For a turnaround situation attributable to strategy we have only to look at Marcor's Mongomery Ward. The now-famous administration of Sewell Avery left the company with run-down operations and ripe for a takeover because it had $325 million in cash as a result of a mistaken retrenchment strategy. A former Sears vice-president took over the ailing company and completely turned it around with a new strategy. The elements of his strategy were to eliminate small stores and go to big ones with a new distribution setup, reorganize around a mass-merchandising concept, invade the new big markets, design good internal planning and control systems, and do all that without substantially endangering earnings.

Strategic planning also encourages integration. It facilitates the systems approach in three important ways. First, the emphasis is on the decision-making aspects in which various levels become involved. Moreover, the strategic plan provides the fundamental premise upon which the developmental plans and the operational plans are subsequently based. That is shown conceptually in Figure 6-1.

Second, a major benefit of strategic planning lies in the involvement of company strategy rather than a document entitled "The Five-Year Plan." In other words, *the process is more important than the plan itself.* The strategic plan serves as a valuable communication device for getting agreement on objectives and courses of action.

Finally, strategic planning is investigative and exploratory in nature as opposed to the short-range profit plan, which is oriented to short-run control of performance standards. The short-range financial plan is not likely to release the long-run thinking and innovative research that is characteristic of strategic planning.

THE APPROACH TO STRATEGIC PLANNING

Not all strategic planning is successful—one chief executive compared its lasting effects to those of a Chinese dinner. His observation reflects

Figure 6-1. Integration of planning and operations.

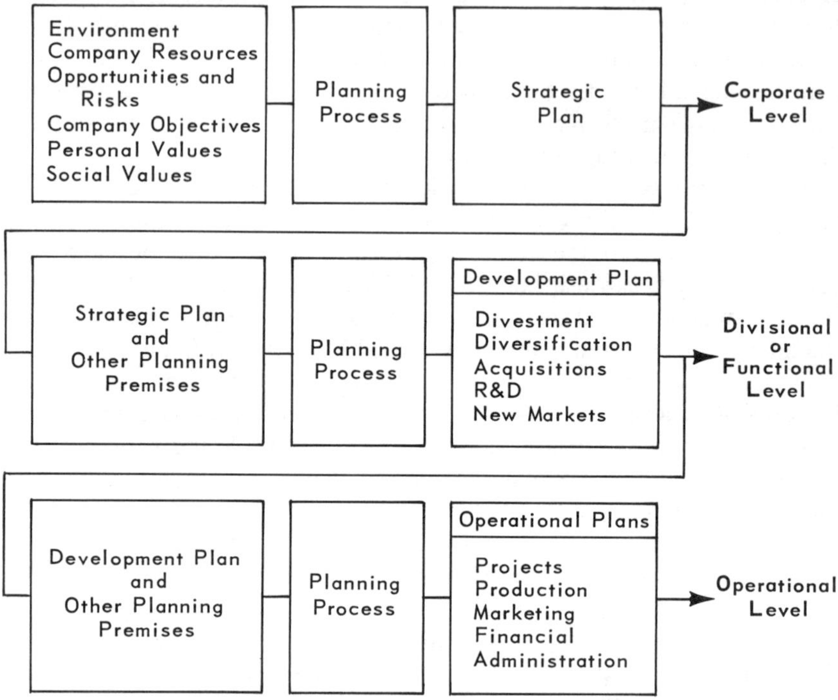

the fate of much strategic planning. Many companies only go through the motions of the process or fail to make the planning meaningful by bringing it down to the level of current decisions. On the other hand, successful companies take a systems analysis approach, one that results in decisions and not just plans. Such an approach has these characteristics:

Formality. Strategic planning is not something that can be scribbled on the back of an envelope. Indeed, one of the most intriguing managerial phenomena of the 1960s and early 1970s was the rapid spread of formal corporate strategic planning. Few managerial techniques have had such impact. The planning has been accompanied by both organizational developments (staff departments) and refined methods. The usefulness of formality is obvious; it forces a structured approach to the setting of objectives and long-range strategy, and it enlists participation of those ultimately responsible for accomplishment.

Integration of planning and control. We have seen in Figure 6-1 how planning can integrate the various vertical elements and horizontal levels of the company. However, unless the implementation of plans is *controlled,* plans are not likely to be fulfilled. Integrated planning and control (IPC) means simply that plans must be utilized as a base upon which the control system is subsequently built.

Futurity. By definition planning is futuristic. However, the trouble with most planning is that it proceeds upon a foundation of existing conditions, policies, products, markets, and organizational structure. Future, innovative, planning asks questions: What opportunities and risks will be present in the environment of the future? What resources will we need to tap those opportunities? The trouble has been that most planning proceeds from the limitations of today, an approach that is likely to perpetuate those limitations.

Modeling. The future holds so many what-if questions that strategic planning is avoided by many executives on the ground that the future is too unsure to be predicted. Modeling helps to overcome that objection. It is a technique whereby the predicted real world is abstracted into a set of relations that can be manipulated to predict various outcomes. That is, for various alternative future conditions, the manager can examine the several outcomes of a particular decision or plan.

Decision orientation. The major weakness of most planning is that it doesn't lead to decisions that must be made *today* to insure the competitive success of the company in the *future.* It is not enough to have a strategic plan—period. It is not enough to do a forecast and stop. It is not enough to project current operations for a five-year period. Something must happen as a result of the plan. *Actions* must first be spelled out and then take place.

STEPS IN STRATEGIC PLANNING

A structured approach to strategic planning, one that will insure organizational integration, is hard to come by. No easy step-by-step or cookbook method is available. The following approach is the one that many businesses take. It is shown schematically in Figure 6-2.

1. *Research the environment.* Identify the existing and future environmental conditions that have or may have an influence on the company. Some of them are:

Economic. Monetary, fiscal, and general business conditions; health and growth of the economy; GNP and disposable personal income; major shifts in demand; foreign competition; labor force and rates.

Competitive. Future of your industry and firm relative to other industries and firms; potential inroads and competitive hazards.

Technological. Major technological trends that will offer both opportunities for new products and risks of obsolescence; capital requirements and availability of production factors.

Governmental. Prospects for regulation, intervention, subsidy; impact of government on foreign competition.

Market. The prospective market for existing and proposed products and services.

From this analysis of strengths and weaknesses will emerge a clear definition of *competitive edge*—a factor of tremendous importance in the subsequent definition of product/market scope.

2. *Identify company strengths and weaknesses.* From an examination of the factors in (1) certain tentative opportunities will emerge. An assessment of company resources, existing and potential, is needed.

Marketing. Identify the marketing strategy, the sales force, the distribution channels, and other marketing forces that are available.

Production. The plant, labor force, capital equipment, location, and stability of production level.

Finance. The capital structure, financial policies, and availability of financing of the required types at an acceptable cost.

Research and development. The talent and organization required for the research and design of new or improved products.

Management. The management depth available to achieve a strategy or to take advantage of opportunities.

3. *Opportunities and risks.* After company strengths and weaknesses are examined in the light of economic and other environmental factors, certain opportunities and associated risks will become apparent. Perhaps new product and service opportunities are obvious, but the company may or may not have the strengths to take advantage of them. This type of assessment will lead to the identification of product and market areas.

4. *Personal values.* The aesthetic, social, religious, and personal alues of top management and influential stockholders exert a significant nfluence on strategy. They must be taken into account. A go-go man-gement may accept certain risks that a conservative management may ot. Some company executives believe that companies should contribute o communities, not just take from them. Others consider profit to be he only reason for a business to exist.

5. *Social responsibility.* The deteriorating image of business, coupled vith the accelerating demand for social responsiblity, requires that any roposed strategy take account of the social aspects. Environmentalism, onsumerism, and governmentalism are among those aspects.

6. *Corporate objectives.* After completing the analysis required by teps 1 through 5, the planner should be in a good position to establish nd/or review company objectives. They should not be stated in tradi-ional platitudes such as "make a fair return for stockholders and pro-ide a nice place to work"; instead, they should be in quantified form hat can subsequently be translated into developmental and operational lans. For a start, the planner would want to identify product lines, rofitability, growth, standing in industry, reputation, capital use, man-gement development, innovation, and employment conditions.

7. *Strategy. Now the big question: what is your strategy?* How do ou get where you want to go? What grand plan should you have to ompete against other firms and surpass them? How can you reach the bjectives of your strategic plan? What should be your corporate char-cter? How will you achieve and finance growth? What should be your narket share and segment? What are your major policies (product, mar-eting, finance, production, personnel)?

8. *Implement the strategy.* Having developed the strategic plan, you mplement it through the traditional functions of more detailed planning, rganizing, and controlling. You are now ready to utilize the classical ools of developmental planning and budgetary (financial) planning. At his stage, you have achieved companywide synergism through the inte-rative device of the strategic plan. Now each manager can relate his articular organizational entity to the whole. (See Figure 6-2.)

The preceding eight-step approach for the development of overall cor-orate strategy can be adapted to the analysis of products, product lines, r divisions. One firm that is following it with enthusiasm is General Electric Co. Strategic business planning is a legacy of the outgoing chair-nan, and it is widely understood that the new president, Reginald H. Jones, was selected for the top spot because of his intimate identifica-

Figure 6-2. A framework for strategic planning.

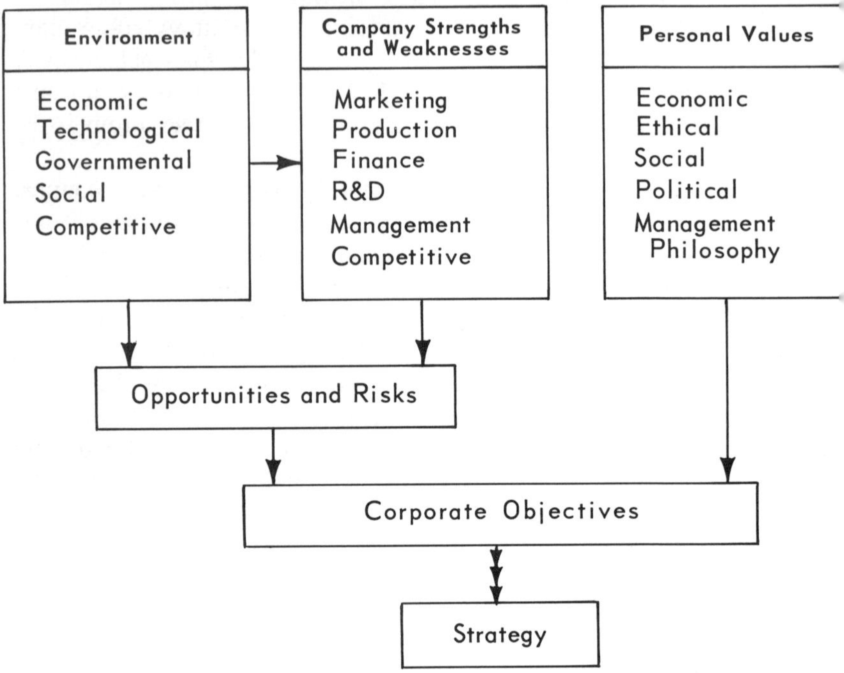

tion with it.[1] The concept involves a continuing in-depth analysis of market share, growth prospects, profitability, and cash-generating power of each venture, product line, or division. These are typical questions: Is the product segment mature? Is it one we should get out of? Is it one we should be investing in and expanding?

Somewhat on the order of Texas Instruments, GE has broken down its operations into 43 strategic business units (SBU), organizational entities or ventures that are capable of performing strategic planning on their own. The logic behind the process is to identify the products and areas with high growth potential, to put money and management attention behind them, and to organize for the effort. With regard to organization, GE's decentralization policy has been criticized in the past because it provides a temptation for managers to go for short-term results. Strategic planning forces the long-range view because managers must now look five years or more ahead. Also, their performance is now rated on adherance to their strategic plans rather than on short-term profits.

The president of a consulting firm that is helping GE implement strategic planning says of the process: "Once it starts, it becomes almost a religion."

BETTER CONTROL SYSTEMS

The classical approach to control has been a three-step process: (1) set standards of performance, (2) measure performance against standard, and (3) correct deviations. Those steps will provide the foundation for the systems approach to control, but the process has had several shortcomings or potential dangers:

Standards frequently have not provided true criteria of performance because progress against achieving overall company objectives has not been measured.

Performance standards that were usually tied into short-run financial planning got short-term results that frequently caused longer-range considerations to be overlooked. Many managers resorted to creative bookkeeping.

Control has taken on a restrictive or constraining connotation that discourages innovation. The persons being controlled have viewed the standard, and not the work itself, as the overriding measure of performance.

Reports were considered control reports to measure the performance of subordinates, not to improve operations or decisions. Subordinates were therefore reluctant to make reports and considered report preparation an unpleasant task. Few managers use reports to manage.

Lateness was a characteristic of deviation or variance reporting. In most cases the lapse of time between a deviation and its discovery precluded action until it was too late.

Synergism was not achieved because performance standards didn't integrate the departments and organizational entities of the company. Indeed, standards between departments were sometimes in conflict. The control process as carried out engendered conflict between the individual and his controllers.

To eliminate these shortcomings of classical control systems and to achieve greater integration of the organization, a modern system should be built around five central ideas: (1) Integrate planning and control. (2) Relate the system to the organization structure. (3) So design the output of the system that it facilitates decision making about the job to be done by the person on the job. (4) Make sure the information to the person on the job is timely. (5) Place emphasis on self-control by the individual on the job.

Although the *integration of planning with subsequent control* is a relatively simple system idea, it is often overlooked in practice. The primary reason why is that most control systems are short-run in nature and measure only routine operational variables instead of achievement of plans.

The central notion of IPC is that each level of plans provides the standards of performance (objectives) for the next lower level of operations. When the objectives of a company are consistent and coherent, the control system should reinforce them by measuring performance against the objective and the cost of the performance.

A fairly common situation results when long-run plans are overlooked in favor of short-term reporting. During the conglomeration era of the late sixties, many conglomerates resorted to creative bookkeeping and paid only lip service to overall corporate objectives in a desperate effort to maintain the upward trend of earnings per share. When the financial house of cards collapsed, many executives admitted that integrated planning and control of operations—not conglomeration—would have yielded much better results.

There are also the related considerations of information overload and the cost of the control system. In this age of complex operations and computer-based information systems, control reports can easily get out of hand. The danger is in reporting everything to everyone and letting a control system expand until it collapses under its own weight. Those possibilities mean that the substantive objectives of the information system must be worked out and must be internally consistent. Purpose, timeliness, accuracy, content, and cost should be specified.

Relating control systems to the organization structure is complex and difficult but necessary. In the past, the effectiveness of organizations has not been achieved because the parts—the functions or organizational elements—have not been related to a whole unified set of objectives. Although copies of the customer's order may have gone to sales, production control, and accounts receivable, those activities were not closely coordinated in either the planning or control process. The information system has been primarily a financial control system built around a chart of accounts. The controls have been concerned largely with cost in dollars and not achievement of objectives.

One reason for failure to interrelate the parts into a unified whole has been the narrow view of the engineer, salesman, accountant, or inventory clerk who will not relate his speciality or box on the organization chart to the remainder of the organization. The result has been a focus on the design of control systems without organizational integration. The problem and solution are demonstrated in Figure 6-3. The heavy solid line indicates the authority relationships, information flows, and control systems of the classical organization. Concern is with formal authority relationships and the chain of command rather than the interrelationship of the parts. The dashed lines show the same organizational structure but with the parts joined together by means of a planning and control information system. Each organizational entity is seen as an information system with the components of input, processor, and output.

Figure 6-3. The organization as an information system.

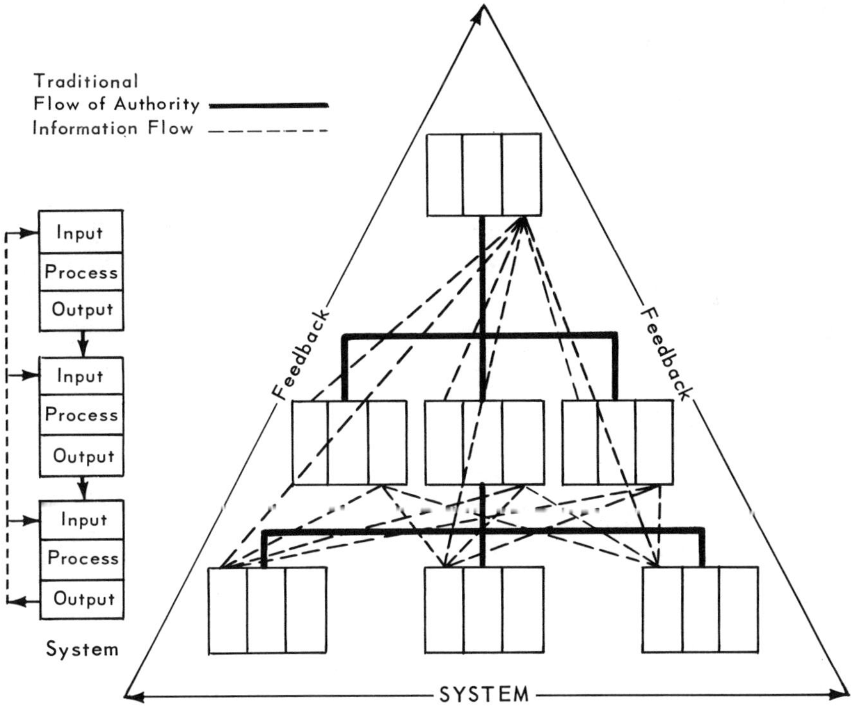

SOURCE: Robert G. Murdick and Joel E. Ross, *Information Systems for Modern Management*, © 1972, p. 172. Reprinted by permission of Prentice-Hall, Inc., Englewood Cliffs, New Jersey.

Each is connected through information and communication channels, and each becomes a decision point that relates to the others.

Another determinant of control systems design is the company's management philosophy. If you are a Theory X manager, run things by the book, and believe that subordinates should be rather strictly regulated, then your system is likely to be more detailed, more evident, and more overwhelming in its approach to the control of the individual. If you are a more participative Theory Y manager who believes in the basic positive aspects of human behavior, your system is likely to be based on exception reporting and a consultative solution to problems.

The control system also should be designed for decision making, not for post facto reporting. That is another way to say that it is necessary to specify the objectives of the system and the magnitude of variance permitted before a decision on a course of corrective action will be needed.

The computer technician, accountant, or systems specialist is likely to state objectives in terms of file structure, retrieval techniques, or reporting times. The manager user must define systems in terms of legitimate information demands for solution of *his* problems and in terms of transactions that are related to an objective. That does not mean processing efficiency or the automation of records.

Timely information is essential to coordinate and synchronize action. The most relevant information on the most critical variables is worth nothing unless it arrives in time for action based on that information to be taken. The ideal system, of course, is the one that provides information in sufficient time for a deviation to be anticipated and corrected *before* it occurs.

FEEDFORWARD CONTROL

A basic requirement of any control system is feedback. Unfortunately, most existing systems rely on feedback *after* deviation from desired performance is discovered. Most managers are being frustrated by discovering too late that actual accomplishments are missing planned goals; they have been dependent on accounting and statistical data that are historical in nature. Variations from optimum inventory levels take months to analyze and correct. Project completion dates are slipped for lack of up-to-date information on progress. Cash budgets are over or under plan because forecasts of variables are not available. All of those corrections from standard take time and cost money while deviations are being discovered, analyzed, and corrected.

By definition, feedback is derived from the output of a system. Since the output—the past—cannot be changed, effective *feedforward control* must be aimed at preventing present and future deviations from plans. Except for a very few applications such as PERT/CPM and a limited number of modeling techniques, *feedforward control* has not been utilized. The idea, borrowed from engineering, is to anticipate the lags in feedback systems by monitoring inputs and predicting their effects on outcome variables. By doing that, action can be taken to change the inputs and thereby bring the system output into equilibrium with desired standards of performance *before* measurement of the output discloses a deviation from standard. If, for example, we can determine the input variables that influence the cash balance in our bank account, we can monitor and manipulate those variables in advance to avoid an overdrawn account.

The approach is not difficult. Through a process of careful planning and analysis the input variables are identified and placed in their relationship to the desired end results (output). Then a model of the control system is developed to show how the input variables affect desired goals. When that relationship is clear, the inputs can be monitored and manipulated in order to achieve desired results *before they occur.*

The feedforward approach to cash budgeting is illustrated in Figure 6-4.

ACHIEVING INTEGRATION THROUGH MANAGEMENT INFORMATION SYSTEMS

The functions of management (planning, initiating, and controlling) as well as the functions of the firm (marketing, production, and finance) are inextricably linked by a common system of information. How well managerial and technical functions are performed is determined in large degree by the quality of the company's management information systems (MIS).

Figure 6-5 is a conceptual representation of the three systems of planning, operating, and controlling integrated into a system of management. The planning system receives as input the planning premises and objectives on which strategies and plans are based, and they in turn provide the input to the operating system. Feedback on performance

Figure 6-4. The feedforward approach to cash budgeting.

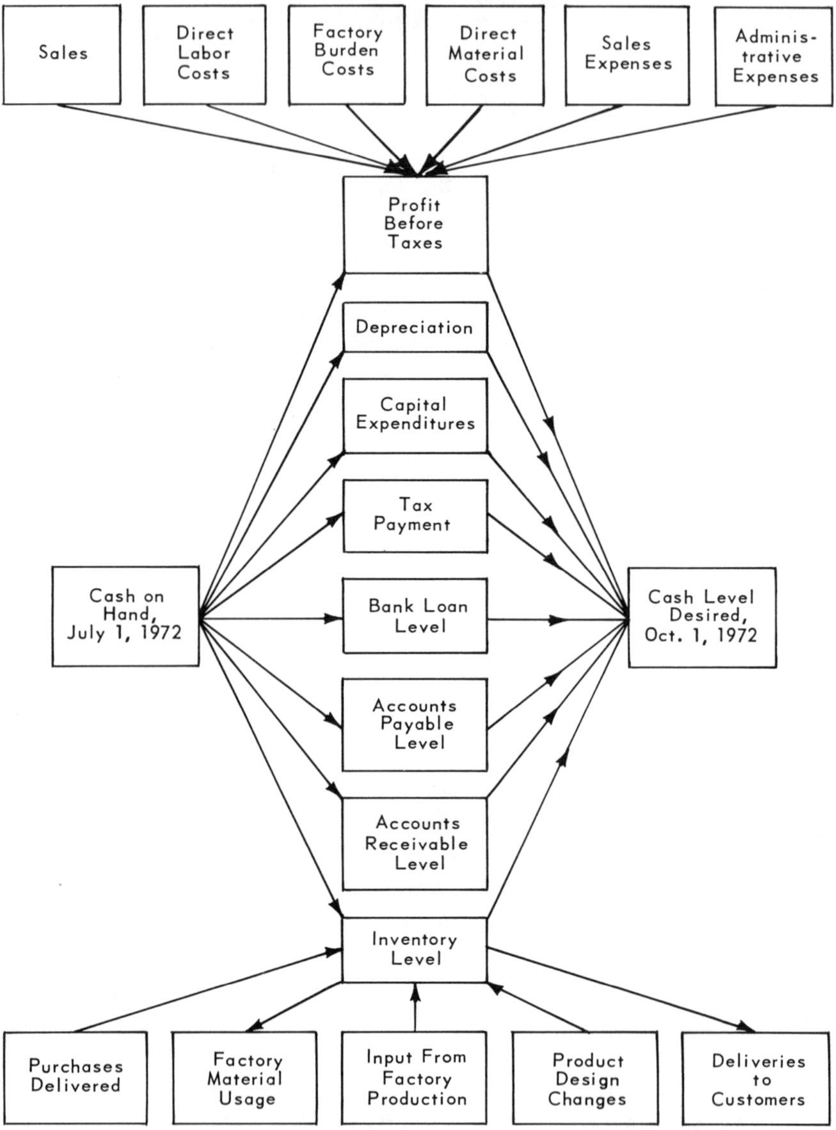

SOURCE: Harold Koontz and Robert W. Bradspies, "Managing Through Feed-forward Control," *Business Horizons*, June 1972.

Figure 6-5. Achieving integration by use of a management information system.

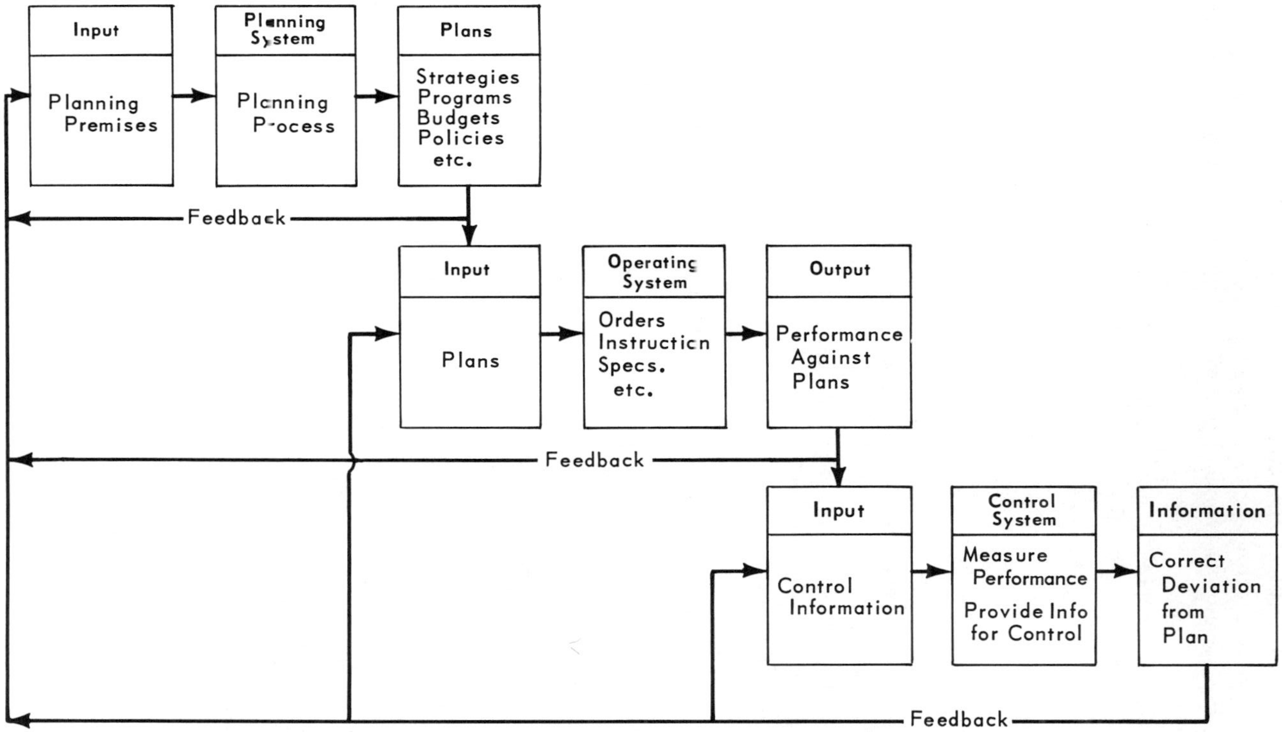

SOURCE: Robert G. Murdick and Joel E. Ross, *Information Systems for Modern Management*, © 1972, p. 174. Reprinted by permission of Prentice-Hall, Inc., Englewood Cliffs, New Jersey.

is obtained through the control system that monitors the operating system and furnishes information as feedback to both it and the planning system. Decisions are made within each system based upon information, and within each system there is a flow of information to implement changes and correct deviations based on feedback from other systems. It is evident that the entire process depends upon the vehicle of a properly designed MIS.

SUMMARY: TAKE A SYSTEMS APPROACH TO MANAGEMENT

We offer ten suggestions that can help you build that elusive synergistic attribute of your organization:

1. *Adopt the systems approach* as a philosophy of management. It is a method of viewing problems in their totality to achieve more nearly optimal solutions.
2. *Review your existing financial planning and control system.* Make sure it provides for measuring the true objectives of the company and that it doesn't encourage a short-run gain at the expense of long-range goals.
3. *Establish a systems climate* that encourages managers to think in terms of the whole organization rather than just the survival of their own organizational units. Put the focus on *company* problems, not departmental ones.
4. *Establish a formal strategic planning system* to identify a competitive edge and provide a product/market definition for strategy implementation.
5. *Relate operational plans and developmental plans* to the corporate strategy. That is the primary method of achieving integration in planning. Moreover, the approach provides a basis for subsequent coordination and control.
6. *Review the organization structure* for better integrative approaches. Check whether task forces, programs, or other innovations can achieve better communications and contributions to common goals. Insure that control systems are based upon system problems and do not restrict interdepartmental teamwork.
7. *Integrate planning and control.* The results necessary to achieve the plans must form the standard against which performance is measured. Planning and control must be closely related.

8. *Design control systems* to facilitate achievement of objectives. Don't let the system itself become the objective!

9. *Design feedforward systems.* When it is possible and appropriate, model the system so that input variables can be monitored and manipulated to head off deviations before they occur.

10. *Review management information systems.* Check whether you are getting clerical automation and systems designed by and for technicians or true information systems for decision making and managing.

7

Your Money and Information About It

In the past he was buried six deep,
But now he's moved up with a leap.
The accountant's gained ground
As firms changed things around,
And he works at the top of the heap.
R.G.M.

Not many years ago, the accountant was considered the historian of the firm, a miser pitted against progress, and a nit-picking penny watcher. Since World War II, his image has changed dramatically as his responsibilities and value to top management have expanded. Today the accountant is decision-oriented. Every activity of the firm, planning or control, ties into the master financial plan. Rapid company moves require skillful financial planning, comprehensive and valid information about internal and external conditions, good cash planning, and most importantly, ingenious tax planning. In both major moves and day-to-day operations, the accountant sits at the heart of two vital systems: money flow and information. What has happened to change the green-eyeshade robot into the most dynamic and fluid figure in modern complex business? And equally important, what do he and his fellow workers think about future changes in business?

THE VALUE OF MONEY

For centuries money lenders have known that a coin in the hand is worth more than the promise of the same coin a year hence, but accountants remained oblivious to that fact until very recently. Upon being drawn into the capital budgeting process and product evaluation projects, they became concerned about different future patterns of cash flow.

It is now common, but far from universal, practice to worry about the time value of money in planning several years ahead, but companies are only just thinking about it in connection with operations budgets. When accountants recognize that operations budgets are related to cash management (discussed below), more attention will be given to timing of expenditures in such budgets. One example should provide an eye-opener, so let's look at Table 7-1. Here are direct expenses for an engineering program extending over a 15-month period. If money costs the company 2 percent per month, or could be invested by the company at that rate, the discounted or present value of all expenses is shown to be $853,500.

Now suppose management applies some very refined planning and decides not to hoard men and materials, but instead to bring them in closer to the time when they will be used. Table 7-2 shows the revised budget with a present value of only $809,400. Doesn't that make more sense than assuming the project will cost $853,500 no matter how the money is paid out? In other words, be your own banker and take profit from the interest.

CASH MANAGEMENT: THE ZERO BANK ACCOUNT

One of the most persistent myths among businessmen and some financial conservatives is that a good-sized cash account is the sign of a robust and healthy company. The primary objective of cash management is to maximize the earnings from every dollar the company possesses and minimize the cost of every dollar the company borrows. The key to good cash management is to forecast and manage cash flow so that cash on hand is kept as close to zero as possible and yet cash will be immediately available to meet needs.

Large companies today have full-time cash managers. Intermediate and small companies should assign the responsibility to someone within the organization. It is fairly easy to measure whether a cash manager is paying his own way by estimating the company's earnings and savings attributable to him.

Table 7-1. Example of first budget.

END OF MONTH	DISCOUNT FACTOR (2%/mo.)	DIRECT MATERIALS AND SUB-CONTRACTS ($000)	DIRECT LABOR ($000)	TOTAL ($000) (col. 3 + col. 4)	PRESENT VALUE ($000) (col. 2 × col. 5)
1	.980	50	12	62	60.7
2	.961	100	18	118	113.5
3	.942	150	25	175	165.0
4	.924	30	40	70	64.6
5	.906		70	70	64.0
6	.888		70	70	62.1
7	.871		80	80	69.7
8	.853		70	70	59.7
9	.837	20	60	80	67.0
10	.820		50	50	41.0
11	.804		40	40	32.2
12	.788		30	30	23.6
13	.773		20	20	15.4
14	.758		10	10	7.6
15	.743		10	10	7.4
Total		350	605	955	853.5

Table 7-2. Example of revised budget.

DIRECT MATERIALS AND SUB-CONTRACTS ($000)	DIRECT LABOR ($000)	TOTAL ($000) (col. 1 + col. 2)	PRESENT VALUE ($000) discount factor × col. 3
	12	12	11.7
	15	15	14.4
	20	20	18.8
50	30	80	74.0
	40	40	36.7
50	40	90	80.0
50	50	100	87.1
100	60	160	136.4
50	70	120	100.0
	68	68	55.7
	60	60	48.2
	50	50	39.4
50	40	90	69.5
	30	30	22.7
	20	20	14.8
350	605	955	809.4

SOURCE (both tables): Robert G. Murdick, "The Time Value of Money." Reprinted from *Machine Design* (January 13, 1972). Copyright 1972 by the Pentagon Publishing Company, Cleveland, Ohio.

Cash Forecasts—Thinking Ahead

Annual and monthly cash flow forecasts are common. The effective cash manager, however, also prepares a forecast of cash receipts and expenditures for each of the next five days. American National Insurance Co. of Galveston forecasts daily cash flow for about two weeks in advance. To implement the forecast cash position and invest unutilized cash, a forecast of the bank balance is prepared as well. Cash management can then concentrate on getting the most value from each dollar by timing its release to, and through, the bank system.

Accelerated Receipts—Vacuuming Up Collections

Three methods are being used to accelerate receipts. The first is to get *quick conversion of receivables* into cash. Pursuing that method often starts a tug-of-war that the company loses to its customers. Careful calculation is required so that cash discounts large enough to motivate payments will be less than the company's earnings on early payments when invested. Computerization of billings makes it possible to handle service charges or unearned discounts promptly so that customers are not antagonized.

The second method is based on the *lock box;* companies that operate over wide geographical areas have established local bank accounts to receive payments from customers. That gets the cash into the company's accounts instead of having it floating around in transport systems. A phone call each day to each bank will keep the cash manager apprised of the cash at his disposal. The third method applies primarily to large transfers of cash; telegraphic transfer is arranged for when routine and repetitive transfers are to be made.

When large, regular collections are being made by a seller, a *preauthorized check* mailed to a bank in the area of the country where the customer is located speeds up the cash flow to the seller. Insurance companies find it to be a very profitable device (in the collection of premiums, for example).

Slow the Outgo

Actual practice in slowing payments varies from the unethical to the very sophisticated. A giant retailer, for example, allegedly pays vendors after 20 days but takes the 2 percent 10-day discount. Some organizations may issue paychecks on Friday on distant banks so that the checks will not clear until after the weekend.

Some more sophisticated methods may be classified as *incremental funding*. One of the easiest and most significant accounts to fund incrementally is the payroll, because it is a stable large account. Further, its timing is fixed. The method consists of first analyzing the pattern in which paychecks clear the bank. Since employees tend to cash their paychecks in the same manner (at their own banks, at creditors, on Friday, or on a certain day in the next week), the distribution of bank clearings follows a consistent pattern. An example is shown in Table 7-3.

Accounts payable to vendors can be incrementally funded owing to the geographical distribution of vendors. Also, it is an amazing fact that, even when the companies are sizable, checks may languish for weeks in vendors' offices before they are deposited. Funding can therefore be based on both distance and account. Checks can be mailed on Wednesday evening and some funding be made on Friday, but most funding may be delayed until Monday.

Another important application of incremental funding is by withholding taxes and payments to governments as allowed by law. Partial payments of sales taxes, social security taxes, and state and federal withholding taxes may be made. As an example, the Federal government allows for a 90 percent payment on withholding and FICA within a quarter. It allows a full month after the quarter for the balance.

Corporate Finance and Cash Planning

In the early sixties it seemed that U.S. companies could finance almost anything, but by 1971 only 58 percent of the cash needed by nonfinancial corporations came from internal sources. AT&T has the greatest need for capital of any company in the world, and its experience exem-

Table 7-3. Payroll releases, funding, and bank clearances.

	PAYCHECK RELEASE, %	FUNDING, %	BANK CLEARANCE, %
Thursday	20	12	6
Friday	80	22	9
Monday		46	51
Tuesday		15	25
Wednesday		5	9
	100	100	100

plifies the change for business as a whole. In the early 1960s AT&T got about 61 percent of its money from inside the company while raising over $1 billion a year in the financial markets. In 1972, it got about 50 percent from inside and had to look for $4 billion outside.

Supertight credit by Federal Reserve, the collapse of Penn Central and the near collapse of Lockheed and a score of other companies, the worst international monetary crises in four decades, and wage-price control effects on profits have had tremendous impact on cash availability. Treasurer John L. Cowan of Continental Oil Co. says he used to spend only 25 percent of his time on making financial deals; now he spends 50 percent of his time on them.

"Hot money" has entered the business world. With rapid inflation, revaluation, and devaluation occurring in many countries and simultaneously throughout the world, cash in the bank raises the question, "What bank?" International companies now find it necessary to have an expert in international arbitrage keep their funds moving from one country to another to avoid shrinking value.

How Are Relations at the Bank?

Small and medium-size companies are not always aware of the advantages of close personal relations with their banks' officers. Often a bank can help place idle cash in the most advantageous place for income. Treasury bills, commercial paper, and special placement may be recommended. The cash needs of large New York banks have necessitated daily borrowings at high interest rates from smaller banks scattered throughout the country. That offers an excellent opportunity for a company to put cash to work on a day-to-day basis by sharing a high interest return with its banker.

IS YOUR FINANCIAL INFORMATION A THREE-DOLLAR BILL?

Management expect its financial information to represent the condition of the firm, the flow of money, the trend of accounts, and significant changes that will occur both short and long range. It also expects information on present and anticipated variances from plans. It does not worry about accuracy to the nearest cent or dollar; it is concerned with kilobucks or megabucks. Now the question: After all the data gathering and cooking in the computer, what may make the resulting management information worthless or, even worse, disastrously misleading? The possibilities are three:

1. The data gathered and recorded are no good in the first place. For example, inventories may only be sampled and obsolete inventory may be counted with the good inventory. Another example might be the evaluation of property in a decaying area. The most common examples are clerical errors. The auditor can assert that financial statements are "fair," but he can never assert that they are true. With that leg knocked out from under him, the manager may wonder who *can* confirm that his financial reports are true. The accountant, internal or external, only guarantees that his manipulation of the data is OK, but we will take a nervous look at that offering further on.

2. The computer gang has garbled the data. Careless inputs and wrong time period inputs are examples. Complex models are often developed for computer processing, and over a period of time new employees fail to understand the model and its limitations. Beware of the electronic garbage pail!

3. Outsiders wander through the "open door policy" computer room or tap into teleprocessing lines. The financial report marked CONFIDENTIAL may be either erroneous, not confidential, or both.

Accountants are concerned with the *validity* of information: Are the conclusions correct, given the assumptions of input? With computerized accounting, new methods have been developed to follow the audit trail. In early computer days, auditors tested transactions around the computer; that is, source documents and summary accounts were traced to each other. If the results were consistent, the computer was assumed to be doing its job correctly.

Now it is more likely that transactions will be tested through the computer or else with the computer. The through-the-computer method involves using a test deck. When update programs are tested, the master file may be damaged, knowingly or unknowingly. Reversing the test transactions incorrectly may also lead to errors in the master file. Auditing with the computer means that the auditor puts his own program on the computer to analyze the company's transactions. The cost of preparing an alternative test program may be quite high.

CAN YOU DEPEND ON YOUR CPA AUDIT?

We believe that U.S. business managers, investors, and the general public have so little understanding of the meaning of the annual audited financial report as to make the report practically worthless for investment decisions. There are at least five reasons for that statement:

Reason 1. Much of the general public believes that the CPA makes a 100 percent examination of all company records.

Reason 2. The public and many managers believe that the statement "in conformity with generally accepted accounting principles" means the CPA has passed on the legality and conduct of the business. That is the same type of error the public makes with regard to the Good Housekeeping Seal of Approval.

Reason 3. Most nonfinancial managers as well as the public take the figures in the financial statements as *absolutes,* as if dozens of financial statements could not be prepared within accepted accounting principles. Abraham Pomerantz, a highly respected attorney in stockholder litigation, was quoted in *The Washington Post* as saying, "It's the bottom line that counts." If that is the nonfinancial expert's view, the public and most managers just don't understand the slop that makes up the gravy. We will touch upon that further on; here we simply ask the manager to reflect on inventory evaluation, depreciation write-offs, and the many little footnotes appended to financial statements as means for changing the bottom line.

Reason 4. Maybe accountants, being human after all, just don't perform to perfection. To illustrate, Peat, Marwick, Mitchell & Co. confirmed healthy profits for Yale Express in 1963 and 1964 that were, in fact, losses. The variance was discovered in 1965, and Yale Express went into bankruptcy.

The audited accounts of Pergamon Press Inc. showed a profit for 1968 of £2.1 million on net assets of £7 million. When another firm, Price Waterhouse & Co., was hired to investigate the affairs of Pergamon Press, many small "adjustments" revised the profit to only £495,000 on assets of £4.46 million.

A question that might arise is how accountants can really audit a company when they must depend on information supplied or withheld by that company. On July 10, 1972, Stirling Homex Corp., a pioneer manufacturer of modular housing, filed for bankruptcy under Chapter X of the Federal Bankruptcy Act. Early in 1971, just before Stirling Homex made a public offering of preferred stock, it changed accounting firms. Harris, Kerr, Forster & Co. was dropped; Price Waterhouse apparently refused to endorse Stirling Homex's accounting principles; and Peat, Marwick, Mitchell & Co. took over. There is considerable evidence that the company withheld vital information from its accounting firm before its sudden collapse.

Perhaps the greatest fraud of the twentieth century was the Equity

Funding case. Haskins & Sells, auditors of Equity Funding Corporation through 1971, and Seidman & Seidman, the firm's "independent auditors" through 1973, gravely assured investors that according to generally accepted accounting principles, $2 + 2 = 4$. Meanwhile Ronald H. Secrist, a former employee of Equity Funding, was having difficulty finding anyone who would accept his description of alleged massive fraud through fabrication of bogus policies by computer-tape modifications. When Illinois state insurance investigators drilled open a Chicago safe deposit vault that was supposed to contain more than $24 million in bonds that Equity Funding listed as security for its policies, the cupboard was bare. On April 5, 1973, a little belatedly, Equity Funding filed under Chapter X of the Bankruptcy Act. Over 100 banks and other institutions were stuck with about 2 million shares of stock. In the last few days of the decline, Equity's stocks were tossed from one institution to another like hot potatoes.

It has been suggested that if the accountants and the investment companies got together and sold the movie rights to this episode, they could have bailed the company out.

Reason 5. The investment in nontangible assets of most companies is growing rapidly in size and importance but is not being recorded on the books. Proprietary techniques, R&D experience, marketing information and systems, software programs, and human resources developed by the company are not accounted for. If we were buying or selling a company, we might pay a lot more for such intangible assets than for the tangible ones. For years, as an example, a big British oil company ran an enormously expensive introduction advertising program in the U.S. Certainly its profits were affected adversely. But if brand loyalty was thereby obtained from a sufficient segment of the market, it would probably be worth more than all the physical assets of the gasoline stations.

Perhaps it would be much better if audited reports were vaguely right than precisely wrong.

FINANCIAL DISCLOSURE—CHANGING RESPONSIBILITIES

The frank and controversial Leonard Spacek, senior partner of Arthur Anderson & Company, laid it on the line when he said:

> My brethren say, just tell the investors what the facts are and let them be on their guard. I say "booby trap." We cannot just present statements to investors and say, "You ought to be able to find the booby traps."[1]

Spacek was also quoted as saying:

> The accounting profession hasn't recognized the fact that public ownership exists. The profession still labors under the impression that it is working for entrepreneurs who know all the details about their companies—the accountant has thought little about what the public investor wants to know.[2]

Indeed, the moneymakers in the Stirling Homex case, for example, were not the public investors at large. Rather, Harper Sibley, who retired from the Stirling Homex board in 1971, is reported to have made $10 million on his total Stirling Homex investment. Other inside investors profited to the tune of hundreds of thousands of dollars by pulling out shortly before the collapse.

Company Collapses Leading to Greater Disclosure Requirements

The accounting profession does not appear to be strong enough to be independent of its clients. As a result, employees, investors, and the public may be misled by the audited annual report. Fuller disclosure has been forced on companies and accountants by angry investors and the SEC under its recent chairman, Willian J. Casey. Occidental Petroleum, Ampex, Westec, Yale Express, and BarChris are examples of insufficient disclosure. In the latter three instances, the accountants as well as the management were sued.

When left to their own devices, corporate managements have little desire to provide full and fair information to their stockholders. There is an underlying fear that such disclosure may result in a competitive disadvantage. That is particularly true with regard to a breakdown by divisions or product lines. Another fear is of the effects on collective bargaining with unions and on investors. Actually, companies often lack awareness of what the investor needs.

The arguments against greater disclosure in quarterly and annual reports are certainly invalid in two respects. Information required by the SEC in Report Form 10-K is proper information for the annual report also. Second, any information that is disclosed to security analysts should be promptly reported to the public.

Can CPA Firms Serve the Public in Secrecy?

The CPA firms have the public responsibility for fair disclosure of the affairs of other firms, but who is to judge them? If CPA firms do not fully disclose their financial status and operations, how can we know the extent to which they are captives of their clients? While the correlation between independence and wealth is not necessarily high, *perceived* independence is important.

The U.S. public, well educated and with rising expectations, is becoming increasingly dissatisfied with the way business operates and the apparent worthlessness of audited reports. The American Institute of Certified Public Accountants has appointed a committee to consider publishing financial and other information by CPA firms. The SEC has issued a regulation requiring all audit firms of organizations that now file with the SEC to file annual financial reports with the SEC.

To summarize, the disclosure of more information in annual reports will continue to generate controversy and meet with resistance by corporations. The odds favor the public in the near future, and wise management will make its preparations now. Table 7-4 shows how some companies are moving.

PROFIT FORECASTING AND THE SOLUTION

As a result of many years of fourth-quarter shock, the investing public is demanding a protective inoculation. Top managers of U.S. corporations are faced with the prospect that they will be required to issue forecasts of earnings. As in the past, their gut reaction has been to fight

Table 7-4. Telling the shareholder more.

DISCLOSURES MADE IN ANNUAL REPORTS	PERCENT OF 100 COMPANIES THAT MADE THE DISCLOSURE	
	1971	1970
Sales by product line	19	24
Sales and earnings by product line	51	32
Financial statistics for 10 years or more	63	67
R & D expenditures	24	17
Concern for corporate responsibility	60	30
Total employment decrease	58	N.A.

SOURCE: "Annual Reports Tell It as It Was," *Business Week,* April 15, 1972, p. 64.

instead of think. A senior vice-president at Armco Steel says, "We're scared to death of the idea of public forecasting." At present, most large corporations prepare five-year plans, one-year plans, and detailed pro forma financial statements for one to two years ahead. Management often gives informal estimates of earnings to security analysts who then pass that information on to clients or investment reports. What, then, is the big problem?

Management Bugaboos

There are several worries for management. Suppose a published forecast of earnings is way off the eventual actual earnings? What is the liability of management in such a case? The answer is that managements have misled investors in previously cited cases by *failure* to inform and have been sued for damages. Wouldn't they be better protected by *disclosure* of anticipated financial changes? True, it might be more difficult to make financial killings at the expense of the public. Also, the honest management would appear to be inept instead of criminal when optimistic projections of earnings failed to materialize. That objection is offset by management's skill at explaining away poor performance, as witness hundreds of annual reports each year.

Another concern is the impact on the stock price of the overoptimism of projected earnings. For example, analysts deduced that Digital Equipment Corp., a minicomputer manufacturer, would earn 40 cents per share in the first quarter of its fiscal year compared with 29 cents in 1971. When DEC reported earnings of 33 cents per share, its stock dropped 17 points to 84 in one day. If management itself were making the projections and publishing them, more insight and care would probably go into forecasts. The public would soon learn in which industries projections are least reliable because of the nature of the industry. The basic question is, shouldn't all investors get the same information the same assumptions and same projections?

Who Would Audit the Future?

Reginald H. Jones, president of General Electric Co., says, "Despite all of the computer models that we have of the company, and all of the sophisticated forecasting techniques that we employ, forecasting is still more of an art than it is a science."[3] After decades of convincing the public that he is an objective scientist, will the accountant now pass himself off as a Picasso? Monsanto's financial vice-president commented, "The idea that your public accounting firm is going to validate these forecasts is the most ludicrous thing I've ever heard. . . . They have no basic training in forecasting. Casey [then SEC chairman] is off his rocker."[4]

Leaders within the Big Eight accounting firms have mixed feelings. Some believe that CPA's will be in the forecast validation business within the next two years; others are strongly opposed to CPA validation on the ground that it would destroy the CPA's independence.

The British Experience

Annual and interim reports in the United Kingdom are similar to those in the United States. For prospectuses of new issues, however, forecasts have been made voluntarily for many years; they have been regarded as necessary to common stock offers. Generally, they have been conservative. For takeovers and mergers, there is considerable pressure on the principals to prepare and publish forecasts.

The accountant apparently attests that forecasts are prepared in accordance with assumptions underlying the calculations rather than with the assumptions themselves. That view is unsettled, however, and some accountants believe that they should question unrealistic assumptions or omitted assumptions.

A Likely Rational Solution

As a noted politician once remarked, "the future lies ahead of us." Certainly, to be equally profound, the future is uncertain. Therefore, why not indicate the degree of uncertainty in projected earnings statements? The accounting and management science people have indeed turned their attention to that process. Theoreticians are concerned with underlying probability distributions of estimates and methods for combining variances analytically or by simulation. The pragmatic manager need not yet concern himself with such esoteric things. A simple crude method that is readily understandable is now available to take him off the hook. Table 7-5 illustrates the basic format. Detailed breakdowns are not given because they would only obscure a simple process.

In practice, management would put its best sales forecasters and corporate planners to work on estimating the most likely value of sales.

Table 7-5. Profit budget, in thousands of dollars.

BUDGET ITEM	FORECAST		
	PESSIMISTIC	MOST LIKELY	OPTIMISTIC
Sales ($8 per unit)	$8,000	$10,000	$11,000
Cost of sales	3,600	4,000	4,100
Gross profit	4,400	6,000	6,900
Marketing	1,600	1,800	2,200
G&A	800	900	1,000
Net income before tax	$2,000	$ 3,300	$ 3,700

A pessimistic forecast would be based on specified assumptions about specified things going wrong. The optimistic forecast would also be based on specified assumptions. Costs would then be estimated by the appropriate functional experts after a systematic analysis. Then three values of earnings would be computed to supply a most likely value and a range.

If the range were very great, management would have considerable protection from liability suits. At the same time, a wide range in the earnings forecast would suggest that management was not too competent. When the dust had settled, management would strike a balance, say, where there was a small risk from stockholders' suits and a small risk of arousing investors and owners.

INDEPENDENT PROJECTION ACCOUNTING

When a need arises, society finds a way to meet it. The need for verifying company projections of profits is apparently just over the horizon. Further, because it is not in our nature to trust other people with our money, we must have a review by an independent party. The independence of the CPA firm and its competence to evaluate forecasts has been questioned by many experts. As a substitute, independent projection accounting (IPA) has been proposed by Edward P. Diggins, chairman of Sprague, Diggins & Ireland, Inc. The function of IPA is not to estimate earnings but to determine whether management has thoroughly prepared its forecast and then report on the adequacy of the effort. Diggins says there are two reasons for establishing a new profession to vouch for earnings projections: credibility and manpower. The IPA would have to be multidisciplinary; he would have to combine the skills of the CPA, securities analyst, market researcher, production engineer, and lawyer. Perhaps a team would be a more realistic approach than a superhuman IPA.

THE CASE FOR INFLATION ACCOUNTING

Inflation is a worldwide problem. A company that had a net worth of $50 million in 1950 in the United States was certainly not the same company in 1972 if its net worth was still $50 million. The decline in value of the dollar is shown in Fig. 7-1. (Inflationary currency that no longer has sufficient gold or other real wealth to back it up has been called "IOU nothing" currency.)

Indiana Telephone Corp. has issued price-level-adjusted figures since 1954, but generally U.S. companies have ignored inflation. LIFO accounting for inventory provides some compensation, since goods first purchased at lower prices are now carried at the "real" value. That is no help to utility companies, of course. Annual reports that show items in the P&L statement as a percent of sales help make comparisons with earlier years more meaningful. Increased dollar sales and increased dol-

Figure 7-1. Decline of the value of a dollar.

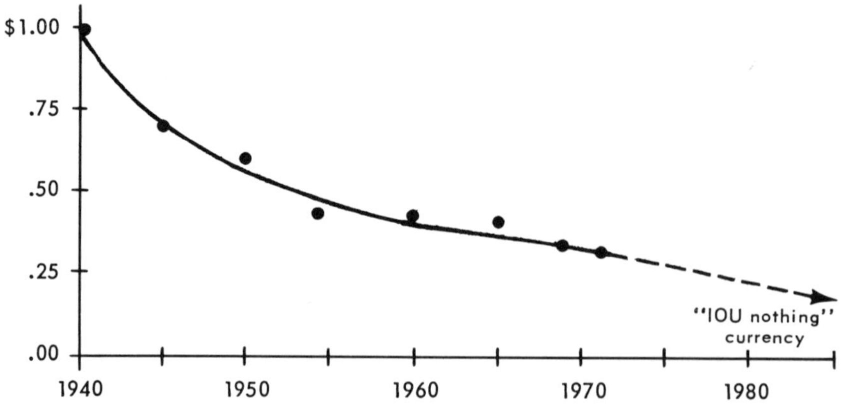

lar earnings are not meaningful unless the inflated values are reduced to a base or comparison year.

Some British companies have established a special asset replacement reserve to counteract the inflated cost of new capital equipment. Many European countries allow companies to depreciate assets very liberally or revalue them frequently. According to one study, capital-intensive industrial companies would suffer most by inflation accounting because their earnings would be shown as drastically lower. On the other hand, service and property companies with large amounts of real estate would fare best.

Right now U.S. accountants are merely watching foreign progress in this field. At an accounting symposium one analyst said, "To me this is a typical academician's impractical theory and practicioner's morass."[5] A number of CPA's and financial executives felt that the concept was interesting, would be difficult to interpret, and would represent a major educational problem. To summarize, we may look for more discussion of the problem but no immediate action.

HUMAN RESOURCES ACCOUNTING

Dr. Rensis Likert, director emeritus of the University of Michigan's Institute for Social Research, has long said that corporations should place a monetary value on human assets. One way to do so is to consider replacement costs for classes of employees. These costs consist of:

1. Recruiting outlay costs, which may vary from $3,000 for an engineer to more than $50,000 for a top manager.
2. Acquisition costs such as moving expenses, physical exams, and personnel paperwork.
3. Orientation and informal training costs.
4. Formal training costs.
5. Experience-building costs—the costs of giving a man experience in new work until he learns enough about it to be worth his compensation.

Another way to evaluate the capital value of human resources is to assume that people are paid what they are worth and capitalize their salaries. At a 10 percent return on capital, a $15,000 per year engineer would be worth $150,000 and a $100,000 president would be worth $1 million.

An argument may be made that, even if it is only a rough approximation, the evaluation of human resources will indicate changes in dollar value from year to year. Further, putting *some* value on human resources is more realistic than effectively valuing them at zero by ignoring them. Once again, it is better to be vaguely right then precisely wrong.

R. G. Barry, an Ohio shoe manufacturer, showed the impact of human resources by providing both a conventional and a modified pro forma statement in its 1969 annual report. The report lists training and development costs as investment rather than expense. Figure 7-2 presents Barry's conventional and human resource accounting statements.

WHAT *IS* THE BOTTOM LINE?

While investors and managers innocently accept the bottom line of the income statement as a true "fact," accountants and economists toss and turn over the meaning of "income." As Dr. Robert T. Sprouse says in his paper, "The Measurement of Income," the primary purpose "is to raise questions, not to provide answers." To provide measurements of income that are useful, it is agreed, we must start with the objectives to be served by the information. The basic objectives of income information are to help make rational investment decisions and to predict future earnings. Sprouse suggests the following concept of income:[6]

> The income of a business enterprise during any given period of time is that amount of *purchasing power* which, if there were no additional investments or disinvestments by the stockholders during the period, could be distributed by the enterprise to its stockholders without impairing the *purchasing power* of the stockholders' equity at the beginning of the period.

The problems of measuring income are largely a result of the artificial segmentation of the life of the business into years that, in turn, creates a need for various methods of measuring depreciation of assets, valuing inventory, and accounting for sales. Widely varying practices for recognizing the timing of revenues are employed. Two cases will illustrate the point.

Case 1: United States Leasing International's income arises from underwriting leases. The corporation participates in the residual proceeds of the leased equipment at the end of the lease. Those "partici-

Figure 7-2. Financial and human resource accounting, R. G. Barry Corp., 1969.

BALANCE SHEET

Assets	Financial and Human Resource	Financial Only
Total current assets	$10,003,628	$10,003,628
Net property, plant and equipment	1,770,717	1,770,717
Excess of purchase price of subsidiaries over net assets acquired	1,188,704	1,188,704
Net investments in human resources	986,094	—
Other assets	106,783	106,783
	$14,055,926	$13,069,832
Liabilities and Stockholders' Equity		
Total current liabilities	$ 5,715,708	$ 5,715,708
Long-term debt, excluding current installments	1,935,500	1,935,500
Deferred compensation	62,380	62,380
Deferred federal income taxes as a result of appropriation for human resources	493,047	—
Stockholders' Equity:		
Capital stock	879,116	879,116
Additional capital in excess of par value	1,736,253	1,736,253
Retained earnings:		
Financial	2,740,875	2,740,875
Appropriation for human resources	493,047	—
Total stockholders' equity	5,849,291	5,356,244
	$14,055,926	$13,069,832

STATEMENT OF INCOME

	Financial and Human Resource	Financial Only
Net sales	$25,310,588	$25,310,588
Cost of sales	16,275,876	16,275,876
Gross profit	9,034,712	9,034,712
Selling, general, and administrative expenses	6,737,313	6,737,313
Operating income	2,297,399	2,297,399
Other deductions, net	953,177	953,177
Income before federal income taxes	1,344,222	1,344,222
Human resource expenses applicable to future periods	173,569	—
Adjusted income before federal income taxes	1,517,791	1,344,222
Federal income taxes	730,785	644,000
Net income	$ 787,006	$ 700,222

SOURCE: R. L. Woodruff, Jr., "Human Resource Accounting," *Canadian Chartered Accountant*, September 1970.

pations in residuals" are recorded as income at their discounted value at the date the lease starts. The auditors give an unqualified opinion.

Case 2. The Superior Oil Co. values its inventories at "market price" and thus recognize earnings at time of production rather than at time of sale. The auditors render an unqualified opinion.

In summary, what we think we see on the bottom line may be nothing like what is really there. The thought brings to mind a familiar verse:

> I met a man upon the stair,
> A little man who wasn't there.
> He wasn't there again today.
> Oh, how I wish he'd go away.

BUY BACK YOUR STOCK AND LOOK BETTER?

"Gamble-Skogmo sets $35.50 bid seeking 500,000 of its shares." (*Wall Street Journal,* December 8, 1972)

"Booz Allen will seek own shares at $10 each." (*Wall Street Journal,* November 28, 1972)

"In recent weeks dozens of other companies have followed Mr. Hogan's example [Standard International], buying up hundreds of thousands of their own shares through tender offers, block purchases from brokers or institutions and stock-market transactions." (*Wall Street Journal,* November 22, 1972)

The reason for those actions was that a number of companies found their cash positions increasing to the points at which long-term investments seemed called for and so were buying back their stocks. There were other reasons for the purchases. Some companies were accumulating treasury shares so that they could offer them in the future for stock options or acquisitions or reoffer them when cash was needed.

Another reason for purchasing their own stocks was simply that the companies knew of no better investments. At current stock prices, some companies claimed, it would have paid them to buy their stocks even if they had had to borrow money to do it. Many companies felt that market prices of 1972 and 1973 did not represent their improved earnings prospects. With fewer shares on the market, earnings per share increase and the market price goes up. If earnings per share are steadily increased, the ratio of the stock price to earnings is believed to rise.

LET THE BUYER BEWARE

In an age when society is quick to disapprove and quicker to pass laws and establish regulatory bodies to monitor business, we might conclude that deception, fraud, and manipulation are on the decline. Instead, like superbacteria that have appeared in response to antibiotics, supermanipulators have appeared in the financial field. Since your company may at some time invest in the stock of publicly listed companies, you should be aware of some of the hazards posed by such financial geniuses.

EXAMPLE: A company treated oil production payments as current income rather than deferring them until the oil was actually produced. It also listed as current operating income nonrecurring profits on sales of oil profits. Nine months after reporting annual earnings of about $5 million, the company was in bankruptcy.

EXAMPLE: The stock of a computer company was driven up to a 386/1 price/earnings ratio. About two-thirds of its "earnings" of 11 cents per share came from a contract with its conglomerate parent.

EXAMPLE: Buying a company with its own assets is a common device of the corporate wheeler-dealer, but minority stockholders should be on the alert for side effects. *The Wall Street Journal* (January 18, 1973) traced a tangled web of manipulations that left the well-regarded First National Life Insurance Co. of America short $1 million. The story reported that the missing money left when the principal stockholder sold control. The terms of the reported deal allowed the buyer to swap a note and some securities of very dubious value for some of First National's high-grade bonds. Part of the proceeds from the sale of the bonds went to pay the seller for his controlling interest and the rest flowed into the pockets of the architects of the complicated transaction.

The moral of those stories is this: Don't depend on audited reports and financial statements when you invest. Check on the management and dig deeper into the accounting methods of the company whose stock you are considering buying.

UPDATE: FINANCIAL ACCOUNTING

1. We all know that money has a time value directly translatable into money. Put that knowledge to work for you.

2. Cash management by forecasting, accelerating receipts, delaying payments, and short-term investment may bring you surprising savings or earnings.

3. Check on the timeliness and validity of your financial information. Every company should have a good financial information system for decision-making assistance.

4. Don't count on your CPA to represent the position of a firm. If you are on a board of directors, you had better make sure you know what is going on by some other method. Otherwise, you may find yourself being sued when your company suddenly goes bankrupt.

5. You might as well prepare to do business without secrets. As long as fraud and insider profiteering continue, the public and SEC will demand fuller and quicker disclosure of all aspects of company transactions.

6. One aspect of fuller disclosure is the requirement for publishing a forecast of profits. A rational way to meet that requirement would be to prepare minimum, expected, and maximum estimates.

7. Financial statements that show earnings in "real" terms over a ten-year period have been urged. Many growth companies have grown only by inflation of the dollar.

8. You should be establishing an accounting system that places a monetary value on your human assets. It is better to have a crude estimate than assign a value of zero and then squander the assets.

9. Neither the accountants nor anybody else have figured out how to specify a firm's income. Don't use the income figure as a single major index of a company's performance.

10. When your company is doing well, you may be getting a good deal if you buy back its stock. It may be earning a better rate of return than anything else you can purchase. In addition, if there are fewer outstanding shares, the earnings per share may rise.

8

The Mess in MIS: Causes and Cures

No development in recent decades holds greater potentenial for improving the process of management than computer-based management information systems (MIS). Yet none has been more misunderstood by managers, misrepresented by manufacturers and consultants, misapplied by computer specialists, and mismanaged by users.

ITEM: RCA Corporation lost $500 million and abandoned the manufacture of computers one year after its chairman, Robert Sarnoff, assured everyone that the product would be RCA's most important growth area in the seventies. General Electric got out after similar losses. Xerox was so anxious to get into the computer business that it paid $1 billion for Scientific Data Systems, a small company whose revenues and profits amounted to only $100 million and $10 million, respectively. After two years, Xerox had kept its losses down to $100 million.

ITEM: Penn Central's computers managed to "lose" several hundred boxcars and in one case an entire train complete with crew. The joke on Wall Street was that the boxcars weren't lost—they were stolen! Macy's lost the computer records that contained $60 million in accounts receivable. Chrysler shipped thousands of cars to the wrong destination because of a computer foul up. The president of a leading New York department store says, "I wish I could put my arms around every customer our computers screw up and say, 'There, there, we'll figure a way between us to make the computer cry, just for once!' "

ITEM: *Business Week* reports that management's romance with computers for their own sake is over. Booz, Allen & Hamilton, management consultants, conclude that, for the most part, third-generation equipment is being used for second-generation systems design. The

National Association of Accountants finds that most companies have achieved a situation in computer applications that can be described as "unrelated islands of mechanization." McKinsey & Company concludes that "in terms of technical achievement, the computer revolution in the U.S. has been outrunning all expectations. In terms of economic payoff on new applications, it has rapidly lost momentum."[1]

CONCLUSION: There's a mess in MIS.

WHAT IS A MANAGEMENT INFORMATION SYSTEM?

Few concepts cause as much misunderstanding and debate as MIS. Some people think it has to do with the mechanization of clerical records, payroll, inventory, and accounts receivable. *That is incorrect.* Others think that it is an all-knowing big brain in a computer that, when the right button is pressed, will output decisions. *That is incorrect.* It is frustrating when, after hours of exposure to the topic, students or seminar participants ask, "What is MIS?" Let's clear that question up now.

MIS can best be understood if its three word components are examined separately: (1) management, (2) information, and (3) system.

Management (for purposes of defining MIS) comprises the processes or activities that describe what managers do: plan, organize, initiate, and control operations. Since we can also say that decision making is a major characteristic of each of those activities, the job of an MIS becomes that of *facilitating decisions* necessary for planning, organizing, initiating, and controlling. That is the purpose of MIS.

Information must be distinguished from data; the distinction is clear and important. Data are facts and figures that are not currently being used in a decision process. Typical data files or records include payroll, inventory accounting records, accounts receivable records, and personnel files. Billing is a typical operation that generates data. By contrast, information consists of data that are being used for decision making and managing. If we take the billing operation as an example, the typical output from the system is a customer's invoice—data. However, if we take the data that comprise the customer's invoice and use them for sales analysis, item analysis, and inventory management, we have then changed data into information for decision making surrounding the planning and control of sales and inventory.

A *system* can be described simply as a set of elements joined together to attain a common objective. A subsystem is a system that is part of a larger system with which we are concerned. Whereas we have achieved a very high degree of automation and joining together of subsystems in scientific, mechanical, and factory operations, we have barely scratched the surface of applying systems principles to organizational or business systems. The concept of synergism (Chapter 6) has not generally been applied to the business organization. Marketing, operations, and finance are frequently on diverse paths and working at cross purposes. The systems concept of MIS is therefore one of optimizing the output of the organization by *connecting the operating subsystems through the medium of information exchange.*

SUMMARY: *The objective of an MIS is to provide information for decision making on planning, initiating, organizing, and controlling the operations of the subsystems of the firm and to provide a synergistic organization in the process.*

CAUSES AND CURES OF MIS FAILURE

Why has MIS fallen so far below expectations? If we can identify the causes of its failure, some of its cures should emerge. Years of experience and carefully organized research have shown that there are ten basic causes of MIS failure. They are discussed, along with some basic cures, in the following subsections.

Lack of Managerial Involvement

Of all the reasons for failure of computer systems, *lack of managerial involvement* heads the list. Remember, computers are too important to be left to computer technicians. In his penetrating book *Up the Organization* Robert Townsend concluded, "They [the computer technicians] are trying to make it look tough. Not easy. They're building a mystique, a priesthood, their own mumbo-jumbo ritual to keep you from knowing what they—and you—are doing."

Now look at companies that have been successful with computer-based MIS—Weyerhaeuser, Pillsbury, and Ford, to name a few. Their success is attributed directly to the fact that manager users are required to become involved in the design of their own systems. Moreover, and equally important, the presidents take a personal interest and participate directly in defining what work the computer should do for the company. Look at any company that has had profitable computer applications and you will find the same thing: managerial—*and chief executive*—involvement. Nothing less is acceptable when computers are becoming the largest single item of capital budgets and have such a widespread impact on all operating systems of the firm.

CURE: *Get two kinds of managerial involvement:* (1) participation in MIS design by manager users and (2) top management support of an MIS master plan and objectives of the computer effort.

Too Many Useless Data

How does a computer specialist measure his performance? He has two ways. First, he wants the computer to be up, or running; from his point of view it is better to have it operating two or three shifts rather than one. Second, he likes to see a lot of output and printout. If left to his own devices, he will gladly output—and print—everything that is in memory or storage. Thus the sales manager who asks for the sales performance report is likely to get computer printout in a stack two feet high that includes historical data on every salesman and district in the company. What he really wants is an exception report that provides information on the performance of individual sales districts that are above or below standard by a predetermined amount.

Unfortunately, the overwhelming majority (estimates range up to 98 percent) of computer applications are for data processing and clerical automation, not for managerial decision making. The manager-user is so overwhelmed with raw data—not information—that he has difficulty sifting out the portion that he needs to do his job.

CURE: *Convert your clerical systems to management systems.* Hundreds of opportunities exist for redesigning and upgrading systems for managerial and operational uses. These are examples:

Clerical System	*Management System*
Ledger accounting	Financial planning
Order entry and billing	Sales analysis and market research
Inventory accounting	Inventory management
Production reporting	Production planning and control

The Communications Gap

The major reason for the clerical instead of the managerial approach in MIS design is the communications gap. We have a long way to go before the computer can talk management's language, and managers for the most part are not about to talk the language of the computer or the computer technician. On the one hand we have the specialist or the systems analyst who has little concept of the process of management or the problems of managers. He doesn't understand *information for decisions regarding planning and control.* He has little knowledge of, or interest in, how information is used to improve operations. On the other hand we have the manager, the user of the system, who is often lacking in knowledge about the computer. Since this lack of expertise makes him apprehensive and uncomfortable, he is not likely to embrace the computer with affection. Moreover, he is afraid that the quantitative approach demanded by MIS will undermine his present style of management, which is largely based on charisma, experience, and ability to sell his own ideas. The result is that he abdicates his responsibility for system development to the computer technician or, worse, practices a form of computer sabotage.

CURE: *Management development.* The manager should be required to know the basic nature and uses of computers if for no other reason than he will then be able to communicate with the computer specialist. The specialist or technician should be exposed to management and decision making. He should learn that his design efforts must relate to information for decision making and not just data for historical records or processing transactions. He should learn to assist with identifying the information needs of the manager-user.

Organization of the Computer Function

In the early sixties, when computer use began to become widespread, applications were mostly clerical and financial in nature. Very naturally, therefore, the computer was assigned to the chief accounting officer. Even today, the majority of data processing systems are financially oriented. According to the most-use principle of organization, EDP operations fall under the controller or the financial function.

Now, the chief accountant's function is an important one, but we can probably conclude that the historical data that are his stock in trade are not generally what are needed for broad forward-thinking decision making. Most of the data generated from the accounting function and the accounting-oriented MIS have application to the planning and control of expenditures.

If the computer is to be used for management information systems instead of historical and financial ones, then it is necessary that the information systems organization be separate from the functional departments. If it remains under the organizational control of the accounting function, there is likely to be a disproportionate emphasis on accounting and related clerical work.

CURE: *Organize for MIS.* Insure that the computer is available to and is utilized by line and operational managers. A rapidly growing number of firms realize the growing importance of the function and are assigning it to or near the chief executive. Many are establishing a new position of vice-president in charge of the information function. There are vice-presidents in charge of the other resources of the firm—marketing, manpower, money, and operations, so why not information? Is it not a major resource of the organization?

Lack of Planning

Although it has transformed clerical and accounting operations, the computer has had surprisingly little impact on the operating problems of management. The disproportionate emphasis has been on accounting and clerical systems. As those applications progressed from payroll to inventory accounting to billing, the natural and inevitable result was the unrelated islands of mechanization. Once the patchwork approach had been allowed to progress too far, many firms found that it was too expensive to start once again from scratch and redesign to an integrated master plan; yet a master plan is essential to obtain integrated systems that can be upgraded into *decision-making* and *managerial* applications.

CURE: *Develop a master plan.* The reasons are simple: (1) A plan will help offset the uncertainty of MIS development. (2) It will improve the economy of operations. (3) It will serve to focus attention on your MIS objective. (4) It will provide a standard against which you can control progress toward goals. The plan should include a *structure* for development and a timetable for *im-*

plementation. The structure, or classification system, can be by level (top, middle, supervisory management), by management function (planning, operating, controlling), by technical function (marketing, personnel, finance), or some other scheme of your own choosing. The design and implementation of MIS according to a master plan lends itself perfectly to the techniques of project management.

Failure to Identify Information Needs

Many a manager expects the computer specialist or systems analyst to design an MIS to help him do his job without making clear what information help he wants. If the name of the game is decision making, the information needs specific to that purpose must be identified. And when he is asked to identify his information needs, it is not enough for him to tell the analyst, "You're the expert, you figure it out." That approach to the problem usually results in electronic bookkeeping or, at best, the automation of an existing manual system. If the manager is to use the system, he must describe what he wants from it.

CURE: *Identify responsibilities and matching information needs.* A favorite method of some consultants is to get the manager-user to write down four or five of his major job responsibilities or objectives and match each of them with a definition of the information needed to do the job. Once that has been done, the most frustrating and difficult part of systems design is complete.

Poor Systems Prior to Changeover

Many people apparently attribute some magic power to the computer; they think that by the computerization of a poor manual system, sometimes called the one-for-one changeover, the results will be improved. If left to his own devices, the specialist will dump the manual system into the computer without change. If he does that, little will be improved except the speed of getting the output from the bad system.

CURE: *Utilize the changeover as an opportunity to review,* redesign, and upgrade the existing system. Although clerical savings and record automation may be desirable objectives from a cost standpoint, they are not the objectives of an MIS.

Reliance on Manufacturer or Consultant

Many companies have spent a lot of money on outside help and done some costly floundering around before settling down to doing their own design work. One such company is Borden, whose vice-president in charge concluded, "You are asking for trouble if you don't have an 'in house' staff doing the job of design and also being available to maintain it."

Some computer manufactures and consultants will try to sell you an off-the-shelf, or turnkey, system that is designed, debugged, and ready for you to push the button. Beware of that approach. First, the chances are good that you will have to spend a lot of the time educating the manufacturer's man or the consultant in your operations. Second, installing the system without substantial preparations is likely to result in chaos. Third, if your staff is not capable of designing your own systems, it is unlikely that it can operate a system after it's "installed" by the consultant.

CURE: *Build in-house talent.* Hire, train, and maintain adequate people to do your own computer design work and operations. That includes manager-users. Naturally, the actions involved in achieving that state of personnel readiness are a part of the master MIS plan.

No Management System to Build Upon

If good planning and control don't exist within the framework of a good organization, no degree of sophistication with a computer is going to produce a payoff. Contrary to what a lot of managers think, an information system is not a substitute for a management system.

A good management system provides the foundation upon which a computer-based MIS is built. When the top executive complains that there is a lack of managerial and operational computer applications, as opposed to accounting or clerical ones, he is tacitly admitting that operations are not well planned and controlled.

Litton Industries provides us with an example. Few organizations had the same degree of sophistication in MIS. However, the backup management system didn't withstand the economic shakeout of the early seventies. The company was concentrating on conglomeration at the expense of managing operations. What's more, it began to believe what the computers were telling it. But the computers couldn't substitute for the planning and control that was missing.

CURE: *Make sure you are practicing basic management.* Check your organization structure and evaluate your system of basic planning and control. If it's OK, then you have a good foundation for designing management information.

Human Acceptance

There is little doubt that personnel acceptance of MIS is second only to managerial involvement as a major cause of MIS failure. Why do people at high and low levels resist the installation and use of the computer? Why do they fight it, sabotage it, or work around it despite what appear to be its obvious technical advantages? Let's look at some common reasons:

Reason	*Illustration*
Threat to status	Salesmen downgraded below production planners upon installation of production control system.
Threat to ego	Manager's job skills become less important.
Economic threat	Clerical personnel fear job loss.
Insecurity	Managers, who formerly relied on personal power, now deprived of personal information and forced to rely on quantitative measures.
Loss of autonomy and control	Production planning and control function now largely being performed by new MIS.
Interpersonal relations changed	Former relationships built on personal information exchange are destroyed.

These selected reasons and illustrations support the conclusion that no system can be sold on the basis of its technical superiority. People are primarily interested in how it affects them personally in their jobs and the way in which they are viewed by others in the social work group.

CURE: *Consider the social and behavioral aspects of systems design and implementation to be as important as the technical or physical aspect.* Remember some do's and don'ts of selling a system:

- Don't design the system first and then try to sell it.
- Don't pay lip service to participation. Involve users and learn how their jobs are affected. Plan for acceptance in the early stages.
- Do consider the social constraints and resistance factors.
- Do begin the initial stages of design by identifying the social system and the constraints it imposes. Pay attention to work group norms, status relationships, and the way people view the system.

HOW SHOULD THE MANAGER BECOME INVOLVED WITH COMPUTERS?

The manager has two major responsibilities with regard to the computer, and they are present whether or not he is directly responsible for the supervision of the MIS function. First, as a user, he must participate in MIS design to support his own operations and job responsibility. Second, he must see to it that the computer and MIS are effective within his department or sphere of operations. Those responsibilities mean that he must close the communications gap between users and specialists to insure that useful, reliable, and economical systems are designed and utilized.

Systems Design

Although MIS design is more complex than the brief treatment in this chapter, the overwhelming majority of systems would be vastly improved if the manager-user would follow a few basic steps that comprise a realistic guide to user participation. By and large, the technicians have overlooked those steps, and their oversight accounts for the one-for-one changeover from manual to MIS. The result has been a patchwork rather than the integrated systems desired. The following are the steps the manager-user should take to guide the effort:

Set system objectives, an obvious step that is frequently overlooked. Such "objectives" as "get the report out on time" or "keep accurate records" are not adequate. Answers must be found for these questions: What is the purpose of the system? Why is it needed? What is it expected to do? To illustrate, a production control objective might be to identify cost variances within one day in order to control overruns. A sales analysis might be to segment customers by size and order frequency in order to direct the sales effort.

Identify constraints on design. Usually the ideal system must be compromised because of constraints or restrictions, which can be external (such as customer requirements) as well as internal (such as management support, manpower availability, and cost). Whatever the constraint, it should be identified in the early stages of design in order to prevent expensive rework. In general, technicians consider only the technical (machine) constraints.

Determine information needs. Although determining information needs is perhaps the most important step in systems design, it is frequently overlooked by the specialist or shortcut by the manager. Yet it is the real reason for having an MIS; it is the means by which system objectives are met. Naturally, both objective and information needs must be stated in specific terms, because the computer will not accept or process such generalities as "weekly cost variances." A more acceptable statement might be "daily exception reports to identify by shop order and lot number the variances in cost and quantity that are over or under standards by 5 percent."

Determine information sources. The next logical step is to determine information sources by an analysis of existing books, records, files, and statistical and accounting documents. Perhaps the design of a new form or other source document will be necessary.

Design the system output format. The design of system output format demands participation by the user, because his information and his system are involved. Moreover, since the output must meet the information needs and is the real reason for having the system at all, it is of the utmost importance to the user. Here are some questions to ask about it: What form are the output reports to take? Should the information be detailed or summarized? Are reports generated on demand, by exception, or on schedule?

MIS Effectiveness

In addition to participation in MIS design, the manager has the responsibility to see that other applications are proper. That involves the review and approval of proposals for new or modified applications and asking the right questions. Some of them include:

Is there a good climate for submission of proposals with potential payoffs? Are people motivated to submit such proposals? An affirmative answer means that profit improvement opportunities have been set.

Is the proposed application economical? Remember that an MIS is supposed to help solve problems more economically than they were solved previously. Before its approval, these questions should be asked:

- Is it *technically* feasible? Is it practical within the scope of available technology and resources?
- Is it *economically* feasible? Does it have a payoff, and will it return more money than it cost?
- Is it *operationally* feasible? Will it be used or will it be resisted and fall into misuse?

Economic analysis means estimating the profit economics of the company and deciding where computer support can help meet the strategic objectives. For example, computer applications might help in marketing, logistics control, product scheduling, financial planning, or risk analysis. If proposed applications have potential earnings in those areas, then the analysis of economics lends itself to the same treatment as any other return-on-investment (ROI) scheme.

Does the proposed application fall within the constraints imposed by the master plan? Have the design and implementation been well planned for subsequent implementation and control? Not only must the proposal reinforce and fit the game plan, but it must be laid out in specific steps, specific responsibility assignments, and a time schedule. The techniques of project management lend themselves very nicely to planning and control of MIS design and implementation.

Is the information being used? Once the hurdles of design and implementation have been cleared and the system is operating, it is up to management to make sure that the output is being utilized in the way intended by design. If planned results are not being obtained, the systems efforts have been wasted. Some *measure of effectiveness* should be assigned to the system to determine whether desired results are being obtained.

SUMMARY: TEN RULES FOR MANAGEMENT UPDATE

In most companies there is a mess in MIS. For the manager who wants to avoid that situation in his own operations, the following suggestions will be helpful:

1. View MIS not as clerical automation but as a management device that provides information for decisions on planning and control.

2. Get involved with MIS design and implementation; don't assign all responsiblity to the computer specialist.

3. Replace your clerical systems with higher-level decision systems.

4. Provide for management development to help close the communications gap between specialists and users.

5. Develop a project master plan for MIS design and implementation.

6. Don't fall into the one-for-one changeover pattern. Use the changeover time as an opportunity to revamp, upgrade, and improve existing systems.

7. Make sure that you have a good management system of planning, organizing, and controlling before attempting to build MIS upon it.

8. Presell the system. Systems won't work unless they are accepted by the people involved.

9. Participate in the design of your own system and the systems in your sphere of operations. Get involved with setting objectives, determining information needs, and designing the output.

10. Personally insure that your MIS program is effective by setting a climate that encourages submission of proposals.

9

Bettering Decisions for Biggering Problems

Q. *How do you reach a big decision?*
A. *Well, I don't know whether I reach any big decisions, but I help once in a while. . . . Finally, I think you'll find you don't make major decisions; they sort of make themselves.*

ROGER BLOUGH[1]

Perhaps the exchange between Roger Blough and an interviewer indicates that executives know little about what they do most, or perhaps it reveals keen insight into organizational behavior. It may be that, in large companies with vast resources and much human talent, great problems are not solved directly but instead trampled to death. It may be that many older, experienced executives have a philosophy of "que sera, sera" as opposed to that of the young Harvard M.B.A. eager beavers. At any rate, the development of new decision-making techniques, the refinement of well-established ones, and the application of both are increasing at a pace that makes one man's experience trivial.

First, we should note that problem solving and decision making are closely related but not identical. There may be several solutions for a problem; a decision is reached when a solution is chosen for implementation. Although generally a problem is solved before a decision to follow a course of action is made, executives could conceivably make decisions without even identifying the problem, much less solving it.

The problems of today are far larger (have more factors) and far more complex (have more and more intricate relationships among factors) than those of 50, 20, or even 10 years ago. The revolution occurred with a change from primarily economic criteria for decisions to social, political, and legal criteria as well. Major transitions in organizational decision processes and compressed time requirements in an exploding technological environment place a premium on systematic, rapid, and good decision making.

Decisions are an integral part of problem solving because they must be made at all stages of problem definition and analysis. They concern:

1. Goals
2. Boundaries of the problem
3. Limits of variables and constraints in the problem
4. Assumed values of the decision makers
5. Premises to be used
6. Data to be used (accept, reject, or search further)
7. Likely consequences of each alternative solution
8. Criteria for evaluation of alternatives
9. Final choice or course of action

SYSTEMATIC APPROACHES TO DECISION PROBLEMS

"Give a manager a problem and he'll give you a decision." The drawback of that supposed skill is that often the answer is for the wrong problem or there are other and better solutions. The "pragmatic" manager terminates his search for an answer as soon as it has begun. There are a number of systematic approaches to decision making that are being used by the well-trained M.B.A.'s. Those methods have become well known by President Nixon's presentation of options in his TV reports.

Case Method

A problem is identified by observing a variance between a desired state of affairs and the existing or anticipated state. The difference has to be significant enough to make somebody feel that action is required. In short, you have a problem if something bugs you.

When the problem situation is complex, like tangled spaghetti, and when the specific techniques for solving the problem are not evident, the problem is said to be ill-structured. (We will talk about well-structured problems under programmed decision making further on.) The general approach to solving such problems, as taught at business colleges and occasionally practiced in business, is as follows:

1. Gather together all readily available data and information that appear to bear upon the problem.

2. Jot down apparent objectives and policies and strategies of the company that appear to bear upon the problem. The values of key people who can influence decisions or implementation should also be listed as best you can. The value systems deal with both ethical and utility values. For example, if the chief executive places a high utility on locating corporate headquarters near a golf resort, that should be taken into account in a problem that involves a new headquarters building.

3. Create a basic framework for analysis of the problem. That means establishing a classification system for organization information and subdividing the problem. Here are some examples:

(*a*) Administrative process
  Objectives of the firm
  Organization
  Planning process
  Implementation of plans
  Control systems
(*b*) Functional areas
  Financial planning and control
  Marketing
  Engineering and research
  Production
  Employee relations
  International operations
(*c*) Individuals
  Key individual or individuals who face the problems
  Managers of key individuals
  Top-level managers
(*d*) Systems
  Management information systems
  Production and logistics systems
  Marketing system
  Human resource system

4. This step may be carried out in either of two ways to yield the same result:

(*a*) Construct a "laundry list" of all apparent problems and then group related problems into a few problem clusters under an appropriate structure from step 3.

(*b*) Identify symptoms of the basic underlying central problem and then define the central problem. Break the central problem down into parts to make the analysis and solution easier.

5. For each problem cluster, develop several feasible alternative solutions.

6. For each problem, establish criteria for evaluating solutions.

7. Develop the advantages and disadvantages for each solution.

8. Evaluate the solutions to each problem; that is, weigh the advantages and disadvantages by applying the criteria established.

9. *Decide* on the best course of of action for each problem.

10. *Reevaluate* all courses of action to determine if tradeoffs will provide a better solution to the total central problem and *decide* on a final total plan of action.

Factor Analysis

Factor analysis is an attempt to force the manager to specify his criteria for decisions and the weight each criterion will have. For that, the method deserves an A. However, it is difficult to include dozens of less significant criteria that, added together, become significant or to include the complex value systems of people involved in the decision process. Factor analysis is more likely to provide a question about a decision than the decision itself. To the uninitiated, it appears to give great precision, which is far from what it actually does give.

Factor analysis may be explained best by a simple example. Suppose that we have a problem of declining sales for a product that has been considered by an aggressive competitor. One of our alternative solutions is to decentralize our sales force by breaking up regional offices into field offices in major cities. That alternative and other alternatives that we are considering must be compared on the basis of criteria that we establish as:

1. Cost
2. Increased market penetration
3. Organizational impact
4. Morale of salesmen

Figure 9-1. Factor analysis of the problem of an aggressive competitor.

	Factor	Wt.	A Establishment of Field Office		B	C	D
1	Cost	7	X2 =	14			
2	Market Penetration	10	X4 =	40			
3	Organizational Impact	4	X1 =	4			
4	Morale of Salesmen	8	X3 =	24			
5							
6							
	Totals			82			

(Alternative Plans)

We list those factors on the left of a chart such as Figure 9-1. Across the top we indicate the alternative solutions. In Figure 9-1 we have shown only alternative A so that the procedure will be easier to follow. In the column next to factor, we place numbers between 1 and 10 to represent the relative importance of each factor in our decision. Thus market penetration (with a weight of 10) is much more important to our decision than any organizational impact (with a weight of 4) of alternative A.

We are now ready to see how well our alternative contributes to the solution of the problem. We use the following scale: excellent, 4; good, 3; satisfactory, 2; poor, 1. For factor 1, our alternative represents an increase in cost that is not small in dollars but is small as a percent of sales. Therefore, we rate our alternative as 2 by that factor. We multiply that rating by the weight of the factor and enter the 2 and 14 in Figure 9-1.

Market penetration will be greatly improved by the decentralization, which will place salesmen closer to the customers. We rate our alternative as excellent and enter 4 in Figure 9-1. We multiply that value by the weight of the factor which is 10, and enter 40 in the adjacent column.

We continue with the other factors and get ratings of 4 and 24. Now we add all the ratings for alternative A to get a total rating of 82 points for the alternative. We proceed in the same way with the other alternatives, and the alternative with the highest point rating is the one that is recommended. Let us review the steps:

1. Establish a list of factors that apply to each alternative solution and that are important to the choice of alternatives.
2. Assign a weight from 1 to 10 to each factor to represent its relative importance in the decision process.
3. Evaluate the first alternative by the use of the first factor on a scale from 1 to 4, or from poor to excellent, respectively.
4. Multiply the factor weighting by the evaluation of the alternative to get a rating.
5. Obtain a rating for each factor.
6. Add all the ratings for the first alternative.
7. Repeat the procedure for the other alternatives.
8. Select the alternative with the highest total rating.

Systems Analysis

Systems analysis has been widely popularized in connection with military and other government decision making under the buzzword PPB: planning-programming-budgeting. It consists of *formal* studies that aid a decision maker in his policy choices. It is characterized by a rational, as opposed to a purely intuitive, approach, which requires that assumptions be made explicit, objectives and criteria be clearly defined, alternative courses of actions be developed, and alternatives be compared by their possible consequences. Quantitative methods are used when possible, but expert judgment and intuition are applied efficiently because of the formalization of the process.

The process consists of five stages. In the first, or formulation stage, the issues are clarified, the scope of the problem is specified, and the elements and factors that make up the problem are identified. In the second stage, information is gathered, classified, analyzed, and interpreted. In the third stage, alternative policies and courses of action are generated. That is the creative stage and the one that is so often omitted by decision makers. The fourth stage is the evaluation of alternatives by applying criteria of cost and effectiveness. The fifth stage is *making the decision,* not letting the decision evolve later without regard to all the preceding analysis.

To maintain a systems approach, which is trading off some gains to get gains in other parts of the system—in short, *optimizing* the total system, iteration of the analytical process is usually required. The entire process is illustrated in Figure 9-2.

Kepner-Tregoe

Kepner and Tregoe, Blake and Mouton, Johnson and Masters, and Batman and Robin—dynamic duos all! Charles H. Kepner and Benjamin B. Tregoe have refined old techniques for attacking ill-structured problems and sold their methods as training programs to a large number of illustrious corporations.

K-T found that companies had no clear idea of what exactly constituted a problem. The K-T definition became: A problem is a deviation

Figure 9-2. Systems analysis cycle.

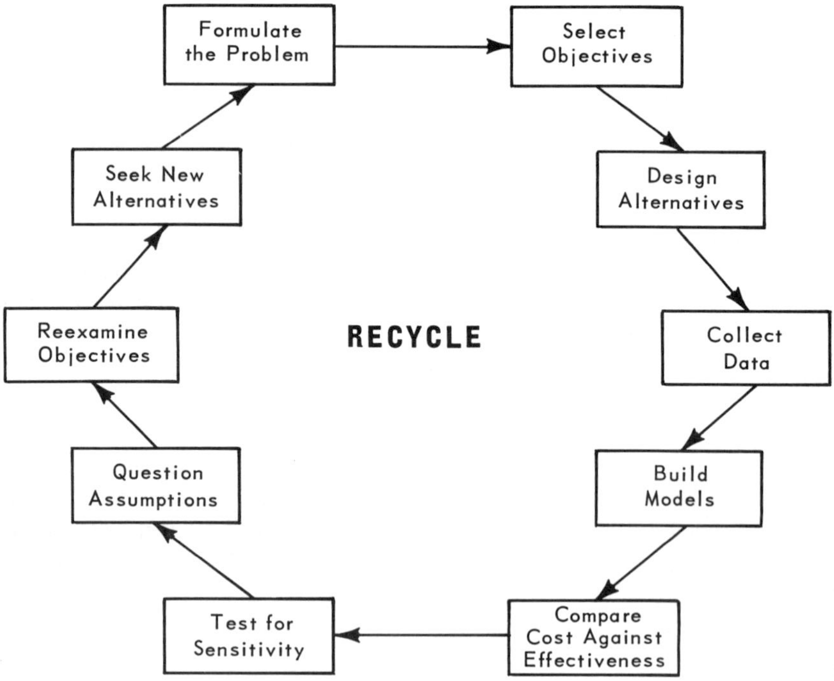

from the expected norm serious enough to make someone want to correct it. The solving starts with breaking the problem down into smaller problems by specifying what, where, when, and how much of the deviation from the norm.

Most problems are caused by change, according to K-T. For example, Viners, Ltd. experienced a surge in demand for electroplated tea sets and trays. The K-T-trained managers used the K-T methods to find a way to meet the surge. The result was a 33 percent increase in output in about 60 days. Basically, Viners took the desired level of production as the norm. Management then looked at where the bottleneck in production would arise. Next, alternative ways of solving that problem were developed. Musts and wants were established for the problem solutions. A must was an increase in production of 33 percent. The wants included economy, immediate application, flexibility, and establishment of a safety stock. Some alternatives were subcontracting, manipulating the work mix in assembly to speed the flow, recruiting additional skilled workers, and finding an incentive system to increase productivity. It turned out that no one of the options would do the job, but three of them together would.

DECISION MAKING: OVER, UNDER, OR AROUND THE PROBLEM

Two useful approaches to decision making have been formalized in flow charts. One is a logic diagram that really lists alternatives at each step of the process. The other, called synectics, emphasizes the role of creativity in finding really different and better problem solutions for the decision maker to select from.

Boerdijk Model

Figure 9-3 shows a process developed by Dr. Ir. A. H. Boerdijk. We introduce it as an update because, despite its great age, it has been too long unknown and unused—consciously, at any rate. At each stage, a very important question is asked. Here are some examples: Is the problem unsolvable? Is a solution useless? Can we avoid the problem? Managers who ask themselves those primary questions can save a lot of grief and many dollars.

Figure 9-3. Problem-solving model.

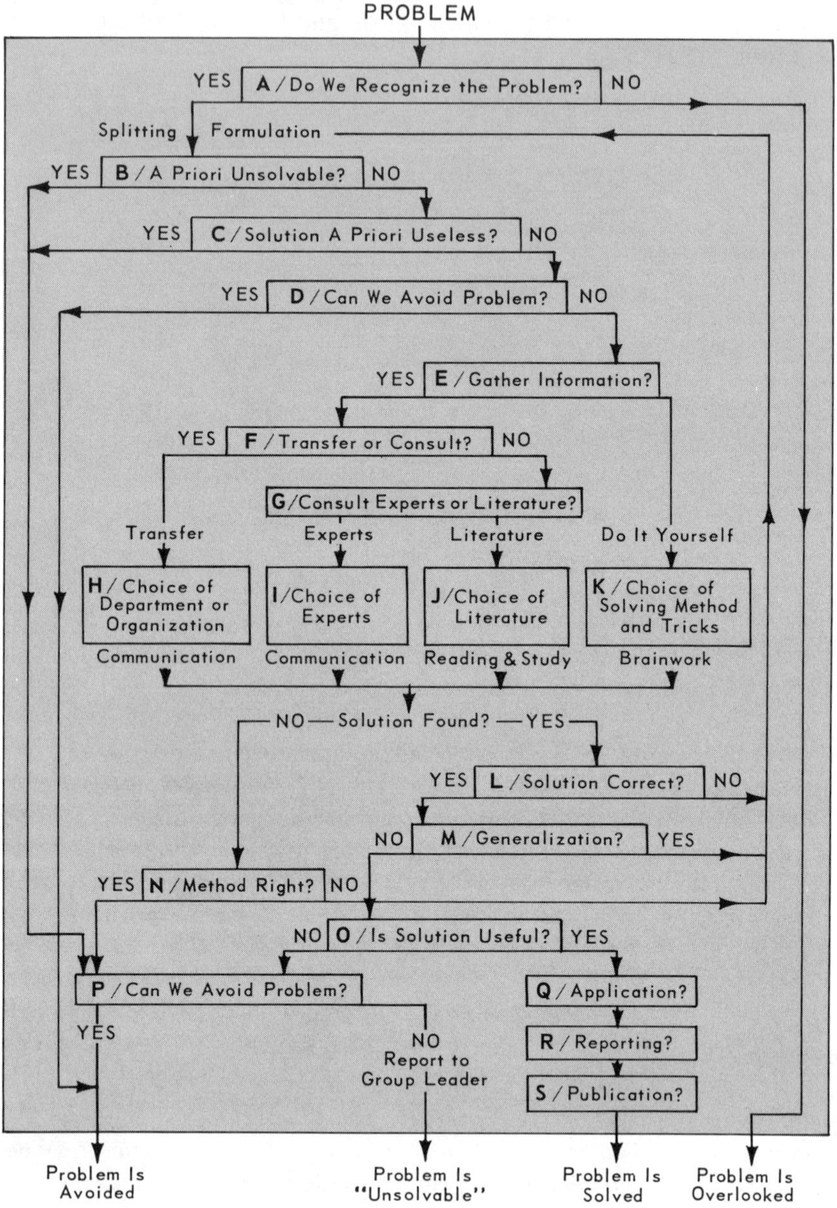

SOURCE: Dr. Ir. A. H. Boerdijk, "Step-by-step Guide to Problem-solving Decisions," reprinted from *Product Engineering*, February 4, 1963, copyright Morgan-Grampian, Inc., 1963.

The next set of key questions deals with who should solve the problem. The manager should not be solving problems if there are experts around who are better equipped to provide him with alternatives.

The total process terminates in the only four possible outcomes at the bottom, and the decision maker should always have his eyes on them.

Synectics

Synectics is a method for alternately stimulating creativity and utilizing analysis in developing innovative solutions to problems. The flow process is shown in Figure 9-4.

The problem statement significantly influences the way a problem is approached. Thus, although we start with a problem-as-given (PAG), we conduct the analytical phase to formulate the problem that we attack. That problem statement is called the problem-as-understood (PAU). Analogy generation permits deliberate distortion of the problem to gain a new look at it. It also transfers the problem to a different conceptual world in which different solutions are available. The entire process is iterative in that the problem as understood is restated if no new viewpoints arise.

FORCING A DECISION

When a manager requires a decision to a complex problem within a short time, he can simplify the decision process as follows:

1. Use a convenient rule of thumb. The three year payback period for a capital investment is a substitute for a refined capital budgeting analysis. The selection of a buffer stock for inventory is a substitute for a probabilistic lead-time demand analysis.
2. Suppress intangible values. Focus on economic units such as profits and costs and use intangible factors only as bounds on the solution. That is, don't dump chemicals in the river, or don't fire any deadwood executives over 60, but retire them in two years.
3. Adopt a short-range viewpoint. For top management, that usually means, "Let my successor worry about any adverse effects of this decision; they won't show up for awhile."
4. Suppress risk. Take a fairly safe path so that risk of adversity can be ignored.

Figure 9-4. Synectics flow chart.

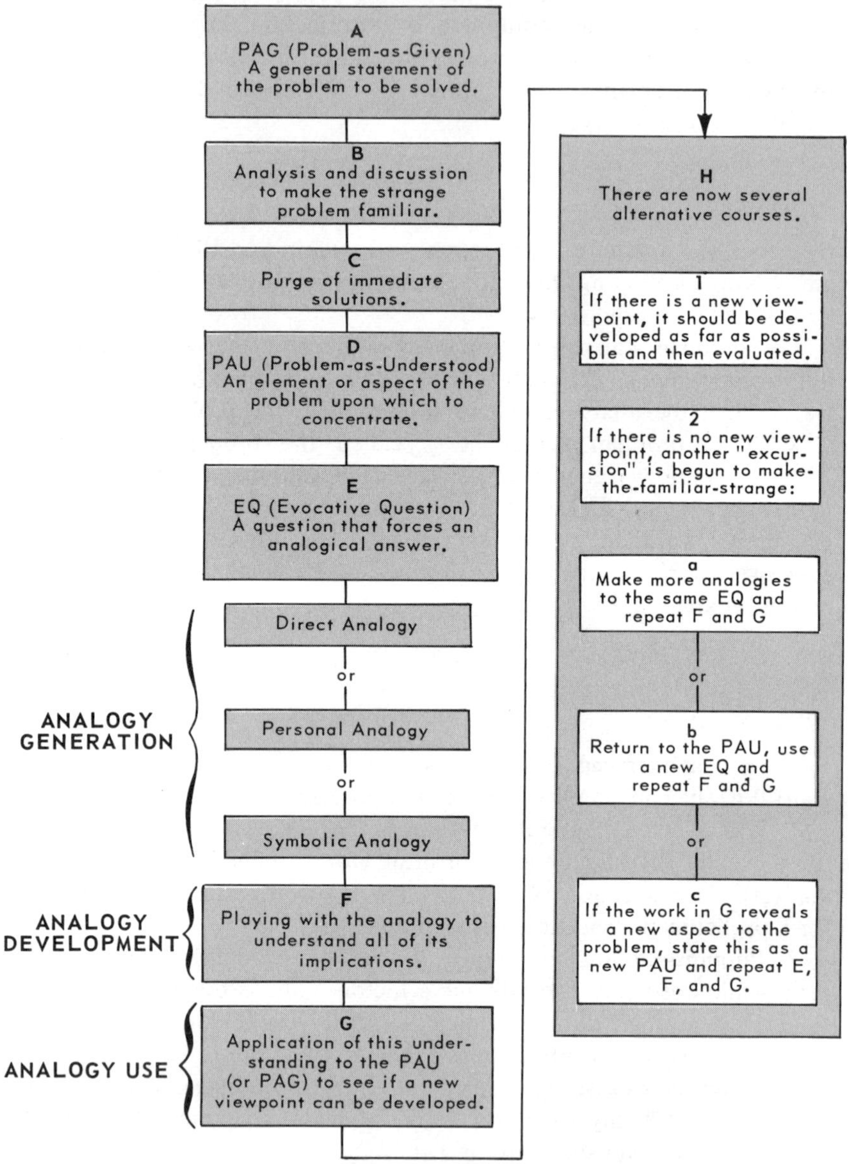

SOURCE: Eugene Raudsepp, "Forcing Ideas with Synectics," reprinted from *Machine Design*, October 16, 1969, p. 138, by the Penton Publishing Company, Cleveland, Ohio.

5. Apply only a quasi-resolution of conflict. Break the problems into parts and treat the parts independently. Treat the individual goals separately or at different times in arriving at decisions. Use an acceptable rather than an optimal level of achievement as a criterion.

6. Employ sequential decision making. Make a decision that reduces the problem, see what happens, and then make another decision. That has the advantage that each decision gets better (theoretically) because more information is available at every stage.

7. Adopt the indifference approach. Every manager knows that he is called upon to make dozens of decisions that he shouldn't be bothered with except for gratification of people in his organization. Those decisions have little impact on the business firm except as they convince people that their manager is really concerned about their problems. To simplify such decision making, one manager reportedly kept a coin in an empty drawer of his desk. When called upon to make an indifference decision, he would yank open the drawer so that the coin rattled around, take a look at it, and say yes if it was heads and no if it was tails. He delivered his decision with an air of great deliberation.

TIME, GENERALITY, AND FUTURITY

Time is becoming an increasingly important factor in business decision making. Planning is actually a means of allowing more time for decisions by making them in advance of their need. The opposite of decision making by planning is decision making by crisis. The two essential elements of a crisis are time and threat. Consider three cases:

1. A fiend has obtained access to your central data bank and erased all the computer tapes. You have no duplicate tapes.

2. A company producing a single product, a soft drink with cyclamates, learns that the FDA has banned such drinks from the market effective at the end of the month.

3. Xerox learns that IBM is going to enter the copier field.

The first rule of crisis decision making, according to Martin Trowbridge, group manager, director of Pegler Hattersley Ltd., is to lengthen the time scale. In case 1, several task forces could be appointed to work in parallel—one to attempt to reconstruct the records, another to establish a new secure system, another to handle customer and creditor inquiries, and others as appropriate. By that temporizing, time in which to determine the best way to get the firm back in business is gained.

The second rule, useful when there is a violent conflict among top-level decision makers, is to get an objective viewpoint. An outside consultant may lend an objective air to the problem and decision.

The third rule is, don't overreact. Just because you are overwhelmed by a surge of orders, don't build a plant immediately. Take time to determine whether the surge is just a fluke.

The fourth rule is, before making a decision, estimate whether the crisis will get better or worse if nothing is done.

Managers recognize that a crisis gives employees a sense of urgency, stimulates greater effort, and facilitates change. It is conceivable that some managers convert problems into crises to effect change.

Time, generality, and futurity of decisions are closely related. Crisis decisions may have little generality and short futurity. They must be revised when more time is available. Managers should be primarily concerned with the *futurity of today's decisions.* Top management should be making only decisions that have a long-range impact on the firm. They are the decisions expressed in plans and strategies.

Executives make two kinds of decisions, one of a kind and general precedent setting. It is important to distinguish between them. If an executive believes he is making a one-of-a-kind decision when he isn't, he will be called upon repeatedly to make decisions in similar cases. If he is actually making a precedent-setting decision, he must be aware that he is establishing a policy that future decisions will follow.

PROGRAMMED DECISION MAKING

Programmed decision making is an automated decision process. The rules are established; and when the data come in, out goes the decision untouched by human mind. The tricky part, of course, is to establish an automated process for complex situations. Prior to the computer, the necessary rules were contained loosely in policies and more specifically in procedures. The computer has introduced undreamed-of power for handling complexity rapidly; it "learns" as past decisions and results are fed into it and improves its "decision" powers. There are five devices for establishing programmed decisions:

1. Logic flow diagram
2. Decision table
3. Analytical model

4. Simulation model
5. Operational process control system combined with MIS

In essence, each of these devices provides a set of decision rules that process information to give consistent decisions.

Figure 9-5 shows a simple example of a logic flow diagram for new product introduction. It provides a step-by-step comparison and decision procedure easily adapted to a computer program.

A decision table is simply a tabulation of factors to consider when making a decision and a combination of conditions for each factor that

Figure 9-5. Logic diagram.

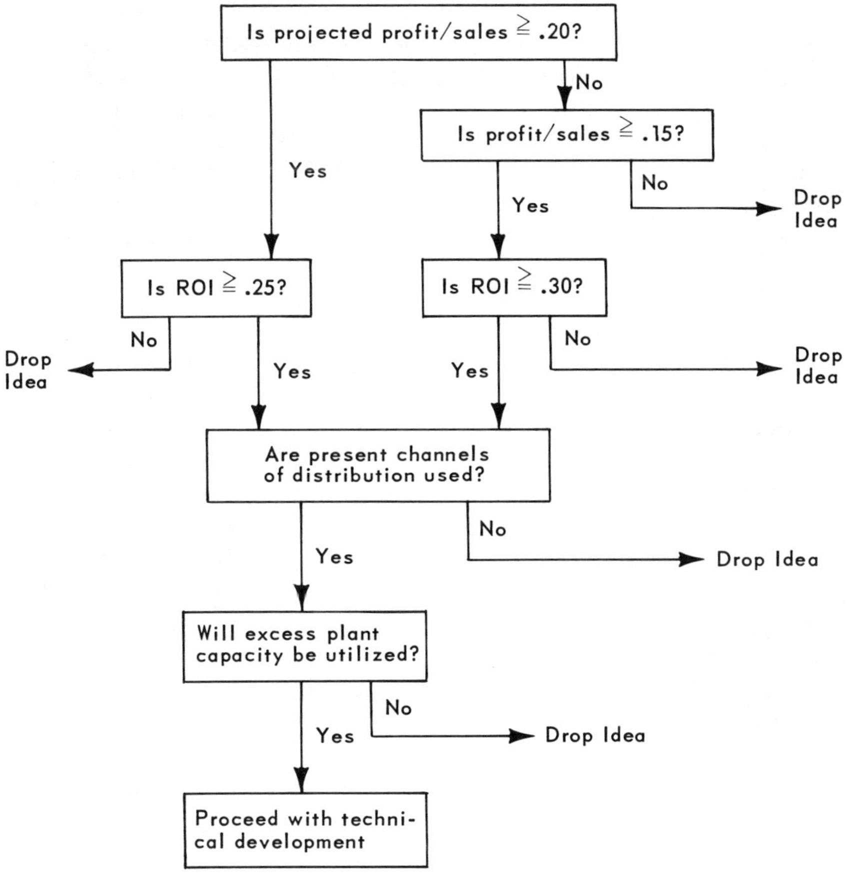

Figure 9-6. Credit approval decision.

	Rule 1	Rule 2	Rule 3
Credit limit OK	Yes	No	No
Pay experience favorable	–	Yes	No
Approve credit	Yes	Yes	–
Return order to sales	–	–	Yes

leads to a specific decision. Figure 9-6 shows a simple credit approval decision table. The first two lines give the factors and possible conditions that may exist for each factor. The last lines show possible decisions. If we read down the right-hand columns, we are actually reading a decision rule. Simple tables may program such decisions as approving or rejecting an insurance application, hiring personnel, assigning work loads, classifying insurance rates, setting up procedures when equipment breaks down, or determining when to mark down stock items.

Complex decision rules and tables may be prepared for computer decision making when many factors must be considered; capital budgeting decisons, plant location, and new product selection are examples. The rules involve, not simple yes-no, but comparisons, numerical limits, and multidimensional attributes. Several tables may be interrelated so that the final decision from one table directs the computer to one of many other tables. Figure 9-7 indicates how complex such decision tables may become for just a subsystem in manufacturing.

Analytical models are generally mathematical representations of portions of the business firm's activities. They may either yield a recommended decision or merely provide information as part of logic systems such as decision tables. For example, in Fig. 9-7, forecasts of sales would be derived by some statistical model. Simulation models, as opposed to analytical models, trace activities of the firm sequentially throughout time. Models will be discussed at greater length subsequently.

Finally, the interfacing of management information systems with process control systems is appearing as a high level of programmed decision making. Information about sales, competition, plant capacity, work force, and many other major management factors is being combined with management judgment and placed in data banks for programmed decision making on what to produce, when, and how. The data are then used

Figure 9-7. Programmed decision making in a manufacturing subsystem.

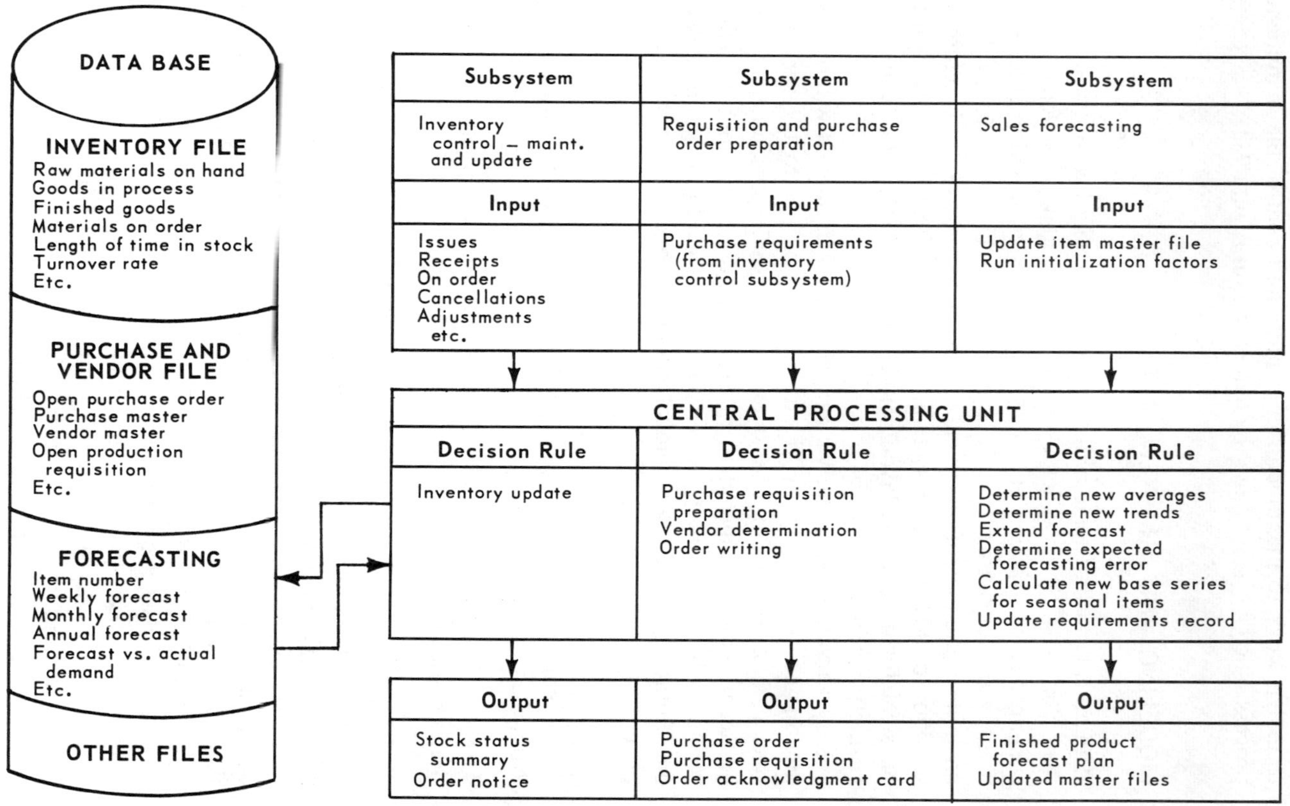

to assign work to manufacturing centers and control the manufacturing process. Such a system might be that shown in Figure 9-8.

MODELING AND THE NEW MATH

If there is a businessman in the United States who hasn't heard the buzzword "model" by now, let us hope he is reading this book. A model is simply an abstraction of reality. Because an abstraction is an abridgement, a model can never *fully* represent the real world; it would require an infinite number of statements to do so. A model is, therefore, a description of a structure or system. It may be in text form, diagram form, physical form (a plant layout model, for example), or symbolic form (usually mathematical).

By varying input data, we can see what will happen without experimenting in real life. After all, it is much cheaper to try variations of sales campaigns, inventory systems, reductions in personnel, or forecasting techniques on paper than to experiment with millions of dollars of resources in hit-or-miss trials. One failure in real life might be a disaster; one failure exposed by a model simply means we throw away some paper.

Analytical Models—Tell Me What Goes In and I'll Tell You What Comes Out

The simplest type of model takes some input data and relates them mathematically to predict a result. For example,

$$\text{sales} = 10 \times \text{advertising}$$

says that if we spend $20,000 for advertising, we'll achieve sales of $200,000. Obviously, in real life the response of sales to advertising decreases as advertising expenditures increase. The modeler therefore develops more complicated relationships to show that. We might say that such models are simple dependency or predictive models that guide the decision maker.

A second class are the mathematical programming models; linear programming, integer programming, and dynamic programming are special cases. Such models tell us what values of inputs will maximize or minimize something important, such as revenue, cost, time, or floor space. Cerro de Pasco Corp. has developed a computerized linear program-

Figure 9-8. Process management control.

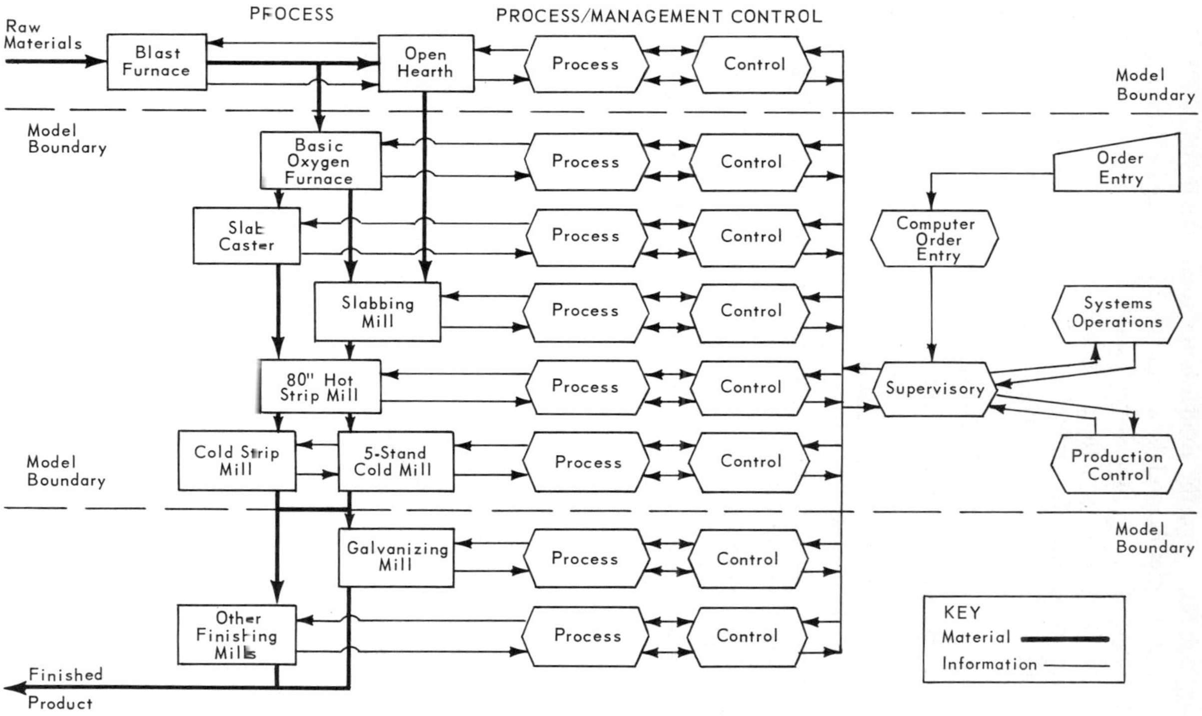

SOURCE: Roger Neil Millen, "An Industrial Dynamics Simulation of the Process Control/Business Control Interfaces of a Large Firm," *IEEE Trans. on Engineering Management*, November 1972, p. 121.

ming model of its entire zinc business. By taking account of such things as metal prices, labor and transportation costs, raw materials, and metallurgical efficiency, the model helps the company decide how much will be sold as metals and how much will be further refined. As one executive said after the model was established, "You don't need an OR guy around. The model practically runs itself."

A linear programming model consists of two parts: the objective function to be optimized and the limitations on outputs. For example, suppose:

1. Profit depends on the number of units of product A, the number of units of product B, and the profit per unit of each.

2. Constraints are the hours available on machines 1 and 2 and the time per unit required on each machine.

3. Linear programming, a series of arithmetical steps or a graph, tells us how many units of A and how many units of B to produce in a given time period to maximize profit.

A third class consists of the tradeoff models, the basic idea of which is illustrated by the graphical representation of Fig. 9-9. In fact, the problem could be solved in practice by graphing the costs of the system.

Figure 9-9. Tradeoff model.

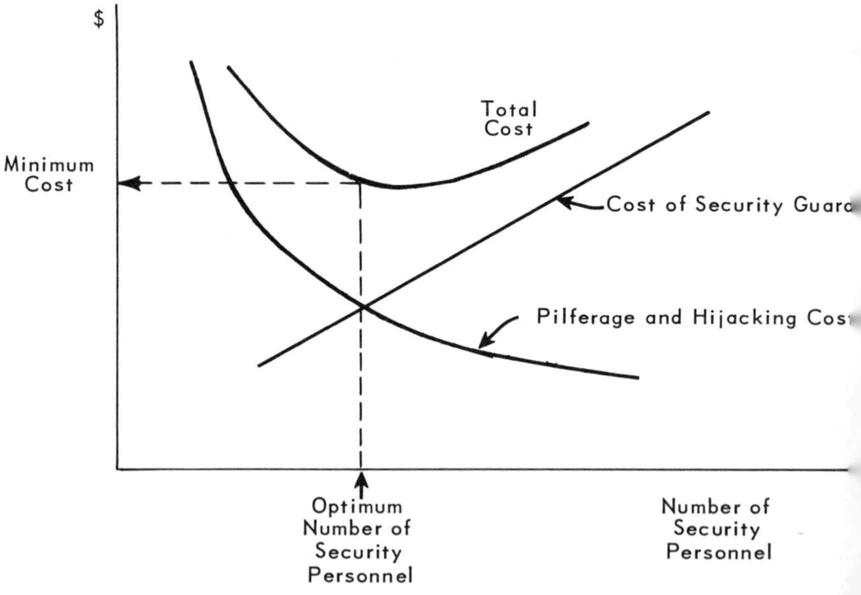

In this figure, the tradeoff is between cost of security measures and cost of goods stolen.

Analytical models are useful for programmed decision making and for obtaining estimates of results under varying conditions to aid the decision maker. They may be simple or very complex mathematically. Their main disadvantage, as deterministic models, is that they do not have random variations in the input or system processing.

Simulation Models—Let's Do It Like It Is

A simulation model usually depends on historical data or management judgment for inputs. For example, the number of machine breakdowns per day may follow some frequency distribution that can be determined. Arrival of repairmen after notification may follow some time distribution. In such a case simulation would follow the actual breakdown and repair of individual machines based upon the underlying probability distributions. Each event in the company is acted out for each time period. Fortunately, the computer plays out the simulation, so that all we need to do is look at the results such as average hours of machine breakdown per week, average idle time per week of repair crew, or average service time per machine. Those results will aid the decision maker in deciding on the number of repair crews or perhaps the replacement of old machines.

Bayesian Decision Making—Getting Managerial Judgment into the Act

If a business is considering developing a new product, management may have no idea how well the product will sell. Judgment is brought to bear by estimating the probability of each of different levels of sales. The probabilities and associated sales may be combined simply to give an expected value of sales. To demonstrate, suppose that sales were judged to be high ($200,000) with probability of 2/10, medium ($100,000) with probability of 7/10, or low ($20,000) with probability of 1/10. Then,

$$\begin{aligned}\text{expected sales} &= \$200{,}000 \times \frac{2}{10} + \$100{,}000 \times \frac{7}{10} + 20{,}000 \times \frac{1}{10} \\ &= \$40{,}000 + \$70{,}000 + \$2{,}000 \\ &= \$112{,}000\end{aligned}$$

The use of a manager's subjective judgment is one attribute of so-called Bayesian decision making; another is that the manager can incorporate later objective information into his estimate of probabilities. For example, suppose a sample survey were conducted to estimate the sales potential of the new product. The probabilities that sales would be high, medium, or low as determined from the study could be combined with management's estimate.

Bayesian decision theory also provides a method for determining the cost and value of information. By applying it, the decision maker can avoid paying more for information than its value to him in making a decision.

COMPUTER-BASED INFORMATION SYSTEMS FOR DECISION MAKING

In the preceding chapter we discussed the management information system and its role in decision making. The MIS is the system that ties together the various topics of this chapter. Humans will always play critical roles in the decision process despite computers and MIS, but the roles will keep moving to higher levels. From the infinite data of the environment, humans will have to select a finite number of relevant data as inputs to the MIS.

WHAT TO LOOK FOR IN THE FUTURE

Changing values and an increasingly well-educated population are producing a change in our culture. The development of the computer will continue to have an increasing impact upon the organization. Present trends of change in value systems and organization may continue as follows:

From	*To*
Drive for achievement and money	Self-realization and fulfillment
Self-control, secrecy, manipulation	Self-expression, openness
Dependence on the company	Interdependence among employees
Rigid hierarchical decision making	Diffusion of decision making
Mechanistic organization	Participative, fluid organization

From	*To*
Company goal in conflict with individual goals	Company goals compatible with workers' goals
Decision making based on organizational position of individual	Decision making based on respect for knowledge
Standardized administration and bureaucracy	Independence of employees

Executives—the New Philosophers

The new executives, instead of professional managers, may become known as public philosophers. Most operational problems will be solved by a loose power system of people who are involved and are technically competent. Many strategic decisions will be produced by simulation and other computer modeling. Making the ethical and political decisions will be the task of top management. Even those decisions will be shared—with government officials, public representatives, labor, vendors, and customers. Stockholders in large corporations will have even less influence than they have today.

The Next Apollo Mission

From a complex control room with thousands of instruments man has guided spacecraft to the moon and back. It does not tax the imagination to picture a group of top executives in a similar operations control room guiding a multinational company. A management information system heavily loaded with operations research models would place status and trends of the company's plants all over the world right at the fingertips of the executives. Proposals, budgets, and strategies could be tested by the MIS as new information indicated future problems. Manager interaction with the computer and television screen and video contact with anyone in the company would be common.

At present, D. W. Phillips International, S.A., has an advanced type of decision room in its Monte Carlo headquarters. Phillips controls a group of 24 companies in 15 countries. Here is a $20 million dollar company that has $300,000 worth of electronic hardware and about $100,000 worth of TV equipment backing up its decision room. President D. W. Phillips expects PI to be a $300 million company by 1980 and says: "We are preparing ahead of time."

10

Marketing in a Changing Society

"The consumer is king. Concentrate on profits, not sales." That is the essence of the marketing concept developed by C. C. Parlin in 1912 and applied by General Electric in the 1950s. The concept took hold in American business only slowly until the consumer movement began to gain strength in the 1970s. Today the mounting cry is "Let the seller beware." Many progressive companies and great merchandisers such as Sears, Roebuck are guaranteeing satisfaction or prompt refunds. Dozens of bills are being passed by Congress and state legislatures to protect the consumer from companies lacking in social conscience. Much remains to be done, and the businessman can expect a continual flow of legislation until it is practically impossible to mislead or bilk the consumer.

WHAT THE MARKETING MANAGER ALWAYS WANTED TO KNOW—BUT WAS SURE IT WAS HOPELESS TO ASK

A department store manager in a large Eastern city says, "Our competition is finished; they can't compete with us any more. They started too late with their systems and now we are getting so much of the business they'll never be able to afford the system to do the job." In contrast, General Foods announced in January 1972 that it had lost $83 million on a hamburger–roast beef fiasco. The cause was lack of marketing intelligence on which top management could base crucial decisions when gaps in operating management occurred.

Companies like Meade Johnson, Pillsbury, IBM, and General Electric are well aware of the importance of information systems that supply marketing executives with tactical and strategic information related to decisions they must make. Such information is obtained by (1) scanning the environment for events of special significance, (2) monitoring key activities, and demographic and cultural changes, (3) conducting market research for special problems, and (4) analyzing and synthesizing data available within the company on company activities.

The MIS is becoming an awesome thing that is available to supply almost any information for any individual style of management. The only person who can negate it is the manager who doesn't know how to use it properly.

THE CHANGING CONSUMER AND CHANGING LIFE STYLE

Long hair, dungarees, sports shirts, slack suits, ankle-length dresses, and miniskirts were seen on TV screens during coverage of the 1972 Democratic National Convention. They were only the external signs of people wanting to "do their own thing." There has been a fragmentation of national values and norms. The multiplicity of life styles will mean that marketers will have to search harder to identify life style leaders. If these are identified, trends may be forecast early.

The nation is becoming one of restless travelers and migrating families that fail to identify with any particular city and its problems. Many young people have almost forsaken all materialistic comforts to live in lonely rooms, communes, or any shelter they find in hitchhiking or cycling about. At the other extreme, there are many families that seek the expensive and superior education, superior health care, and recreational facilities available today. Those families have a strong desire to move upward within the "establishment."

Another type of family may eventually be the dominant one. It is the transitory family. The divorce rate among couples under 30 years of age has been estimated at 50 percent. Many couples live together, break up, or establish families with children and never marry. As a result, many individuals opt for few or no children, a choice made easy by medical science and more liberal laws. There are "group" families of couples, satellite relationships apart from a stable partnership.

Will the family disappear by the year 2000? Changes in social mores are only one factor affecting the traditional family unit. Human semen has been frozen and used successfully after two years of storage. Artificial wombs with eggs ready for fertilization have already been developed. Will child production be an occupation instead of a natural outgrowth of marriage? Who will do the buying? Who will make buying decisions? What new products and services will be in demand? While we cannot forecast the answers to those questions, each company should study and evaluate its own future business and strategy under various assumptions about the future.

GETTING READY FOR THE SERVICED SOCIETY

"If you can buy it, you can rent it" is the slogan that ushered in the age of selling services instead of selling goods. Services in 1972 claimed 44 percent of personal consumption expenditures, provided 68 percent of the jobs, and made up 64 percent of GNP. Contract window cleaning, credit cards, lawn services, multimedia self-learning systems, service contracts on TV, autos, and homes, and off-track betting are a few examples.

To sell services, companies must learn how to sell systems. The pioneer example is IBM, which concluded that its business was not selling or leasing hardware, but developing complete systems of hardware, training programs, personnel, and procedures. Another example is General Electric. When it sells an X-ray unit, it may provide the hospital with ways to link all its services—X-rays, blood analysis, and so forth—together to prevent duplication. Even products contain more built-in services; frozen and prepared foods, self-cleaning ovens, and cordless power tools come to mind. By 1980, consumer spending for services will approach $419 billion per year.

Top management in a company today must examine its products to determine how they must be modified or fitted into a service system to meet tomorrow's demands. The sales force must be retained for the more difficult task of selling services instead of isolated products or components.

The Checkless Society

We are creeping up to the checkless society. For the marketer, the big question is who will take the risk. If banks or credit card companies take it, the company consumer credit organization may disappear. If retail businesses take it, nationwide computer-linked credit status data banks may appear. Computer foul-ups of catastrophic proportions are a potential hazard.

RETAILING BEATS SCIENCE FICTION

Will underground conveyer belts someday deliver food to homes? By 1975 shoppers will be speaking over Bell's Touch-Tone phones to order from stores that are really warehouses. Already customers may shop by sitting in their cars, pressing buttons for grocery orders, and receiving their goods while their gas tanks are being filled.

By 1980, shoppers will be whisked by mass-transit systems to retailing skyscraper shopping centers. A wide range of products, services, and entertainment will make the centers a sort of commercial Disney World. Medical facilities, motel facilities, movies (with Huxley's feelies of *Brave New World*), and even revolving stores to match today's revolving restaurants are all on the way.

Capital investment will be much higher for the retailer. Service costs may be down, however, since salespeople may operate from a central room by means of two-way TV or videophone to answer shoppers' questions. Checkout personnel may be unnecessary because the credit card may both release a product from an affixed position and charge the purchase.

In 1972 a Japanese company developed a vending machine that will accept a credit card—just one of many signs that the preceding paragraphs are not some kind of science fiction. Another sign is the trend toward the super supermarket. Floor space of the high-volume supermarket was 34,000 square feet in 1972 compared with about 21,000 square feet in 1965. Kresge has recently opened a K-Mart store in Boca Raton, Florida, with 84,000 square feet of floor space. In addition, the National Retail Merchants Association is working on a single system of merchandise identification to permit full use of the computer. It will soon be possible for the president to press a button and get a balance sheet report and a P&L statement for any specified period of time. Large retailers such as Sears already have store–to–district office on-line sales recording and end-of-day financial statements. Rapid changes in movement of goods will be promptly noted so that inventory can be kept in balance but reduced while turnover is increased and employee productivity can also be increased.

SHOPLIFTING IS WIPING OUT PROFITS

The number one threat to profitable retailing, particularly of food, in the United States is shoplifting and employee stealing. Shrinkage of 3 percent is generally considered to be the peril point for a supermarket. One dishonest checkout employee working with an accomplice can destroy a store.

Stores are meeting the threat to security in a variety of ways. Special guards are common. Videotape systems as well as dummy cameras are employed. Five closed-circuit TV cameras at a cost of $500 each have reduced robberies to zero at Super Valu stores in Minneapolis.

CONSUMER GOODS ITEMS

Unit-price labeling that tells you how much an item costs per ounce, pound, gram, or quart is gaining in popularity. Dating of dairy products, grocery products, and meat is being required in some areas. Soon labels will tell you the number of calories and the amount of protein, fats, and carbohydrates in grams per unit volume, under order of the FDA.

A new U.S. law, effective July 12, 1971, requires stores that advertise special prices to make the advertised items conspicuously and readily available. What is needed now is a law to insure that when customers flock to a sale at a department store, they won't find that all the items were sold to employees before the store opened.

PHYSICAL DISTRIBUTION

A national pallet pool system is about to begin operations. Any shipper will be able to utilize pallets on a three-year lease at 1.5 cents per day, with all repairs and replacements handled by National Pallet Leasing Systems, Inc.

For the shipper, the 1970s represent the container revolution. Containerization of shipments has been coordinated among shippers, truckers, railroads, and merchant ships. Levi Strauss International states that containerization has achieved major savings by reducing pilferage, breakage, insurance costs, and the need for special export packaging. It has improved customer service and lowered warehousing and inventory costs by making handling more expeditious.

Huge costly ships for containerized goods are now so efficient that the disaster of a rate war threatened the seven main Atlantic Ocean shipping lines. A cartel has now been formed to pool revenues, but it has come under legal attack on several fronts. Without it, the shipping lines fear they will go under because of overcapacity.

The computer is making big contributions to physical distribution. In the warehouse, computer-controlled order-picking systems may fill orders from goods stored randomly and remembered by the computer. That will speed up order filling and reduce pilferage in the clothing industry, since employees won't be able to locate clothing sizes easily.

Computer and mathematical techniques have saved IBM $700,000 in design of warehouses and $150,000 by eliminating unnecessary conveyors and lifts.

SELLING AND SALES MANAGEMENT

Every time a salesman made a call on a business in 1972, it cost his company, on the average, about $50. As a result, sales managers were trying to schedule routes for greater efficiency, utilize the most advanced technological innovations, and train salesmen in the psychology of buyer behavior. The marketing manager of Ennis Business Forms, Inc. sent out a bevy of miniature robots to replace a disgruntled field salesman who quit. "Push me forward, close my lid, I'm all prepaid," the robot said at the end of its sales pitch.

The fastest growing trend in industrial selling is the use of audio-visual aids such as film strips, movies, and videotape cassettes. Less-experienced salesmen can make better and quicker presentations with such aids. The modern salesman is now part of an otherwise invisible team. Back at the plant, market researchers, engineers, accountants, and sales promotion people are providing him with integrated information and support.

On-line management information systems permit a branch manager to query a central data bank about customer records, sparing him from wading through voluminous information. Analysis of sales and share of market by counties and by products requested of a computer showed a metals distributor that he had overlooked quite a bit of territory when he checked with customer listings.

ADVERTISING AND PULSATING MADISON AVENUE HEADACHES

"Honesty" is not a happy word on Madison Avenue. The Federal Trade Commission is showing increased enthusiasm for cracking down on the advertising of products with dubious value. Specifically, it charged J. B. Williams Co. with advertising Vivarin, claimed by the FTC to be little more than caffeine, as being able "to improve one's personality, marriage, and sex life and solve marital and other problems."

A number of consumer advocates have proposed that antiadvertising time be given on TV to follow and correct allegedly false advertising. The FTC itself has proposed that the producers of Bufferin, Anacin, and Bayer aspirin spend about 25 percent of their total $80 million budgets to "correct" claims made in previous ads. It has also moved to eliminate $73 million in advertising by cereal makers that stifles competition and is "probably fraudulent" as well.

Honesty is beloved, however, when a company can really identify a competitive edge. Brand X is on the way to becoming obsolete in advertising as companies try to show up competitors. Schick, Inc. claimed in its advertising that its electric shaver outperformed shavers made by Norelco, Remington, and Sunbeam. Mazda, in its commercials, showed its automatic transmission model streaking away from the clearly named and identified Chevrolet Vega and Ford Pinto.

The large agencies are also taking blows to the solar plexus from customers and new competitors. Customers are balking at the flat 15 percent fee and setting up their own in-house services such as research. They claim better control, better results, and lower costs. The big company that has a large advertising budget also has a large computer. It is able to invest in software particularly suitable for its own selection of a media mix. At the same time the more creative admen are tending to break away from the large cumbersome, authoritarian agencies and are either free-lancing or forming small, fast-moving agencies that are more responsive to customers' needs.

For the consumer, the future of advertising looks good; for the admen and some of the nation's largest corporations, it looks dim. When Aileen Cowan was working for the Center for the Study of Responsive Law, she wrote 70 corporations for scientific data to back up their advertising claims and they refused to supply it. It is doubtful that the American public will tolerate such an attitude for long.

PRICING

The problems of pricing remain with industry as always. Pricing new products, despite sophisticated quantitative techniques and marketing research, must be guided by the value the consumer places on the product. The number of units sold is important in both spreading development costs and lowering manufacturing unit costs.

OVERALL: MARKETING UPDATE

Marketing theory is advancing on all fronts. The most difficult area, now being cultivated intensively, is consumer behavior. Environmental aspects, cultural characteristics, and the socio-psychological behavior of individuals in product decision situations are being integrated in descriptive as well as mathematical models. The main points for the manager to keep in mind are:

1. Marketing information systems are being developed to extend the ability of the decision makers. Marketing research, on-line equipment, and environmental scanning are putting a wealth of useful up-to-the-minute information right at the call of the marketer.

2. Rapid changes in consumer life styles have greatly affected consumer preferences and buying habits; they have reflected back from the retailer to the manufacturer to the industrial goods producer. Such changes must be closely monitored by most companies to prevent disastrous surprises and losses.

3. Products are increasingly appearing on the market with services built into them. Modern society is extremely time conscious, so that prepared foods, self-cleaning devices, self-maintaining machinery, easy billing and payment systems, and service contracts are in demand. Your sales force must be prepared to sell intangible service, not just products. Your company must direct itself to finding product improvements that save *time*.

4. Retailers are introducing newer, bigger, and more expensive concepts. Bigger stores, bigger pilferage, more rapid recording of sales transactions, more problems of identifying consumers' change in preference. Better managers, better-trained managers, are needed to handle great new complexities. That thin margin of profit on sales is more exposed to adversity than ever.

5. Consumerism is producing a completely new marketing scene. The customer has been designated as king for some time, but he is finally being crowned and enthroned. He is demanding and getting exact information about the goods he is purchasing. It may be that puffery and misleading information will disappear from consumer goods labels

and advertising. Consumer goods, that is, may be promoted as industrial goods are.

6. The problem of rapidly rising costs of physical distribution has not been solved, but lots of effort is going into work on it. Palletization, containerization, new methods of shipping, analysis of competitive shipping methods, and computerized approaches to such analysis are in progress.

7. The lonely salesman on the road is changing into the point man for a highly trained team of specialists. Sophisticated promotion and marketing analysis prepare the way. Meanwhile, back at the plant, technical and financial people supply supporting information for selling or negotiating.

8. More aggressive, informative, and truthful advertising is on its way. A more educated population is getting fed up with the juvenile pap that jams the airways.

11

Manufacturing

When the government talks about increasing productivity, it usually means output per man-hour in the factory. For top management, the productivity of the factory is crucial. Three trends make possible an increase in shop productivity:

1. Development and application of the systems concept in an ever more sophisticated manner.
2. Increased motivation of workers by means of job enlargement, self-measurement, and worker control of quality.
3. Technological progress along with more intensive capital investment.

If you aren't planning and implementing intensively in those three areas, you are falling behind in the race for survival.

"SYSTEM" IS THE WORD

- Where are the parts for that rush order?
- Why do we keep trying to fit one rush order on top of another?
- Why are the subassemblies for the Oppo order piling up outside the lathe department
- Why do only half the units passing through the shop have cost tickets?
- Why do we have N/C multiturret drill presses in one department and massive overtime labor in the next?
- Why in the devil is the paperwork for production control always fouled up?
- Why are some men working at their machines at a breakneck pace while others seem to be idle half the time?

At Western Electric's Kansas City plant, the answer to such questions was to use computers to interlock five major areas:

1. Merchandise control for integration of order processing, shipping, warehousing, and stock items.

2. Production planning and control for generation and control of shop orders and machine allocation.

3. Material ordering and control for production, stock, and inventory control and investment data.

4. General accounting, with emphasis on exception reporting.

5. Metal part production scheduling by use of a network of telephones in the shop to report the status of jobs. Each telephone has associated with it a deck of prepunched dialing cards that identify machine tools and another deck for orders being worked on. Information is obtained by inserting cards in the telephone equipment to give order status, machine use, and operator's time.

At Xerox, a modular approach has produced dozens of planning and control systems. About five of them are linked together to plan and report production activity.

This is the age of the system. No longer does the manager study his problems as small unique headaches. He looks at a problem in its total setting. He recognizes that solving one problem in isolation may produce half a dozen problems elsewhere. The manufacturing manager of today must view the entire manufacturing process as an organic system. All activities must be integrated. Increased automation—mechanical routinization—must be continually pursued.

Manufacturing is now viewed as two systems, one imposed on the other. The first system to be designed is the operating system, the flow and processing of the work. It is a system primarily of men and machines and technical communication. The second system is the management information system, which provides the planning and control for the operating system as a whole. (See Chapter 9).

MOTIVATION, WORK ENLARGEMENT, AND QC

At the Volvo plant, in Sweden, a pilot program involves job rotation for 700 people on assembly and paint lines. The purpose is to introduce variety in work and enlarge skills so that productivity will be increased. At the Cummins Engine Company, in Indiana, hourly workers took their skills and knowledge to a meeting with processing engineers. As a result the cost of a part was reduced from $4 to $1.18. A Cummins pilot program includes rotation of eight men on a production line so that each learns three jobs.

There are two basic tenets of factory productivity:

1. Since much of the work is basically dull, management must seek innovative ways of creating interesting task combinations. If workers could be motivated to do their best, productivity would increase far beyond the possibility of any capital substitution known today.

2. About 5 percent of the workers cause 95 percent of the problems. Therefore, if those people could be screened out in hiring and placement, large sums of money could be saved.

The keys to increased productivity have been demonstrated by research but rarely applied in the shop. First, management must recognize that lots of the actions it takes don't motivate people to produce more; they only prevent extreme dissatisfaction. Lack of clear policies, unfair administration of policies, poor working conditions, and wages are examples.

If workers are to be motivated, their minds must be captured by challenges that are difficult but possible to meet. They must be working at things they like to work at. Finally, a job well done must get recognition. At the same time, it must be recognized that a satisfied worker is not a motivated worker. Ways to keep the worker's aspirations ahead of his achievements and rewards must be found.

Obviously there is no standard formula for implementing the preceding concepts. Today, however, progressive managers are restructuring jobs to provide variety and fuller responsibility. Job enlargement as a concept has been around a long time, but now it is getting a better audition. Workers are being given responsibility for both producing and controlling the quality of their work. That has the immediate effect of reducing quality control inspection costs, since production and testing may be integrated as a system process.

If workers can be allowed to set their own goals (provided they at least meet what management has in mind) and set their own means of achieving those goals, their work becomes more challenging. Recognition, status, and bonus plans will reinforce such new attitudes.

N/C MEANS CONTROL BY THE NUMBERS

By using numerically controlled (N/C) machines, the Ford Motor Company makes thousands of templates, hundreds of wood models, and many lines of auto body dies. The result, says a Ford spokesman, is the shaving of up to 4 months from the traditional 21 to 22 months it once took to tool for a new model run.

Fortunately we don't have to motivate machines. All we have to do is make machines smarter and more versatile. N/C, has transformed machines from tools into robots. When computers and N/C machines are completely integrated with automatic materials picking and finished goods storing or shipping, the production revolution will be completed.

Over 15,000 numerically controlled machine tools are now used to provide a wide variety of metal working and assembly tasks. Punched cards or tapes guide these expensive and complex machines. A single "island of automation" may perform, say, eight operations in sequence with the machine or the material untouched by human hand.

It is not surprising to find N/C machines in the auto industry or at Boeing, Bunker Ramo, or IBM. It is a sign of the times that they have been developed by Gerber Scientific Instrument Co. for the difficult task of cutting fabrics to patterns in the garment industry. Although the costs are high for such machines, top managements have found the savings higher. Also, the outgoing quality is improved.

THE AUTOMATIC FACTORY VERSUS THE AUTOMATIC MAN

General Electric has ushered in the automatic factory with its ComManDir* Numerical Control System. From production preplanning to numerically controlled machinery, the computerized system takes command and is monitored from a central control station. General Electric claims that machine output can be improved by as much as 100 percent, debugging can be reduced to minutes instead of weeks, and errors, quality costs, and maintenance problems can be greatly reduced. (See Figure 11-1.)

Back at the production line, automation is increasing at a furious rate. General Motors has set up its Vega line to produce up from 30 to 100 cars per hour. One two-stage Unimate machine in the line bangs out 130 welds in 4½ seconds!

For top managements who have always wistfully longed for the automatic man, the millenium is almost here. Those troublesome workers on the assembly lines who just can't seem to drive in 50,000 screws a day without getting bored, disruptive, sick, or prone to errors may not be needed much longer. Professional computer programmers and a few machine tenders will be the new production crew. The modern

Figure 11-1. General Electric CommanDir* system operation.

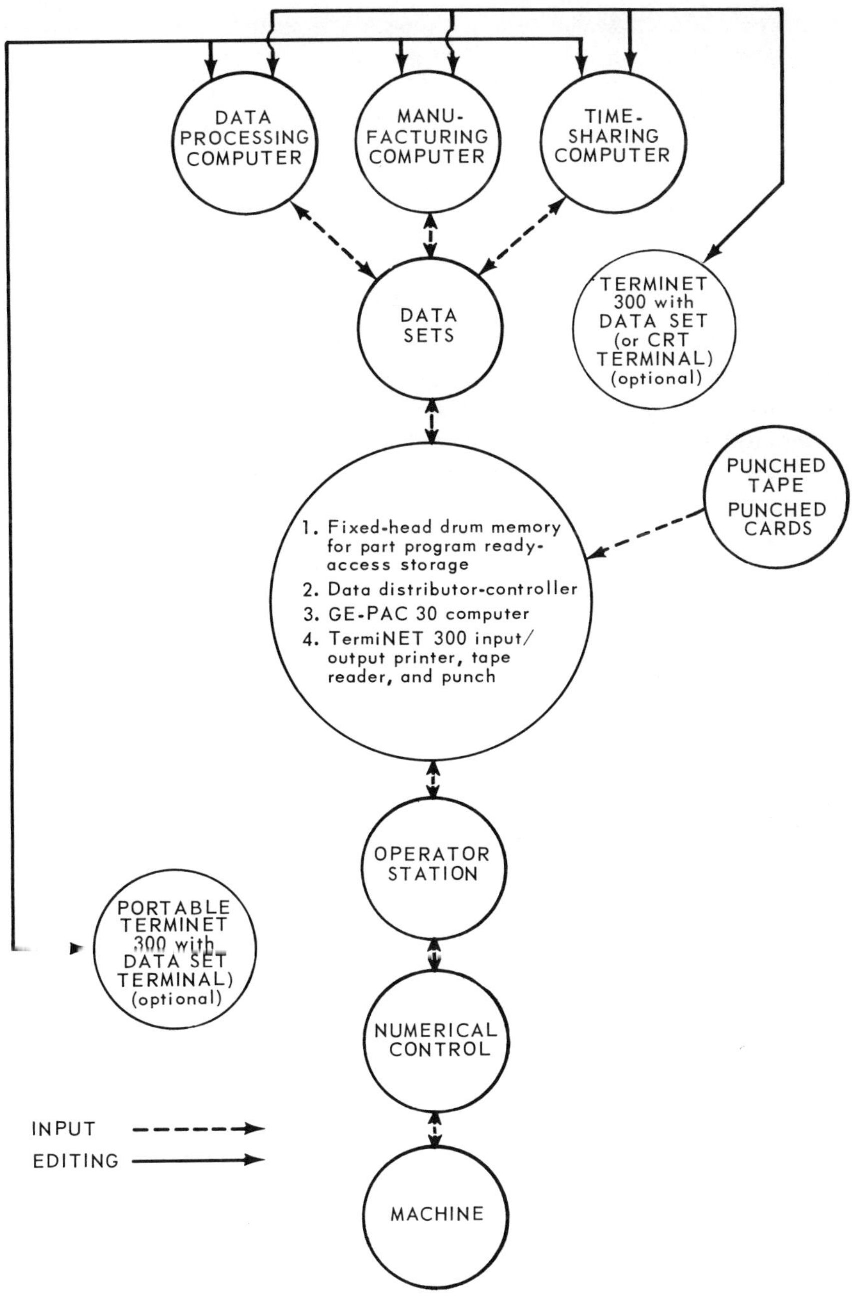

SOURCE: General Electric Company.

era is being born of N/C machines and a central computer. Just as a process control computer juggles the flow rate of crude oil in a cracking tower, adjusts pressures and temperatures in the stills, and regulates the output mix from heating oil to jet fuel, so computers will command total plant output (Figure 11-2). For managers who want to look at specific applications, the Ford Pinto production line, the Schlitz beer plant at Winston-Salem, the Sarah Lee cake plant at Deerfield, Illinois, and the Dan River textile plant at Benton, Alabama, offer a diversity of operations.

HOW TO GET LOADED IN THE 1970s

Fifty-foot high shelves, random storage, and computerized control of order picking will offer cost savings in the future. As noted in Chapter 10, random storage of styles and sizes, with only the computer knowing where to locate items, will reduce pilferage in the garment industry.

Also, as noted in Chapter 10, national pallet leasing through an inter-industry pallet pool promises dramatic savings. National Pallet Leasing Systems has recently announced that it has obtained financial backing to start operations. Companies that have found pallet shipping expensive or difficult before will be able to take advantage of such unit-load shipping. Without the problems of ownership and with the pallets readily available, more companies will want to use the pallets.

Figure 11-2. Total automation.

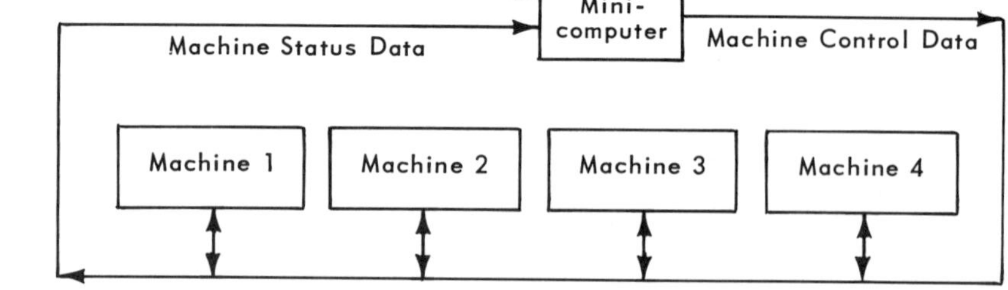

A tremendous growth in pallet load shrink wrapping over the next decade will be an outgrowth of the spread of palletized handling. Plastic shrink film offers the promise of increased load integrity, reduction of damage, lower material cost, and more product per cubic volume. For some types of products, it will even be economical to use shrink wrapping without a rigid base.

THE CAPITAL INVESTMENT—A SMALL STEP FOR SCIENCE, A LONG WAY TO GO

When the Playtex girdle came out, a large competitor invested and lost millions of dollars in production facilities because of intrinsic manufacturing problems related to the molding of the latex stretch material. Du Pont lost about $80 million over an eight-year period because it could not bring the manufacturing cost of Corfam down sufficiently.

The capital investment decision is what business is all about. Essentially, top management is betting its stockholders' money on a particular product, production method, or auxiliary support facility every time it makes a capital investment. The capital sunk in a production process can generally be recovered only by the sale of products at a profit. Yet many top managers sit around an executive table, look at a superficial proposal with costs only—and those rounded to the nearest million, twiddle their thumbs and then stare at the ceiling to find the right decision. A capital investment in production is a long-range decision and as such should be part of the company's carefully developed long-range plan (Figure 11-3).

Progressive companies are utilizing probability methods in their forecasting of both costs and profits in order to make capital investment decisions. One of the authors recently made a study of the project evaluation forms and procedures of such companies. Syntheses of the short and long forms used are given in Tables 11-1 and 11-2 (pp. 192–193).

The application of the computer to models of the factory and to simulation of the entire manufacturing system is growing. In addition, the time value of money, long recognized by bankers and academicians, is finally being recognized by top managers. The concept of risk as a correlate of a particular capital investment now appears in specific form on project evaluation sheets. In short, many of yesterday's M.B.A.'s have reached top management today, with the result that more sophisticated tools are being used to plan the production activities.

Figure 11-3. Capital expenditure management in the long-range planning process.

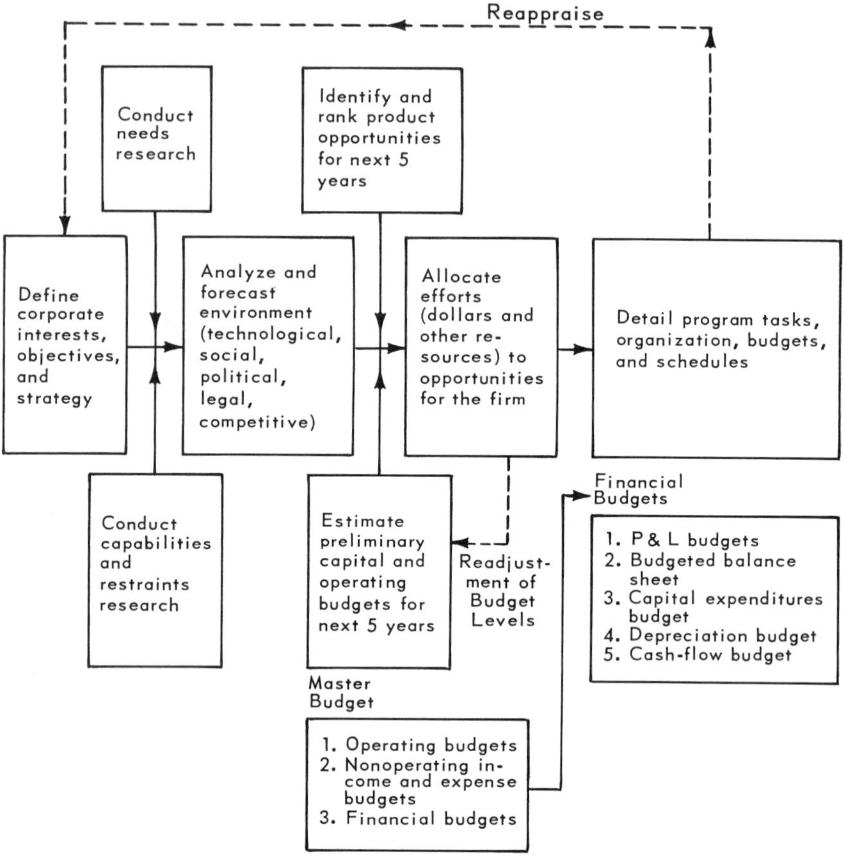

PRODUCTION CONTROL—WHERE THE PROFITS ARE BURIED

When an aggressive venture company acquires a formerly profitable but now decrepit company, it uses the financial statements as the guide to trouble spots. Whether the major problem is in marketing, engineering, key managers, or tough competition, there are almost always great immediate gains to be had from getting good control of production. The old-time techniques are still being used to good advantage:

1. Get rid of old work rules, introduce incentives, and let the union in on the state of the company to obtain cooperation.

2. Junk obsolete equipment and develop high-production layouts.

3. Balance assembly lines better.

4. Sequence operations, when possible, so that high-labor and high-cost material are introduced at end-of-the-line operations. That reduces investment in work-in-process inventory.

5. Use management science techniques to forecast demand on the shop, to order economic lot sizes of materials, and to make economic lot-size production runs.

6. Use statistical quality control methods.

7. Search for down-time problems, idle labor problems, frequent overtime work.

8. Scrap and reject analysis.

The new techniques for seizing control of manufacturing costs are:

1. Use of the computer for analyzing and forecasting demand by individual product and model.

2. Use of the computer for maintaining inventory records and reordering.

3. Use of the computer for developing the master schedule for each week. That includes the parts explosion system required for scheduling.

4. Use of the computer to assist with loading of machines and assignment of workers.

5. Use of the computer to assign daily job priorities.

6. Use of TV for factory surveillance (if allowed by the union) and of central electronic monitors to warn of machine breakdowns and to measure down time.

7. Finally, and most importantly, a management information system that keeps foremen and key middle managers aware of deviations from plans, schedules, and budgets. The MIS should also aggregate production and cost information and promptly supply information on significant variances to top management. Top management must be kept aware of any upward trend of cost of production as a percent of selling price.

ECOLOGY AND PROFITS

In April 1972 the Supreme Court ruled that federal judges have a broad mandate to consider all claims of pollution victims, even beyond the remedies that Congress provides. That means that businesses are subject to damage suits for water and air pollution even if they are complying with all federal and state regulations. Besides, adverse publicity can cause a company to lose customers and lead to stronger legislation. By 1975, the Clean Air Act of 1970 will provide heavy penalties for polluters.

The cost of making old factories and processes pure is usually, but not necessarily, high. The amounts required by various industries are shown in Table 11-3.

Three courses have been adopted by companies to meet the public

Table 11-1. Project evaluation factors, short form.

- I Identification and Objective
  - A. Project name, number
  - B. Date
  - C. Department or division
  - D. Product line
  - E. Class of development
    1. New product line
    2. Line extension (new product in existing line)
    3. Product new to the company but not new to the market
    4. Maintenance development to catch up with competition
    5. Cost reduction
- II Summary Technical Analysis
  - A. Outline of investigation and technical objectives
  - B. Manpower requirements each year for the first three years
  - C. Labor, materials, and subcontract costs each year for the first three years
  - D. Capital investment required for the project by engineering
  - E. Projects that must be postponed if this project is approved
- III Summary Marketing Analysis
  - A. Estimated total annual market each year for the first three years
  - B. Estimated company sales in units for each of the first three years
  - C. Estimated company selling price per unit
  - D. Competitors' sales-price range
  - E. List of competitive products
  - F. Manpower requirements for each of the first three years of the project
  - G. Labor, materials, and subcontract costs for each of the first three years
  - H. Capital expenditures required
- IV Summary Manufacturing Analysis
  - A. Additional floor space required, if any
  - B. Tooling and equipment required and its cost
  - C. Lot size
  - D. Training required
  - E. Labor, materials, and subcontract costs for the first year of production
- V Summary Economic Analysis
  - A. Total sales in dollars, three years
  - B. Cost of sales, three years
  - C. Gross profit
  - D. Operating expenses
  - E. Operating profit
  - F. Capital investment and working capital required
  - G. Return on investment

SOURCE (Tables 11-1 and 11-2): D. W. Karger and R. G. Murdick, "The Art and Science of Costing New Product Payoff," *Machine Design*, September 30, 1971.

Table 11-2. Project evaluation factors, long form.

I Identification and Objective
(Same as for short form)

II Status Report
Brief summary of progress and expenditures to date

III Technical Phases
- A. Engineering analysis
- B. Engineering exploration
- C. Development model design
- D. Development model construction
- E. Development model test
- F. Production model design
- G. Pilot production test
- H. Final engineering design and manufacturing drawings
- I. Costs for each phase broken down by direct labor, direct materials, indirect expense, and general and administrative expense
- J. Estimated start and completion times for each phase
- K. Anticipated development problems
  1. Unproved concept
  2. Unsatisfactory concept of approach
  3. Lack of personnel
  4. Lack of facilities
  5. Unsatisfactory definition of requirement

IV Marketing Characteristics
- A. Types of customers that comprise the market, their needs, their buying practices
- B. Size of market
- C. Market trend and growth
- D. Customer loyalty
- E. Market share
- F. Marketing practices: pricing, distribution, servicing, warranties
- G. Competitors: strength and weaknesses
- H. Anticipated marketing problems
  1. Unsatisfactory sales forecast
  2. Competitive situation
  3. Customer make rather than buy
  4. Indefinite requirements

V Operations Characteristics
Key skills, techniques, facilities; labor content; geographical considerations; proprietary and patent considerations; regulations

VI Manufacturing
- A. Available facilities
- B. Capital equipment requirements
- C. Manufacturing skills matched against requirements
- D. Inventories required
- E. Anticipated manufacturing problems
  1. Undeveloped process
  2. Lack of personnel
  3. Tooling cost estimate too high
  4. Lack of facilities: plant, equipment, tooling
  5. High facility cost
  6. High manufacturing cost
  7. No cost estimate available

VII Finance
- A. Sales in dollars each year for three years
- B. Cost of goods sold: labor, materials, burden, each year for three years
- C. General and administrative expenses
- D. Marketing expenses
- E. Target annual profit for each of first three years
- F. Capital expenditures required
- G. Working capital required
- H. Inventories, in dollars
- I. Return on investment

VIII Degree of Certainty at Each Stage
- A. Certain, and no anticipated problems
- B. Certain, but anticipated problems
- C. Probable (over 50% chance of success), but anticipated problems
- D. Possible (under 50% chance of success), but anticipated problems

Table 11-3. What it costs to clean up pollution.

INDUSTRY	TOTAL INVESTMENT REQUIRED, MILLIONS OF DOLLARS*	EXPENDITURES, MILLIONS OF DOLLARS				PERCENT OF TOTAL CAPITAL SPENDING		
		1971 actual	1972 planned	Percent change, 1971 vs. 1972	1975 planned	1971 actual	1972 planned	1975 planned
Electric utilities	$ 6,190	$ 565	$1,027	+ 82	$1,188	4.4	7.2	7.0
Petroleum	2,690	527	542	+ 3	462	9.0	8.2	6.0
Paper	1,980	257	494	+ 92	224	20.6	29.8	14.5
Iron and steel	1,780	217	206	− 5	870	12.8	13.0	32.7
Nonferrous metals	1,670	111	269	+142	149	10.3	21.7	10.7
Chemicals	1,250	282	445	+ 58	419	8.2	12.2	10.7
Commercial†	1,200	234	224	− 4	315	1.3	1.1	1.5
Stone, clay, and glass	780	112	173	+ 54	195	13.2	14.1	15.6
Machinery	560	95	381	+301	239	3.4	11.3	6.4
Food and beverages	550	101	158	+ 56	208	3.8	5.2	6.2
Mining	470	61	192	+215	157	2.8	6.8	5.4
Rubber	410	45	53	+ 18	100	5.4	5.0	8.0
Fabricated metals	400	89	119	+ 34	74	7.1	7.4	4.9
Instruments	260	60	74	+ 23	119	9.0	9.5	13.5
Electrical machinery	240	70	70	0	91	2.3	3.2	3.6
Gas utilities	220	49	79	+ 61	82	2.0	2.8	3.2
All business	$22,760	$3,245	$4,906	+ 51%	$5,378	4.0%	5.3%	5.3%

* Total required to meet pollution control standards in effect as of January 1, 1972.

† Commercial category includes stores, insurance companies, and banks.

SOURCE: *Business Week,* May 13, 1972, p. 77. Cost estimates made by the McGraw-Hill Economics Department.

and legal pressures for a cleaner environment. The first has been to continue dumping acids and other wastes into a stream or river and mount a big advertising campaign about cleanup complete with pictures of the sparkling stream. That has proved to be only a temporary holding action until some environmentalist finds that the waste-disposal point is downstream from the advertised clean water point.

The second course has been to start a gradual program of cleanup that stretches over the years and meanwhile seek delays in legal enforcement so that annual capital expenditure for antipollution equipment is held to a relatively low level.

The third course, which is not open to all manufacturers, is to recycle liquids or gases or reclaim waste and sell portions as byproducts. That is, mercury, sulfuric acid, and powdered metals, instead of being dumped into streams, are recaptured by use of appropriate equipment and put into salable form. Some companies claim to have broken even while cleaning up their environments.

SUMMARY: MANUFACTURING

1. The big push in manufacturing is toward the complete system. That includes production planning and control and automation of materials handling and processing. All those are coordinated and synchronized by the manufacturing information system. Such "automatic" planning, operating, and control are directed toward increased efficiency and lower manufacturing costs.

2. The human factor in production is being recognized in practice, not just in theory, as possibly even more important than all the advances in the systems approach. Management is making an effort to get employees committed to their jobs by creating a better working climate and establishing more self-fulfilling goals for the worker.

3. Numerical control of machines coupled with computer control of the production process promises to make the repetitive work of the factory disappear.

4. Many developments in palletization such as plastic shrink film are lowering materials handling and inventory carrying costs.

5. Capital budgeting consists of making the nearly irreversible major decisions in business. Modern techniques such as computer simulation for product payoff and probabilistic capital budgeting are giving a competitive edge to progressive companies.

6. Production control using the computer, mathematical programming, scheduling algorithms, and simulation is yielding increased manufacturing effectiveness and efficiency.

7. The ecology movement may be a blessing or a curse. Smart managers try to turn uncontrollable events into opportunities. In this case, the payoff from cleaning up the environment may come from reuse of waste products or entry into production of products that reduce pollution.

12

Engineering and Research

There's nobody else to follow anymore.

YUJIRO KOIKE, *a director of Matsushita Electric Industrial Co. research institute*[1]

Technological innovation is the driving force behind economic growth in the United States. Economists estimate that 50 to 80 percent of the real growth in GNP is attributable to gains in productivity, nearly all of which flows directly from new technology.

ROBERT A. CHARPIE, *former President Electronics Division, Union Carbide Corp.*[2]

We need only look at a few of the miracles of engineering and research to remind ourselves of their impact on companies and industries. Consider how General Electric realized one of man's age-old desires, the production of man-made diamonds. The failure to grow crystals and other blind leads led to speculation on subjecting graphite to pressures of 1 million pounds per square inch at temperatures of 700 degrees. In 1954, four years after the start of the project, the first truly identifiable man-made diamonds were produced.

Bell Labs, another bastion of applied research, has produced wonder after wonder over decades in an unflappable manner. A routine announcement recently reported a breakthrough in magnetic bubble computer memories, a technology that may shrink the size of computers two thousandfold. Only a few months earlier, Bell Labs unveiled a miniature laser that operates at room temperature without the usual costly cooling equipment.

Top management should be aware of trends in expenditures and the relationship of research expenditures to sales and profits. Where should your company put its money— on research, development, or engineering? What are the differences between these activities; that is, do you really know where your money is going? Are you at the point where there is nobody else to follow, or can you skip research and copy the Japanese?

New management techniques are closing the discovery-to-design gap. The time compression requires major adjustments by the marketing organization and tighter integration of all functions by top management. Such new techniques include methods of organizing, planning, and control of technical development. Sophisticated technical information systems are being developed to speed research and engineering.

The increase in computer capability and the parallel software development have begun to raise this question: Can computers design products? Perhaps they can. Computer-aided design is now being combined with computer-aided manufacturing.

Finally, questions of social and legal responsibility are beginning to filter down from top management to involve the engineering function.

Table 12-1. Federal R&D expenditures by function (estimated in millions).

FUNCTION	1972
National defense	8,998.1
Space research and technology	3,109.4
Health	1,348.4
Commerce and transportation	761.5
Education and manpower	621.7
Natural resources	277.7
Agriculture and rural development	262.2
Community development and housing	141.7
All others	191.0
Total	$15,711.7

SOURCES: National Science Foundation, *Federal Funds for Research, Development and Other Scientific Activities,* Fiscal Years 1970, 1971, 1972, NSF 71–35, Vol. XX (Washington, D.C.: U.S. Government Printing Office, 1972); and *Statistical Abstract of the United States,* Section 20 (Washington, D.C.: U.S. Government Printing Office, 1972).

Figure 12-1. R&D expenditures and the future; 1980 projections.

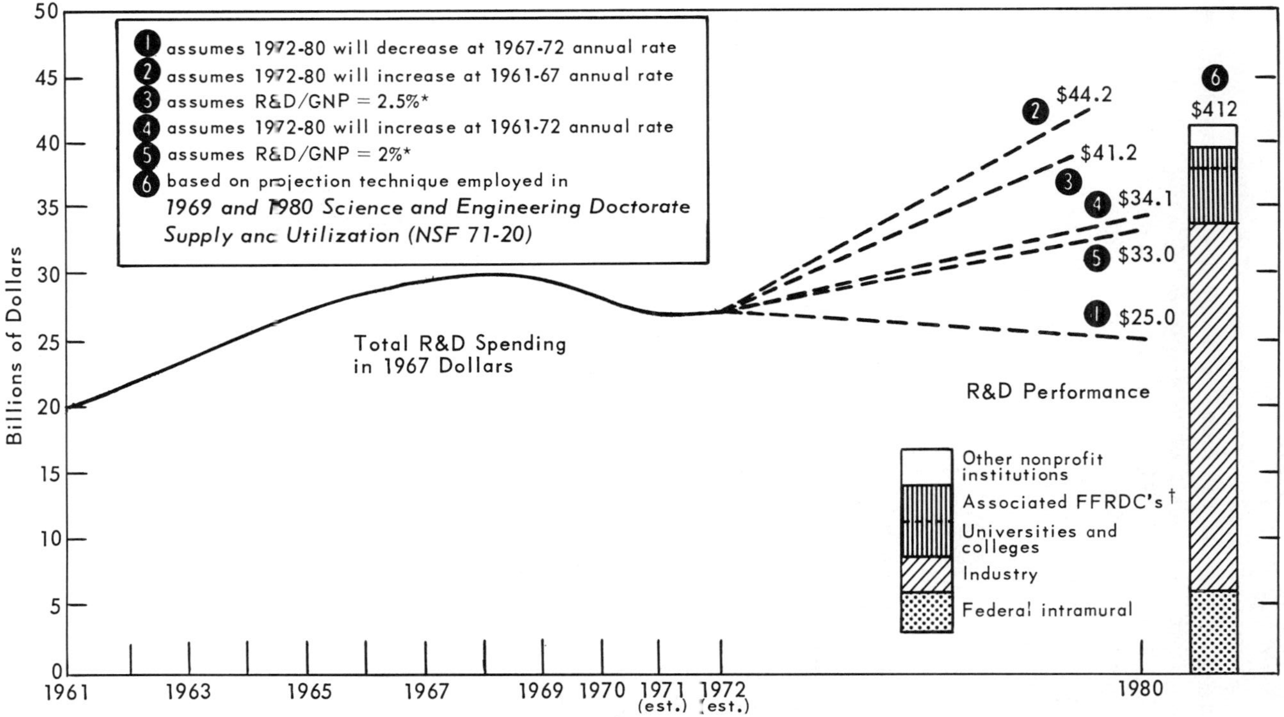

* Based on 1980 GNP in 1971 dollars projected at $1.6 trillion.
† Federal funded research and development centers.

SOURCE: *National Patterns of R&D Resources, Funds & Manpower in the U.S., 1953-1972*, National Science Foundation, 72-300, 1972.

National policy goals determine to a great extent how much will be spent on research in this country and on what it will be spent. Of about $30 billion spent on R&D in the United States in 1972, the federal government supplied about 53 percent of the funds and private industry 42 percent. Despite many promises and strong statements of support for R&D on health, mass transportation, pollution, and other social problems, the Department of Defense, NASA, and the AEC receive the bulk of R&D support. The breakdown of major recipients for 1972 is given in Table 12-1, page 198.

The trend of expenditures for R&D will be upward as it has been in the past (see Figures 12-1 and 12-2), but at a declining rate. President Nixon has, in the opinion of many key scientists in government, failed to implement the kind of R&D program which the country needs.

Figure 12-2. Downtrend in R&D resource allocation in relation to GNP 1961–1972.

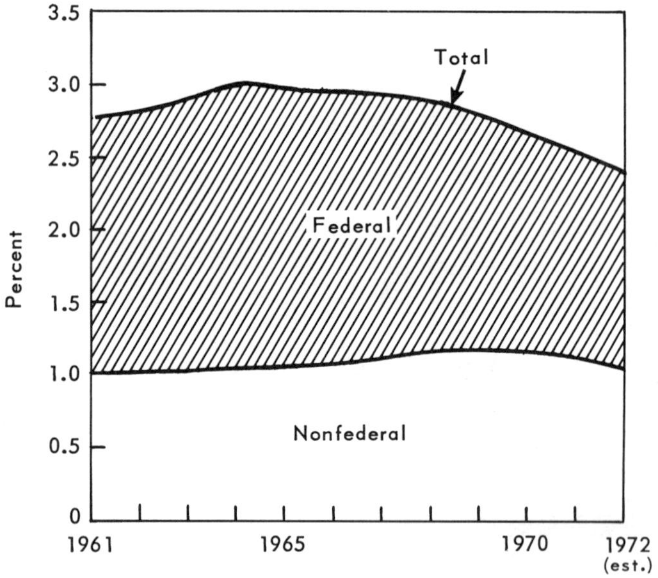

SOURCE: *National Patterns of R&D Resources, Funds & Manpower in the U.S., 1953-1972*, National Science Foundation, 72-300, 1972.

Therefore, unless the Defense Department continues to obtain increases in funds for R&D, it is unrealistic to project large amounts of money going to social programs or being supplied by industry. The inflationary effect on R&D also means that less R&D will be obtained for the money spent.

As a manager, you may ask, "So what?" United States industry has always led the world in technology and applications, if not in the more fundamental research area, you may say. While U.S. executives boast about their technological lead, the facts apparently contradict them. Figure 12-3 will give you a glimpse at what is really happening.

WILL YOU KNOW WHERE TO BET YOUR MONEY?

In the past two decades, research and development has emerged from an obscure and little-understood activity to a major factor in the life of every industrial enterprise. In today's highly competitive environment, with an ever more sophisticated buying public, R&D cannot take place in a vacuum. At American Standard, as in most of our dynamic industrial corporations today, the doctrine of relevance of R&D is of paramount importance. Specifically, this means that our efforts in technology must be keyed, as closely as possible, to current and future products, product line, and processes.

MILTON B. HOLLANDER, *Vice-president, Technology, American Standard*[3]

This section is not intended to guide you to technical areas but rather to help you distinguish among degrees of research and development. Often, untutored management invests in low-level engineering design under the impression it is putting money into applied research. It keeps wondering why its "new products" are obsolete before they hit the market. For strategic as well as budgetary reasons, top management is getting more curious about what to expect from R&D expenditures.

The National Science Foundation distinguishes basic research as that which seeks increases in scientific knowledge and has the primary aim of developing a better understanding by the researcher rather than having a practical application. Applied research, on the other hand, is directed toward practical application of knowledge. Development is the

Figure 12-3. The United States falls behind; how other nations are gaining in the technological race.

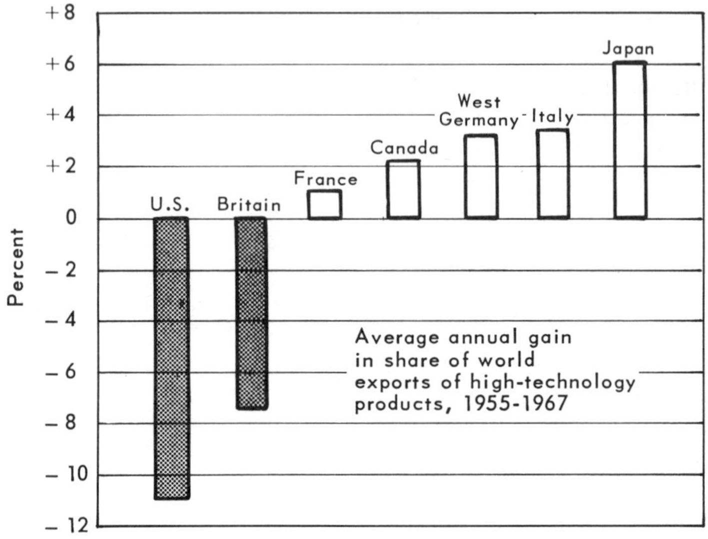

SOURCE: "Making U.S. Technology More Competitive, *Business Week*, January 15, 1972.

systematic use of scientific knowledge directed toward the production of useful materials, devices, systems, or methods. The study of refraction in crystals, the study of a system to produce a fine beam of homogeneous light for power concentration, the development of laser devices for operating on the retina of the eye or for cutting steel are examples of the several levels of one R&D subject. A more useful classification for top management is shown in Figure 12-4.

FROM THE LAB TO THE MARKET—A HOP, SKIP, AND A JUMP

One of the challenges that top management must face is the shortened time span from a laboratory discovery to a marketable product. That means that decisions must be made more rapidly, studies must be made more quickly and be better, and risks will be higher. Within a shorter interval, management must decide whether it wants to develop a commercial product or pass the opportunity by. If it does decide to convert an applied research discovery into a product, it must plan the manufacturing and marketing program practically in parallel with the technical design process. Figure 12-5 shows how the development period has been compressed for several technical products.

PROJECT MANAGEMENT—THE HANDLE TO ENGINEERING PAYOFF

> *The greatest advances in the practice of management, as opposed to theory, in the twentieth century have been the development and application of project management and the refinement of project management techniques.*
>
> R.G.M.

Project management is such an important concept in this day of large complex projects that it is well worthwhile for top management to learn about some of its major concepts and details. Basically, it is a philosophy of systems action, a method of planning and control, and a form of organization that ties tasks to individuals under a project manager. The goals of the project are specific; the time and cost limitations are clearly defined; and the resources to be employed are negotiated between the project manager and his manager.

Projects are broad in scope in most cases, so that they cut across many disciplines and draw widely upon company resources. They deal with systems or complex products, so that systems management or program management is sometimes employed synonymously with project management.

Avoid Trouble by Use of Project Management

There are certain situations in which project management should be used to prevent disaster. The most important use is on projects when the company has limited technical resources and consultants, vendors, or suppliers must participate. When a large project that will disrupt the current work schedules of the organization is accepted, project planning is necessary to achieve efficient use of resources and prevent bedlam. It is similarly necessary when compressed time schedules and fixed fee

Figure 12-4. Matrix for developing universal definitions of research and

I—PERIOD	II—PEOPLE	III—PLACE
A. BASIC RESEARCH Fundamental research Pure research Academic research	Creative, curious, unrestrained individuals motivated by scientific tradition	University or nonprofit foundations, government laboratories, and a few industrial laboratories
B. APPLIED RESEARCH Invention Technological research	Creative, curious individuals of varied backgrounds externally directed by market needs	Industrial, university, and commercial research laboratories
C. DEVELOPMENT New product development New process development Major improvements or new uses Evolutionary inventions Testing Evaluation	Teams of scientists and engineers, with planning and organizing skills, who work well together	Industrial laboratories and pilot plants
D. TECHNICAL SUPPORT Application engineering Cost reduction Product maintenance Product engineering Foreign intelligence Technical information Quality control	Scientists, engineers, and other technicians	Industrial laboratories and production facilities or in the field

SOURCE: Maurice S. Newman, "Evaluating Research and Development Activities". Reprinted by permission of *Management Services*, March-April 1966, by the American Institute of CPAs.

development.

IV—PURPOSE	V—PROCESS	VI—PROCEEDS
To understand the unknown and to contribute to general knowledge	Investigating new scientific phenomena, discovering secrets of nature, and verifying theories of the physical world	Research papers to be presented or distributed to, and evaluated by, a group of scientific peers
To explore practical possibilities of creating new products and processes; to satisfy heretofore unsatisfied wants	Creating, inventing, or discovering new components, devices, compounds, or processes or modifying and combining existing components, devices, compounds, or processes to produce a new application	Theories or knowledge about natural or industrial materials and processes, tests of all areas of uncertainty, and proof of technical feasibility
To create a reliable and satisfactory new product or new process	Using professional teams with varied skills and greater resources to resolve major technological aspects of new products or processes	Technical specifications and production requirements for a new product or process
To maintain a competitive position in the industry	Using highly trained people and substantial resources to meet varying requirements of the marketing and producing departments	Technical services or reports as appropriate

SOURCE: Maurice S. Newman, "Evaluating Research and Development Activities." Reprinted by permission of *Management Services,* March-April 1966, by the American Institute of CPAs.

Figure 12-5. Science-to-discovery gap.

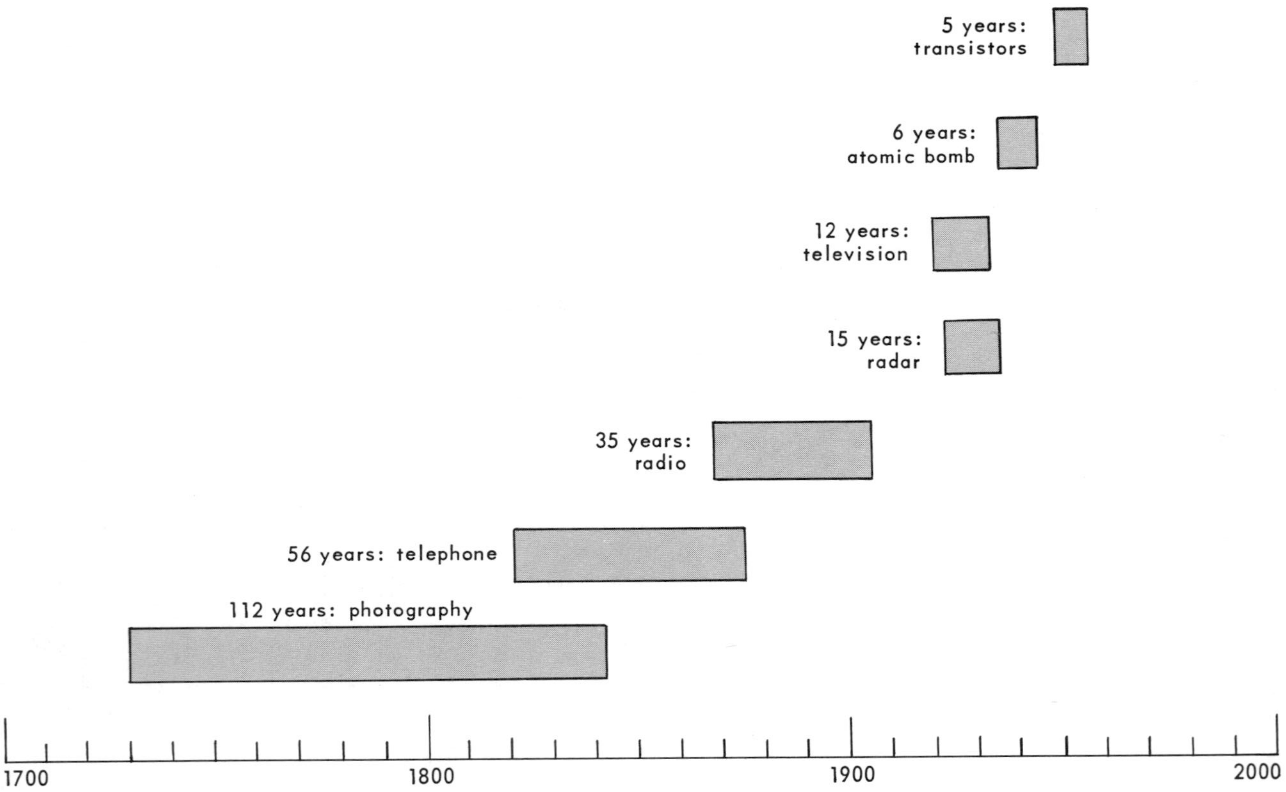

or penalty contracts require extremely close control of quality, time, and cost.

The diplomatic term for flubbing R&D planning and control is "cost overrun." Recent classic examples have been provided by Lockheed Aircraft Corp. management. The Lockheed C-5A transport aircraft order of 120 planes experienced a cost overrun of $882 million, of which about $382 million was attributed to technical problems and $500 million to inflationary factors.

Step 1: Establish Project Objectives

The establishment of objectives seems to be ordinary prudent good management, but project management calls for something more: it requires that *specific* performance objectives be set. In engineering, that means quantitative specifications; for management in general, qualitative objectives are often acceptable. Also, the performance specifications must be established for the life of the equipment and cover supporting systems as well. Top management exercises control by making sure that such qualitative specs appear in all proposals for contracts and requests for funds.

Step 2: Establish the Work Breakdown Structure

The work breakdown structure (WBS) is essentially an outline. Major tasks are determined; subdivisions of those tasks are established; and subtasks for each subdivision are defined. The subtasks usually represent end items, but for support work such as thermal or stress analysis they may represent only engineering proof tests. Similarly, supporting functions that extend over the life of the project, such as value engineering and quality assurance, contribute to end products.

Each subtask is defined by a work package, which describes what is to be done and the labor, materials, and supporting services required to do it. When the time and cost to complete each work package have been estimated, a network diagram showing precedence of those subtasks may be prepared.

Step 3: Establish the Network Plan

Often a given task cannot be started until several other tasks have been completed; the sequencing interrelationships among the tasks are usually complex. The simple network shown in Figure 12-6 illustrates tasks or events (circles) and activities (arrows). IBM explains the network as follows:

> [An activity] cannot be started until the first event has been accomplished. The second event connected by this activity cannot be considered accomplished until all activities leading to the event are accomplished.
>
> Each activity is defined by its initiating and terminating events. Activities require manpower, material, facilities, space, or other resources. Activities, therefore, represent work; events represent specific accomplishments that are the result of work. Some users are activity-oriented in their planning and control operations while others are event-oriented. (*For source, see Figure 12-6.*)

When the time durations and costs are attached to the activities, we have a program evaluation and review technique (PERT) system of planning. The longest time path from start to finish, called the critical path, may be shortened by making tradeoffs between cost and time for activities in the critical path.

Much more sophisticated than the PERT networks are the graphical evaluation and review technique (GERT) networks. Look forward to seeing them in greater use in the 1970s. They allow feedback loops for iteration and probabilistic outcomes when, for instance, parallel lines of attack on a research project are to be followed.

Step 4: Develop the Management Information and Control System

The PERT network supplies you with the management and technical plan; now your problem is to find a way to stick to that plan. The big point to keep in mind is that you must control performance, time, and cost. They are interrelated as shown in Figure 12-7, and you should burn that eternal triangle into your mind. In regard to time, top management faces a problem that technical managers don't face. Technical managers must control time within the life cycle of the project; top management must plan and control on an annual basis as well as from a profit standpoint. Whereas technical management wants to make certain a required capital facility has been purchased early enough to insure meeting schedules, top management wants to postpone capital expenditures as long as possible because of the time value of money and the relationship of such expenditures to cash flow budgets.

Since the early sixties, certain PERT networks have been standard-

Figure 12-6. Activity layout.

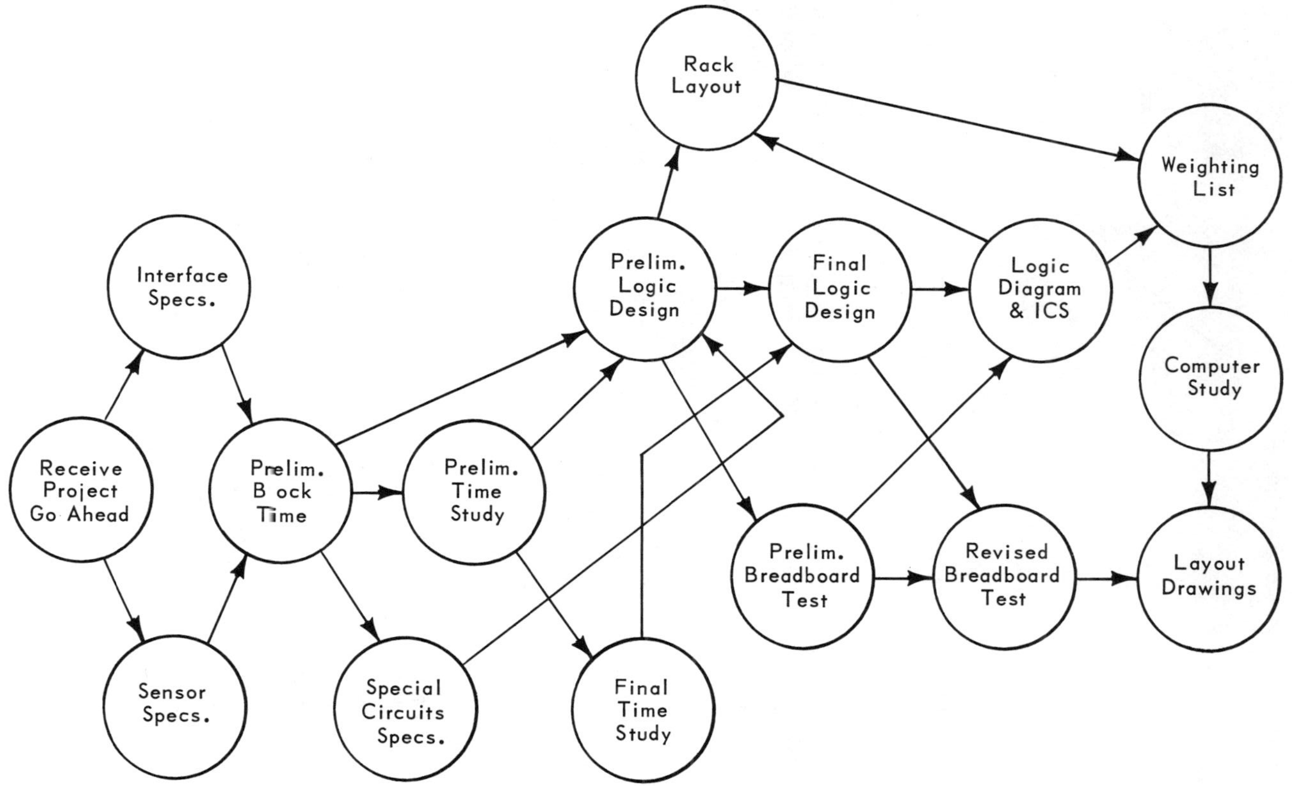

SOURCE: *PERT: A Dynamic Planning and Control Method*, IBM (undated), p. 6.

Figure 12-7. An eternal triangle.

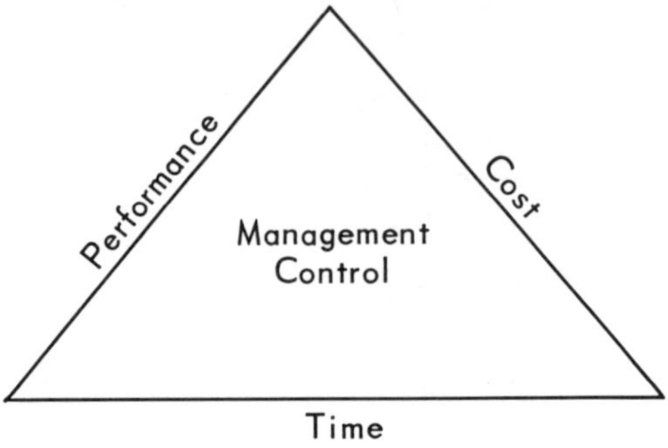

ized, PERT plans and progress reports have been computerized, and a variety of charts have been developed. In each case the purpose was to provide management with information on trouble spots in time to take action. Figure 12-8 illustrates one such modern chart. A computerized output is not shown because it would be gibberish without a lengthy technical explanation.

Besides such charts, the usual financial reports are required: monthly expenditures by labor and materials for each subtask and task with variances from planned amounts shown. Such monthly reports are usually computerized and issued within one week after the last day of the month. Projected annual variances are also included with such reports.

Organization

Organization for project management has been kept until last for a very good reason: The organization for a project is matched to the tasks. That is just the opposite of a functional organization in which jobs are moved from one organizational component to another to be performed. In the line project organization, the project manager has complete responsibility for all performance, time, and cost once management has established or accepted the quantitative goals for that triumvirate. Under the project manager are section managers, each of whom is responsible for a specific subdivision of the total project. In the next line of the hierarchy are managers; below them are the engineers and technicians. Each engineer is given complete responsibility for a well-defined subtask or portion of a subtask.

Figure 12-8. Planning and control form: cost schedule and manpower by skill categories.

WS No. xxx　No. 1　Rev. No. 0

Contract No. xxxxx

Large Solid Motor　Dated 2-2-73　Prepared by ______

No. of Personnel

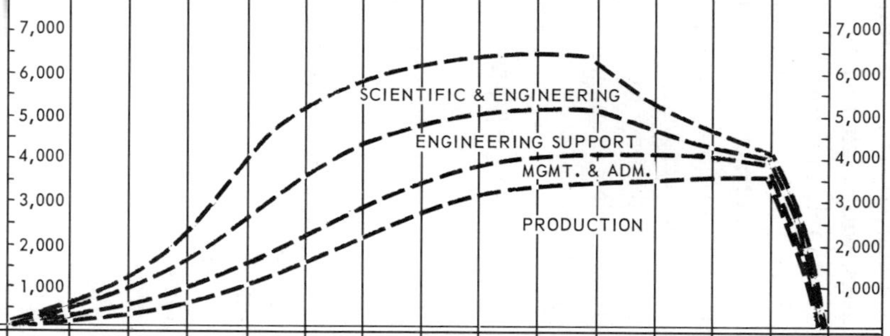

Description	Program Number	1972 1	1972 2	1972 3	1972 4	1973 1	1973 2	1973 3	1973 4	1974 1	1974 2	1974 3	1974 4	1975	1976	Total
COSTS ($000)																
Scientific & Engineering		250	500	775	1,575	1,600	1,625	1,500	1,400	1,375	1,200	650	400	150	100	
Engineering Support		175	350	675	1,325	1,350	1,400	1,275	1,050	1,025	1,000	500	300	100	50	
Management & Administration		75	150	300	500	600	650	700	700	700	700	700	600	500	350	
Production				250	600	1,450	1,825	2,525	2,850	2,900	3,100	3,150	3,200	3,250	3,000	
Total Costs		500	1,000	2,000	4,000	5,000	5,500	6,000	6,000	6,000	6,000	5,000	4,500	4,000	3,500	

SOURCE: Adapted from Howard M. Carlisle, "Systems Approach to Integrating Costs and Technical Data," *Management Services*, July-August 1967.

The project organization has a characteristic growth pattern. During the concept formulation and proposal stage, the organization consists of a few key engineer-managers. It expands rapidly during the feasibility design stage and levels off during much of the detail design stage. Toward the end of the detail design stage and during the operational test stage, it tails off. Management then faces the problem of insuring that new projects are started. High performers in earlier projects may be given key positions with high responsibilities; low performers may be shuffled into more suitable positions.

Another approach to project organization is the matrix structure. Project managers act as contractors to "buy" services from permanent functional engineering organizational components. The method produces more conflicts than line project management. In addition, we find that engineers are essentially reporting to two or more people: their functional managers and the project managers.

THE COMPUTER—HALF ENGINEER

In general, custom design poses one of two problems:

1. Given customer performance specifications, what combination of components will make up the total end product?

2. Given a customer need for a product whose design requires research beyond the present state of the art, what are the performance and design specifications?

It is because problem 1 can be solved by means of the computer that we say computers are becoming engineers. IBM has programmed computers to design logic circuits. General Electric uses a special input form to have the computer figure out capacitor designs. Computers have also developed designs for airplanes and ship hulls.

Problem 2 points up that it will be some time before the computer will completely replace the engineer. Each product has two characteristics: degree of innovation and degree of complexity. The capability of computer design is moving extremely slowly in each of those directions.

The question that is raised today is, "What is engineering?" Much cookbook design of the past can certainly be performed by computers. How rapidly will the computer encroach on what is still believed to be engineering? So-called creative design consists most frequently of definitions of forms that are modified by new information. Today practically every complicated design requires interaction between the human and the computer. In fact, just as some designs could not be developed without human intervention, so some could not be developed without use of the computer. Will the real designer please step forward?

The term computer-aided design (CAD) is often used to describe the entire electronic paraphernalia associated with engineering design. The cathode-ray tube upon which the engineer may sketch with an electronic pencil and have visual sketches converted into accurate geometry is one example. The *X–Y* plotter that draws graphs, lettering, or forms of any kind as outputs of computer programs is another aid.

The top manager had better keep an eagle eye out for developments in this field or he may fall out of his nest.

THE MARRIAGE OF CAD TO CAM

Will computer-aided design be linked to computer-aided manufacturing? At McDonnell Douglas Corp. it already has been. The design process begins when the aerodynamicists decide on an overall outline or shape for the plane. That shape is translated into a numerical description for storage in the computer. Detail designers work with ligh-beam pens on cathode-ray tubes to sketch supporting structures within the outline. N/C programmers eavesdrop on the CAD computer to prepare for manufacturing the parts by a computer-controlled system of N/C machines. (See Chapter 11 for a further description of N/C.)

HOW MUCH IS AN ENGINEER WORTH?

The compression of salaries between the new engineer and the 20-year man to a narrow differential is becoming more and more inflammatory. Unless management finds a fire retardant, the engineers will be driven into unions that will impose severe constraints on management's actions.

Despite popular myths, however, the engineer does quite well compared with craftsmen. The median rate for an engineer with four years of experience is equivalent to the "usual" weekly earnings of plumbers, based on Labor Department statistics for 1970 as shown in Table 12-2.

Frank Hayes, a Delaware consulting engineer, put together a table based on the National Electrical Manufacturers job evaluation plan. He estimated the points for each factor and used 348 evaluation points to

Table 12-2. Average 1972 labor rates.

TRADE	HOURLY RATE	RATE WITH BENEFITS
Bricklayers	$7.70	$8.71
Laborers	5.41	6.29
Carpenters	7.16	8.29
Electricians	7.96	8.67
Painters	6.73	7.48
Plasterers	7.29	8.19
Plumbers	7.91	9.49

SOURCE: Data are abstracted from a table in Francis J. Lavoie, "How Much Is An Engineer Worth?", *Machine Design* (May 4, 1972), p. 69.

represent $8, the electrician's rate. All other job classifications were based on that anchor point. Table 12-3 shows the result.

LIABILITY AND RELIABILITY START HERE

Hammer's law: "An unsafe product will bring corrective action or drive its producer out of business, thereby raising the safety level of all such products." So says Willie Hammer of Hughes Aircraft Company.

In the past, in total dollars and number of claims, automobile liability cases have represented the largest categories. Product liability claims may soon move into the same size class. That is due to consumer education and the courts' view of privity of contract. As a result, suits are being brought not just against the vendor of the product but against the manufacturer as well. Claims for product injuries have grown from 50,000 in 1963 to a rate of 700,000 per year. In one well-publicized case, a housewife was awarded $93,000 when she was blinded by the explosion of a can of drain cleaner. A child scalded by a vaporizer that tipped over was awarded $150,000. In Cook County, Ill., in 1966 there were eight cases for which the combined amount awarded was $906,640. The new phrase is "Let the manufacturer be careful" instead of "Let the buyer beware."

Table 12-3. Job evaluation of engineers and some tradesmen.

JOB CLASSIFICATION	POINT RATING	CALCULATED MONTHLY RATE	ACTUAL MONTHLY RATE	1939 RATE	1913 RATE
Laborer	150	$595	$920	$104	$54
Mason tender	160	660	945	121	54
Roofer	177	710	1,610	216	95
Cement finisher	187	745	1,080	216	95
Reinforcing ironworker	201	805	1,500	275	121
Painter	210	840	970	194	85
Bricklayer	240	950	1,460	285	126
Carpenter	290	1,160	1,530	216	100
Structural ironworker	303	1,200	1,490	285	126
Steamfitter or plumber	310	1,235	1,690	250	109
Sheetmetal worker	319	1,275	1,630	285	126
Electrician	348	1,385	1,540	260	114
Beginning engineer	—	—	810	125	60
Engineer 15 years experience	—	—	1,580	500	250

SOURCE: Francis J. Lavoie, "How Much Is an Engineer Worth?" Reprinted from *Machine Design,* May 4, 1972, by the Penton Publishing Company, Cleveland, Ohio. Table developed by Frank Hayes.

Top management must institute procedures to demonstrate in court that reasonable prudence was taken at every step of design, manufacture, and field testing. Design for safety and reliability are the responsibility of the company and engineers. Written rules should be prepared and kept by each engineer.

1. Emphasis should be placed on methods of hazard elimination and accident prevention, rather than on damage containment and emergency equipment, which should be used only for backup purposes.

2. All safety devices must be subjected to stringent analyses and be designed to minimize secondary failures.

3. Whenever possible, emergency equipment should be extraordinarily foolproof and simple in design and use.

In descending order of priority, the design criteria for accident prevention should be these: eliminate the hazard, limit the hazard level, isolate the hazard with interlocks, use fail-safe (active or passive) designs, or anticipate failure with monitoring systems. To minimize the risks once an accident has occurred, have a carefully prepared procedure for hazard isolation, personnel protection, escape, and rescue.

Any safety device must have certain fundamental characteristics:[4]

1. It must perform its function at the highest practicable reliability level.
2. It must be effective under operational conditions that exist where it will normally be used, not merely under controlled laboratory conditions.
3. It must be accurate, quick-acting, and easy to maintain, calibrate, and check. Procedures to test or calibrate the device should be provided.
4. Failure of the safety device must not produce damaging effects or hazardous conditions. The use of airbags for protection in automobiles has been questioned in this respect.
5. When failure of the product would cause loss of power, the safety device should be provided with an independent power source. That is why many safety devices are gravity-operated.
6. The energy level of a safety device must be less than that which will create or contribute to a hazard in the product being protected.
7. Circuitry within the safety device should not provide a path for possible operational degradation or failure of the product being protected.
8. The design should insure that efforts to circumvent operation of the safeguard would be impossible or extremely difficult. [See the story in the box on the next page.]

SUMMARY: ENGINEERING AND RESEARCH

1. Costs of engineering and research, both salaries and support costs, have been rising rapidly. You should carefully analyze how to spread your money—on research, development, or engineering. One high-priced engineer may be worth three mediocre engineers.
2. You can expect the government to spend less on R&D and to place more emphasis on social projects. That may mean less cheap technological fallout or fewer contracts for your company. New opportunities may be available for companies interested in pollution control, mass transit, and land use.
3. The time span from laboratory concept to commercial product is being shortened. You must move fast if you have a good product concept.
4. Project management and its increasingly sophisticated techniques

HOW SAFE IS HALF-SAFE?

During January 1967, the Air Force launched an unarmed MACE missile on a practice flight from one of its Florida bases. MACE had been an intermediate-range missile before it was designated obsolete and converted to use as a drone. It resembled a pilotless aircraft.

Soon after launch, the guidance and control system failed and the missile veered off course. As it approached the safe-flight boundaries of the range, the Range Safety Officer attempted to blow it up. A destruct system aboard the MACE was designed to activate an explosive charge when the RSO initiated a suitable command by radio. Unfortunately, the destruct system also failed to work.

The second safeguard to terminate wild flights was an aircraft loaded with air-to-air missiles, which accompanied the drone. The pilot launched two of his missiles in an attempt to knock down the MACE. One missile exploded soon after leaving the aircraft; the second missed the target.

The chase aircraft pilot then fired 1,000 rounds of 20-millimeter cannon ammunition at the drone. It sailed serenely on down the Gulf of Mexico, and over the tip of Cuba. It finally landed exhausted 900 miles from where it had been launched; probably (and luckily for U.S.-Cuban relations) in the Caribbean.

The Air Force cannot be faulted for the precautionary measures taken. The incident is cited to show that even extremely low probability events are not impossible.

SOURCE: Willie Hammer, "Design for Safety—Or Else!" Reprinted from *Machine Design*, March 23, 1972, by The Penton Publishing Company, Cleveland, Ohio.

are being used to solve a wider variety of business problems. Project management requires the development of objectives, the preparation of a work breakdown structure and work packages, a network plan to sequence the work, and an information and control system to keep the performance, time, and cost on targets.

5. Computers are replacing engineers in many areas of design. To the degree that engineering consists of logic and analysis, computers will continue to take over more functions of the engineer. If your engineers are still doing modular design of an established product, you are behind the times.

6. Computer-aided design is in the process of being linked to computer-aided manufacturing.

7. A continuing problem for management is to develop career paths for engineers instead of dead-end jobs. Companies cannot pay engineers more than the value of their contributions. Companies must utilize their engineers more fully by developing progressively increasing responsibilities for them.

8. Engineering plays a critical role in protecting the company against liability claims. Engineers should be assigned greater responsibility in that area and held accountable to their increased responsibilities.

REFERENCES

CHAPTER 1

1. As reported in *Nation's Business,* February 1965, p. 68. See also Frederick Haas, *Executive Obsolesence* (AMA, 1968).
2. Abraham H. Maslow, *Motivation and Personality* (New York: Harper & Brothers, 1954).

CHAPTER 2

1. Max Ways, "Business Needs to Do a Better Job of Explaining Itself," *Fortune,* September 1972, p. 85.
2. Philip Kotler, "What Consumerism Means for Marketers," *Harvard Business Review,* May–June 1972.
3. "Living With New Labeling Rules," *Business Week,* February 3, 1973.
4. "Radicals in the Board Room?", *Forbes,* May 15, 1972, p. 61.
5. "The Pressure Is On for Safer Products," *Business Week,* July 4, 1970.
6. Conrad Berenson, "The Product Liability Revolution," *Business Horizons,* October 1972
7. Kotler, op. cit.
8. Henningsen v. Bloomfield Motors, Inc., 161A.2d 81–84 (160).
9. R. L. Thornton and D. C. King, "Ecology—The Fear Appeal in the Public Sector," *MSU Business Topics,* Winter 1972.
10. "Is Doomsday Really That Close?" *Business Week,* March 11, 1972.
11. "Milton Friedman Responds," *Business and Society Review,* Spring 1972, p. 10.
12. Peter Drucker, "The Shame of Marketing," *Marketing/Communications,* August 1969, p. 64.

CHAPTER 3

1. "How Business Faces a Hostile Climate," *Business Week,* September 16, 1972, p. 70.
2. "Social Responsibility, Time to Take Stock," *Personnel Administrator,* January–February 1972.
3. *Business and Society Review,* Autumn 1972.
4. Gilbert Burck, "High Pressure Consumerism at the Salesman's Door," *Fortune,* July 1972, p. 70.
5. "Accounting and the Road Ahead," a speech made by Harold S. Geneen at the annual meeting of stockholders, International Telephone & Telegraph Co., May 10, 1972, in Memphis, Tennessee.
6. "Faces Behind the Figures," *Forbes,* December 15, 1972, p. 59.
7. *The Wall Street Journal,* January 8, 1973, p. 26.
8. "How Social Responsibility Fits the Game of Business," *Fortune,* December 1970.
9. "Corporate Reformers Rearming for '73," *Industry Week,* May 29, 1972.
10. Paul Samuelson, "The Businessman's Shrinking Prerogatives," *Business and Society Review,* Spring 1972, p. 38.
11. "Corporate Reformers Rearming for '73," op. cit.
12. "Industry Rates Itself," *Business and Society Review,* Spring 1972.
13. Max Ways, "Business Needs to Do a Better Job of Explaining Itself," *Fortune,* September 1972, p. 85.
14. Samuelson, op. cit.
15. Daniel Yankelovich, "Business in the '70's: Decade of Crisis," *Michigan Business Review,* November 1972.
16. *Business Week,* April 29, 1972, p. 25.
17. "How Social Responsibility Fits the Game of Business," op. cit.
18. Robert Estes, "Contemporary Challenges to American Business Society Relationships," speech presented at conference sponsored by the General Electric Company, University of California at Los Angeles, 1971.
19. Dan H. Fenn, Jr. and Raymond Bauer, *The Corporate Social Audit* (New York: Russell Sage Foundation, 1972).
20. Ibid.
21. J. S. Shulman and F. Gale, "Laying the Groundwork for Social Accounting," *Financial Executive,* March 1972.
22. "Corporate Reformers Rearming for '73," op. cit.
23. "How Business Tackles Social Problems," *Business Week,* May 20, 1972.

CHAPTER 4

1. Donnie Radcliffe, "Zumwalt—Embattled Admiral," *Miami Herald,* December 31, 1972, p. 4E.

2. Douglas McGregor, *The Human Side of Enterprise* (New York: McGraw-Hill, 1960).
3. Chris Argyris, *Personality and Organization: The Conflict Between System and the Individual* (New York: Harper & Row, 1957).
4. Chris Argyris, *Management and Organizational Development: The Path from XA to YB* (New York: McGraw-Hill, 1960).
5. "Supermarkets Stocking Up on Psychology," *Miami Herald,* May 24, 1970, p. 18G.
6. Michael Beer and Edgar F. Huse, "A Systems Approach to Organizational Development," *Journal of Applied Behavioral Science,* Vol. 8, No. 1 (1972), p. 82.

CHAPTER 5

1. *Michigan Business Review,* July 1972, p. 6.
2. "Management Itself Holds the Key," *Business Week,* September 1972, p. 142.
3. R. M. Fulmer, "Profiles of the Future," *Business Horizons,* August 1972.
4. Ibid.
5. Robert Levy, "The Rites of Business," *Dun's Review,* September 1972.
6. Harlan Cleveland, *The Future Executive* (New York: Harper & Row, Publishers, Incorporated, 1972).
7. *The Wall Street Journal,* December 7, 1972, p. 1.
8. Warren Bennis, "Organizational Developments and the Fate of Bureaucracy," *Industrial Management Review,* Spring 1966, p. 52.
9. C. Peter McColough, "Lessons of Leadership," *Nation's Business,* September 1972, p. 46.
10. Marshall McLuhan and Barrington Nevitt, *Take Today: The Executive as a Dropout* (New York: Harcourt Brace Jovanovich, 1972).
11. "Second Thoughts on the 'Office of the President,'" *Business Week,* October 3, 1970, p. 42.
12. Y. K. Shetty and H. M. Carlisle, "A Contingency Model of Organization Design," *California Management Review,* Fall 1972.

CHAPTER 6

1. "GE's New Strategy for Faster Growth," *Business Week,* July 8, 1972.

CHAPTER 7

1. "What Are Earnings? The Growing Credibility Gap," *Forbes,* May 15, 1967, p. 34.

2. "Accountants Turn Tougher," *Business Week,* October 18, 1969, p. 128.
3. "Business Fears Profit Forecasting" *Business Week,* November 4, 1972, p. 49.
4. Ibid.
5. Quoted in John C. Burton (Ed.), *Corporate Financial Reporting: Conflicts and Challenges* (New York: American Institute of Certified Public Accountants, 1969), p. 56.
6. Robert T. Sprouse, "The Measurement of Income," in Burton, op. cit., p. 204.

CHAPTER 8

1. Rodney Brady, "Computers in Top Level Decision Making," *Harvard Business Review,* July–August 1967.

CHAPTER 9

1. *Nation's Business,* September 1967.

CHAPTER 12

1. "The Flaw in Japan's Boom," *Business Week,* July 10, 1971, p. 42.
2. *Applied Science and Technological Progress, 1967.* Washington, D.C.: National Academy of Sciences, 1967, p. 357.
3. Milton B. Hollander, "Get the Most Out of R&D," *Research/Development,* December 1970, p. 18.
4. Willie Hammer, "Design for Safety—Or Else!" *Machine Design,* March 23, 1972, pp. 112, 113.

INDEX

LIBRARY
and
LEARNING RESOURCES

UNIVERSITY OF WISCONSIN-OSHKOSH. WISCONSIN FOUNDED A.D. 1871

University of Wisconsin
Oshkosh